"The voices speaking in *Been There. Done That. ?* heal the wounds of the aching soul, ending isolation while shining the light of introspective understanding to people with autism, by people with autism. It's lovely to see our voices as the experts while others who care so greatly for us serve the authors in a consultative role—as it should be."

—*Dena L. Gassner, MSW, Program Director of Center for Understanding, Board Member of GRASP, and Advisory Board Member of Autism Society of America*

"Resonating profoundly with my own difficulties, the Aspie mentors within this book validate our challenges from their personal experiences. By giving positive practical advice, the Aspie mentors better equip us for many aspects of our everyday living. This is an outstanding guide that every Aspie should own!"

—*Barb Cook, Editor-in-Chief of* Autism Aspergers Network Magazine *and co-founder of Australian Autism Aspergers Network Inc.*

"Clear, concise, well-structured, and an easy read, *Been There. Done That. Try This!* is an accessible compendium of wisdom from Aspie forebears and the dedicated bridgekeepers who have empowered them. Non-preachy, warm, often funny, the host of positive role models offer up a vast range of healthy choices for a new generation. This collection addresses all the major issues facing Aspies today and is the long-awaited instruction manual gifting future generations of Aspies with the ideas, strategies, and understanding that will empower them in their own diverse journeys."

—*Donna Williams, author, artist, autism consultant, and public speaker*

"Under the auspices of the venerable Asperger's expert Dr. Tony Attwood, leading self-advocate Anita Lesko, and 'community organizer' Craig R. Evans comes a full chorus of voices from the autism spectrum: young, old, male, female, and global. Together, these self-advocates offer perspectives, life stories, and advice for not only living, but thriving in an often inhospitable world. *Been There. Done That. Try This!* addresses every major stressor in the life of a young adult with Asperger's, from the personal to the interpersonal, from schools to offices, from trying to 'pass' to disclosing a diagnosis. Each issue has its essayists' anecdotal advice matched with Dr. Attwood's professional insight, rounding out a comprehensive approach to meeting and defeating the challenges we face."

—*Daniel Heinlein, Host of* I Am Autistic, The Autism Channel *by the same authors*

The Complete Guide to Asperger's Syndrome
Tony Attwood
ISBN 978 1 84310 495 7 (hardback)
ISBN 978 1 84310 669 2 (paperback)
eISBN 978 1 84642 559 2

Asperger's Syndrome
A Guide for Parents and Professionals
Tony Attwood
Foreword by Lorna Wing
ISBN 978 1 85302 577 8
eISBN 978 1 84642 697 1

Pretending to be Normal
Living with Asperger's Syndrome
Liane Holliday Willey
Foreword by Tony Attwood
ISBN 978 1 85302 749 9
eISBN 978 1 84642 210 2

The Asperkid's (Secret) Book of Social Rules
The Handbook of Not-So-Obvious Social Guidelines
for Tweens and Teens with Asperger Syndrome
Jennifer Cook O'Toole
ISBN 978 1 84905 915 2
eISBN 978 0 85700 685 1

Finding a Different Kind of Normal
Misadventures with Asperger Syndrome
Jeanette Purkis
ISBN 978 1 84310 416 2
eISBN 978 1 84642 469 4

Been There.
Done That.
TRY THIS!

AN ASPIE'S GUIDE TO LIFE ON EARTH

EDITED BY TONY ATTWOOD, CRAIG R. EVANS AND ANITA LESKO

The Mentors
Qazi Fazli Azeem, Garry Burge, James Buzon, Bob Castleman, Mitch Christian,
Debbie Denenburg, Charli Devnet, Temple Grandin, Ruth Elaine Joyner Hane,
Paul Isaacs, Dr. Know, Karen Krejcha, Henny Kupferstein, Anita Lesko,
Richard Maguire, John Makin, Larry Moody, Lisa Morgan, Jennifer Cook O'Toole,
Lars Perner, Jeanette Purkis, Mary Robison, Steve Selpal, Dr. Stephen M. Shore,
Dr. Patrick Suglia, Liane Holliday Willey, Alexis Wineman

Jessica Kingsley *Publishers*
London and Philadelphia

First published in 2014
by Jessica Kingsley Publishers
73 Collier Street
London N1 9BE, UK
and
400 Market Street, Suite 400
Philadelphia, PA 19106, USA

www.jkp.com

Library of Congress Cataloging in Publication Data
Been there, done that--try this! : an Aspie's guide to life
on earth / edited by Tony Attwood, Craig R.
Evans, and Anita Lesko.
    pages cm
  ISBN 978-1-84905-964-0 (alk. paper)
 1. Asperger's syndrome--Patients--Life skills guides.
2. Autistic people--Counseling of. 3. Autistic
children--Life skills guides. I. Attwood, Tony. II. Evans, Craig R. III. Lesko, Anita.
  RC553.A88B438 2014
  616.85'8832--dc23
                        2013048194

British Library Cataloguing in Publication Data
A CIP catalogue record for this book is available from the British Library

ISBN 978 1 84905 964 0
eISBN 978 0 85700 871 8

Printed and bound in Great Britain

The greatest wisdom on Autism Spectrum Disorders such as Asperger's syndrome resides within those who have an ASD. If you have, or someone you love or support has, an ASD, seek the wisdom of those who have an ASD and you will understand.

Dr. Tony Attwood

We *can* all thrive with autism. The heroes herein, contributing their life-earned wisdom to future generations of Aspies, are living proof. I'm dedicating this book to the delightfully warm, talented and brilliant young man who introduced me to the amazing world of autism—Nolan Parks.

Craig R. Evans

I dedicate this book to all the Aspies around the globe. For only another Aspie can truly know what it's like to walk in these Aspie shoes.

Anita Lesko

Give a man a fish and you feed him for a day.
Teach a man to fish and you feed him for a lifetime.

Chinese proverb

Contents

Preface

Dr. Tony Attwood

Working on this book has been enlightening, inspiring and, most of all, fun. The original idea was to explore and apply the great wisdom on Autism Spectrum Disorders (ASDs) that has not been published in academic journals or textbooks but has been acquired over the lifetimes of those who have Asperger's syndrome. They are the great Aspie mentors who know ASD from the inside; they have "Been there, done that," and from their wisdom say, "Try this!" They provide advice and encouragement that has far greater credibility, empathy and value than the advice of neurotypical parents and clinicians. Read this book and be enlightened.

Craig R. Evans

In 2003 I met my first (amazing) Aspie. His name was Nolan. At 13 he was reciting Latin genus species names of animals and lining then up in rows based on size, color, foods consumed or just alphabetically (in English or Latin). He'd phonetically sounded out the animals' names and learned their stories after reading about them on his Animal Facts cards. At the same time, Nolan was creating different combinations of mythical (futuristic) animals on a website called SPORE. And he was drawing astonishing cartoons of his favorite pets (Australian sugar gliders). The zoo was his second home. I was learning that Nolan is a lot like his mother: artistic, brilliant, funny, creative and loving. But unlike his mom, Nolan is challenged. Between allergies, sensory issues and severe anxiety, daily life was a battlefield. After raising two neurotypical kids in my first marriage, I'd never experienced anything like this before. I needed to find some answers.

An in-depth scan of the web turned up little more than a few autism associations, notices of fund raising walks and sketchy discussions of possible causes and the hope for a cure. Oddly, there was nothing about living with autism. In order to learn how to deal with Nolan and the explosion of children like him, I needed to change that.

Nolan became my stepson in 2007 when I married his wonderful mother. In 2008, I launched Autism Hangout, an online discussion forum that reports news, complies facts and community-submitted personal experiences, and invites ongoing discussion to discover insights on how best to deal with the daily challenges of autism. My mission was simple: I wanted to find ways for Nolan—and others like him—to "thrive with autism." And those messages needed to be shared with a shell-shocked autism community. So my journey as a journalist began.

I decided to videotape my findings in short (under ten-minute) video reports. After posting a few, my instincts were confirmed. The videos were getting hammered—some garnered more than 1000 views in a 24-hour period. Today, there are close to 500 videotaped reports at Autism Hangout, not all mine. But all focused on relevant, positive, helpful messages.

I've interviewed some amazing people along the way: authors, autism experts, medical professionals, occupational therapists, teachers, caregivers, speech and language pathologists and successful/inspirational/thriving people with autism. Two things I immediately noticed they all had in common: hope and a positive attitude. So in capturing their messages (on video) and putting them out there, I knew it was going to be possible for all of us to learn to thrive with autism. And then I met another person who rocked my world: Dr. Tony Attwood.

Sometime around 2009, I'd written Dr. Tony (in Australia) and invited him to record answers (via Skype) to questions about autism that were submitted by Autism Hangout members. He immediately agreed, acknowledging the importance of dispersing encouraging findings, techniques and treatments as quickly as possible. The "Ask Dr. Tony" show became a reality. Many of those programs have since received tens of thousands of views.

And the grateful comments from hundreds of viewers confirm their helpfulness…and hopefulness.

During one of those recorded conversations, Dr. T brought up the concept of "Aspie mentors"—someone older with Asperger's/ High Functioning Autism (HFA) looking to help younger spectrum dwellers face the same challenges they encountered and overcame earlier in life. Talk about hopeful! I jumped on it!

We were pretty sure, starting out, that we'd be able to locate "qualified" Aspie mentors. Our "qualification" was simply someone diagnosed with Asperger's (or HFA) who had found satisfaction in life. Satisfaction could be defined many ways: a good job, money, a fulfilling marriage, and peace. But we discovered something else that provided enormous satisfaction. Something remarkable.

Almost without exception, the mentors who took part in this work were *already* mentoring. Having lived through the proverbial dark ages of ignorance towards their needs and predispositions, without exception, this group was already actively engaged in giving back in order to help others like themselves avoid stress. Mentoring is one of the many ways they find fulfillment.

Initially, the thought was to assemble Aspie mentors in cities across the country. Monthly meet ups could be arranged where junior Aspies could meet with senior Aspies and learn (from their life's experiences) how to navigate common Aspie-related issues (such as anxiety, self-esteem, making and keeping friends) to avoid stress. But I quickly found out that the databases necessary to make that sort of event happen were years away. However, it wasn't long until I arrived at the idea of a book—a "primer"—of Aspie mentor wisdom, which might someday help pave the way for meet up groups.

So here, with this first book of Aspie wisdom, we start. For me, Dr. Tony and Anita and hundreds of thousands of next-generation Aspies, this book is a dream that's come true.

I'm hopeful the insight and wisdom of the compassionate, brave, persevering souls that contributed to this book is clearly communicated to those on the spectrum following in their footsteps. And I'm more hopeful the love—from Aspie to fellow Aspie, clearly present in this act of selflessness—is noticed by the world. This is compassion in print.

Thank you, *thank you*, Aspie mentors, for genuinely making the world a better place. And thank you, Cherri Saltzmann, Mitra Ahani, Kathleen Tehrani and Theresa and Frank Gustafson. None of this could have happened without you.

Anita Lesko

I went the first 50 years of my life with Asperger's syndrome. Only I didn't know it! I heard of it two years ago from a co-worker whose son just got diagnosed with Asperger's. I stood in shock as I read all the signs and symptoms of it. All the pieces of the puzzle suddenly fell into place. The whole picture of my life now made sense! I never fit in. I always knew I was different. I simply never knew why.

It seemed my invisible disorder created endless obstacles. Somehow I managed to develop strategies to overcome them. Perseverance was the biggest one. It has taken me to great heights—15,000 feet to be exact! I got a flight in an F-15 fighter jet in 2006. One of my special interests took me there. In 1988 I graduated from Columbia University. A Master of Science in Nurse Anesthesia has enabled me to have a great career. I've been working the past 25 years as a Certified Registered Nurse Anesthetist.

The night I discovered I have Asperger's, I went to the bookstore. I purchased every book they had about it. Dr. Tony Attwood's *The Complete Guide to Asperger's Syndrome* was the first one I read. To this day it remains my Bible of Asperger's. It's as if Tony knew me from the second I was born!

I then went for a formal diagnosis. There was no support group in my area, so of course I started one. I wrote my memoir/inspirational book *Asperger's Syndrome: When Life Hands You Lemons, Make Lemonade* during a two-week vacation. After seeing my manuscript, Dr. Temple Grandin called to ask about including me in her new book. *Different...Not Less* was published in April 2012, and I am Chapter 7.

Someone told me about a great website: autismhangout.com. Wow! Indeed it was great. There were hundreds of educational video clips in short eight- to ten-minute segments, and included there was Dr. Tony Attwood, in a series called "Ask Dr. Tony." I sent the founder, Craig R. Evans, a copy of my book, and he then contacted me to do an interview. I admired Craig for all he was doing for autism. I later expressed my desire to help others on the spectrum. I wanted to do something on a global level. Craig said he might just have what I was looking for.

Two weeks later I received an email from Dr. Tony Attwood. He, too, had a dream on a global scale, to gather all the "older" Aspies to provide their wisdom to the younger ones. We had "been there and done that," and now would share our wisdom to "try this!" I was ecstatic—the project was going to be me, Craig and Dr. Tony.

We immediately went to work. First we assembled a list of categories of issues that most affected Aspies daily. A survey was then created based on these categories, and field tested on 50 Aspies. I became quite proficient at rounding them up. Dr. Tony participated in this as well, tweaking the survey with more categories.

Now the survey was ready for launch. I recorded a video clip explaining the need for this project. I got it everywhere Aspies would see it. We had over 322 responses, which was strong statistical data. A never-before-conducted study had been accomplished.

Meanwhile, I was assembling the group of Aspie mentors. I gathered quite an impressive list—a "who's who," in fact: Dr. Temple Grandin, Dr. Stephen M. Shore, Dr. Lars Perner, Alexis Wineman, and many more. I started with Aspies with whom I was already connected, and Kathleen Tehrani (autismbrainstorm. org) directed me to other appropriate mentors. Instructions for the mentors were then prepared. Each was to write a minimum of four essays, choosing from the 17 categories. The essays were to be a maximum of 600 words, which would provide quick, concise wisdom to the reader.

Now came the really exciting part—the essays began arriving. I was thrilled from my Aspie point of view, and started feeling really connected. This was incredible advice from successful Aspies, like a global support group.

Most of the Aspie mentors were diagnosed late in life. Like myself, they all managed to succeed despite the obstacles. It is the wisdom that we gained in managing to do this that we want to pass on to the young Aspies. It is a different, more complex world today; our youth need all the help they can get. This book will unite Aspies around the world in a historic movement. This is only the beginning.

Equally important is educating the public about Asperger's. The term "Asperger's" has now been removed from the Diagnostic and Statistical Manual of Mental Disorders (DSM-5) and replaced with the term "Autism Spectrum Disorder," but we shall always be Aspies! This book will provide insight into the Aspergian mind. People will finally see how we experience the world around us. We have many gifts, and with those we've made this a better world; we have created electricity, motor vehicles, computers, and many conveniences of modern life. However, the severity of the sensory issues will truly become apparent, and I hope that people will now recognize just how profoundly we are affected. This book is not only for other Aspies. It's for parents, educators, therapists and medical personnel—anyone having contact with Aspies.

This book, full of Aspie wisdom, is a dream come true. I set out to help hundreds of thousands of Aspies around the world. This is only the beginning, the first step to unite us. We have a voice that wants to be heard: here come our first words, which will resonate around the globe. We are connecting with each other and, even more far-reaching, we are allowing the world to see we have hopes, dreams and feelings too. We belong on this planet, just like everyone else.

Addendum: Words are only one form of human communication. In addition to the submitted essays, Aspie mentor artists from around the world freely contributed artwork to this book. This is included in color towards the center of the book, between Chapters 9 and 10. It is our hope that through both reading and seeing how stressor issues feel to someone on the spectrum, all of us will come to a deeper, more compassionate understanding of what daily life is like.

REFERENCES

Attwood, T. (2008) *The Complete Guide to Asperger's Syndrome*. London: Jessica Kingsley Publishers.

Grandin, T. (2012) *Different...Not Less: Inspiring Stories of Achievement and Successful Employment from Adults with Autism, Asperger's and ADHD*. Arlington, TX: Future Horizons.

Lesko, A. (2011) *Asperger's Syndrome: When Life Hands You Lemons, Make Lemonade*. iUniverse.

THE 17 RANKED ISSUES THAT CAUSE THE MOST STRESS TO SOMEONE WITH ASPERGER'S/HFA*

Ranking of issue by stress caused

Percent of respondents living with issue

#1 Anxiety 98%
#2 Self-esteem/self-identity 95%
#3 Aversion to change 87%
#4 Meltdowns 87%
#5 Depression 87%
#6 Sensory issues 86%
#7 Making and keeping friends 86%
#8 Personal management issues 85%
#9 Intimacy, dating, sex and marriage 85%
#10 Emotional availability 85%
#11 Faking it 84%
#12 Getting and keeping a job 83%
#13 Disclosing a diagnosis 79%
#14 Bullying 77%
#15 Choosing a career 76%
#16 Empathetic attunement 75%
#17 Being diagnosed 67%

Aversion to change 87%
Anxiety 86%
Meltdowns 83%
Sensory issues 83%
Making and keeping friends 82%
Self-esteem/self-identity 80%
Emotional availability 80%
Faking it 78%
Intimacy, dating, sex and marriage 77%
Depression 76%
Disclosing a diagnosis 73%
Personal management issues 72%
Bullying 72%
Getting and keeping a job 69%
Being diagnosed 61%
Choosing a career 58%
Empathetic attunement 58%

*Based on proprietary research conducted by Craig R. Evans in 2012–2013. See Appendix for more information.

CHAPTER 1

Overcoming Anxiety

Stress Ranking: 1

Ranking of issue by stress caused

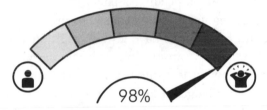

98%

Percent of respondents living with issue

86%

People with Asperger's/HFA may have issues with anxiety. Some examples of anxiety include: feeling fear in social situations, feeling anxious when going to the doctor/dentist, being physically overcome by a sensory issue that causes discomfort and/or pain, and having a change forced on you when you're not ready for it. Do you have concerns about anxiety?

Mitch Christian

The list of anxieties over my lifetime starts with an intense fear of the dark as a child. I couldn't enter a room without the lights being on, and would stop at the doorway as if there was a physical barrier stopping me. Over the years, the problem went away gradually, but I was well into my thirties before it was pretty much gone. I also had a peculiar anxiety about men with beards when I was growing up, probably caused by an uncle who startled me by accident. Large dogs have always frightened me, and I've never been comfortable around big animals in general. My fear of heights is somewhat less intense than it used to be, but I still avoid getting near ledges and windows that are too far above ground. As a teenager, I developed anxieties about leaving the house and being outside in general. Learning to drive was very stressful, and driving continues to be something I only do when necessary, although like many of these issues it has become less severe over the years.

Social anxieties have been the biggest issue, though. It comes from being uncomfortable with too much eye contact, the proximity of other people, and noise levels, as well as having trouble filtering out background sounds. I avoid crowds, and I also stay away from shopping malls at peak traffic times. At work, I'm able to keep meetings at a minimum, and usually find a seat near an exit or at least in the back when I'm attending a larger gathering. This reduces the fear that I might get trapped in the throng of people when the meeting is over. When I am around other people, I strive to keep general conversations brief, but not so short as to appear rude. My job allows me to work on my own projects and I'm able to use email or phone calls to communicate with co-workers most of the time.

As an adult, the way that I've found to keep overall anxiety levels under control is to make periodic retreats away from the stressors that come from the requirements of daily life. That includes having plenty of alone time at home with a minimum of interaction with other people. When I bought my house I looked specifically for one with a finished basement where I could have a room that gave me a place I could go at the end of the day, where I could reduce and control sound and light levels. I turned it into a small home theater room where I can watch movies and television, play games and browse the internet. I try not to spend too much time there, though, by keeping on a schedule of chores that requires me to leave the room periodically, or to leave the house for short trips on the weekends. I also take time to read books upstairs in front of a window at the back of the house in order to get some regular exposure to sunlight. Plenty of sleep, regular amounts of moderate exercise, and a diet free of junk food help regulate my general anxiety, as well.

Bob Castleman

Anxiety is a destroyer. It destroys productivity at work. It turns simple things like doing the laundry into insurmountable obstacles. It paralyzes the mind and prevents making decisions, or worse, prevents even correctly assessing situations so you can make good decisions. This is true for everyone, but especially for anyone with autism. Anxiety forms a feedback loop into the sensory and processing differences we experience, magnifying their effects and often escalating the anxiety to crisis levels. My best defense against anxiety comes down to a few simple, but powerful techniques.

One is simply to take care of myself. Diet, exercise and sleep habits need to be an inviolate part of my routine. Exercise is especially important. And for me, at least, it has to have sufficient intensity to allow me to stop thinking about all the things that create anxiety in my head. I need the kind of exercise that demands focus and intensity. Some like to exercise at a pace that allows the mind to fall into a reverie, drifting around in a free-floating stream of consciousness. This type of exercise isn't about exercise as much as it is a form of meditation. But for me this is entirely insufficient. My mind is constantly active. It is overstimulated and distracted by a tsunami of information. This alone is enough to create anxiety, and at times I need nothing less than a complete shutting off of that flood. For me, the best anxiety-reducing exercise requires complete, 100 percent focus and intensity. It's the only way to shut down the overactive cognition that plagues me. This isn't even about the type of exercise. Jogging leads to a meditative state, but running wind sprints until your quadriceps burn and your lungs ache requires focus and intensity. There's one very nice thing about exercise. It helps regulate sleep. And to exercise at the intensity I need, I need to be conscious of nutrition. It all fits together.

Another anxiety slayer is awareness—both awareness of my triggers and awareness of what I am experiencing in the moment. While I'm not sure this is valid from a clinical perspective, I divide anxiety into two separate categories—future and present. I even go as far as to call present anxiety agitation. For me, cognitively at least, anxiety is worrying about what might happen and agitation is about what is happening right now. Anxiety includes an element of anticipation. Agitation is happening in real time.

Agitation is easier to deal with. If I am in a noisy room, I know to leave. If there are distractions at work, I can usually make adjustments. But this takes a level of self-awareness that isn't always easy to learn. I have to actively self-monitor and have some sense of when my agitation levels are increasing. I have to proactively adjust as much as possible to prevent escalation. And it helps tremendously to not place myself in agitating environments.

Anxiety is more problematic. Anxiety, as I experience it, is deeply rooted in anticipation. If I am required to go somewhere that I know will be potentially agitating, then I can fall into an endless sequence of "what ifs" and theoretical scenarios. What is critical here is the word "theoretical." What do I know for sure about an upcoming event? What value is there in mentally rehearsing multiple scenarios? How much of my anxiety is simply transferring negative past experiences into these scenarios without any real evidence? I have found that if I stick with what I actually know about an impending event (which turns out usually to be much less than one would think), then I can dump all my anxiety-generating scenarios into my "conjecture box." Conjecture has little weight in my cognition. Conjecture is something requiring additional data and further analysis. I am much less likely to be anxious about something that cannot be solved due to lack of data. To me, in a very real sense, knowledge is power. The more I know about a future situation, the more I can anticipate the agitating factors and prepare myself. The more I know about what I don't know, the more I can successfully move the future into my conjecture box, and remove some of its anxiety-producing power.

Garry Burge

As an adult on the Autism Spectrum I have always had to endure anxiety. When I was much younger, I experienced anxiety by encountering a sense of dizziness. When at school, a change of sound would make me feel disorientated and detached from my physical body. As I got older, I experienced phobias which would include a fear of fainting and being in enclosed spaces. This also happened within the school system, and teachers and authority figures could not relate to the experiences I encountered, nor could I find the necessary tools to deal with them. As I grew and developed into an adult, I experienced anxiety at sometimes very high levels. I did my best to avoid certain situations and people so as to avoid certain scenarios that may prove difficult.

Anxiety became a problem in employment, and working full time especially meant that managing anxiety became a vicious cycle. Often I would experience insomnia, resulting in having to take sick days off from work, and then have to deal with the thought that by not working, I was somehow guilty of being lazy. I also found work spaces challenging and had to do my best to cope.

The way I overcame anxiety was to imagine it as being like a lion in a cage. I had to learn how to tame the lion. For a certain period of time, I did try antidepressants. I was on Cipramil and it managed to remove a lot of anxiety, but I felt as though I couldn't think and concentrate properly. I realized I needed to do something myself about my anxiety levels, and found what was useful was to avoid stressful situations altogether. Once I became an autism advocate I found it easier to deal with anxiety as I knew exactly why I was different to other people. It helped me to come to terms with who I am and find ways of dealing with anxiety. I also developed an interest in deep breathing and meditation, and learnt some deep breathing techniques. Along with deep breathing, exercise has also helped reduce my anxiety. I go to the gym at the university and undertake cardiovascular exercise. I find this helps me to control my breathing flow which is especially important when I find my breathing becoming very shallow due to anxiety. Controlling my breathing helps me to minimize my anxiety.

Within employment and everyday life, I still find dealing with anxiety challenging at times, but I try to look for events and situations which may trigger it. Compared to when I was younger, I have found that I am managing anxiety levels better, but at times, anxiety can become difficult. I rely on my emotional tool kit which Dr. Tony Attwood once described, to use if anxiety levels are hard to manage. As an adult with Asperger's syndrome, I have managed to hold down a job in a university library and start a support group for adults on the Autism Spectrum called "Aspie Support." It is good to be able to give something back to the community and to know that I am helping others at the same time.

Liane Holliday Willey

Anxiety has taken its toll on my body and my mind. Panic attacks have sent me to the emergency room, as I feared they were heart attacks. Doctors remind me that anxiety played a hand in my irritable bowel syndrome, my diverticular disease and the loss of a chunk of colon and my gallbladder. Sleepless nights are my norm as my brain races around my obsessive thinking and my habit of trying to predict my tomorrow. I perseverate over faux pas I've made and I worry whether I've collected enough facts about any issue I have to deal with. My visual thinking brings images to my mind that I really, really need to erase but cannot. By the end of every day, my mind's hard drive is spent and my body is exhausted. But I cannot sleep. It's a twisted circle I'm on, and anxiety shadows my every move.

I regularly forget to pay my anxiety the proper respect it needs, the respect that will get it out of my life. But I'm a work in progress and these are the things I do to remove as much anxiety as I can.

- I do my best to relax. I sit still, breathe slowly and deeply, count each breath until a rhythm flows, and I fill my mind with a soothing picture, which for me is a view of me walking my horse in circles.

- I try to eat nourishing foods, though sugar is hard for me to do without. I try to exercise until my heart rate gets elevated properly and my muscles get used. I also stretch, especially my neck and shoulders, as I know anxiety creates particular tension in those areas.

- I turn to my animals and my favorite interests because they soothe me and remind me I have lots to be happy about and many nice experiences to continue enjoying. I might sit in my horse's stall, pet my dogs or look at photos of architecture. I might read a fantasy novel or watch an old western. The point is, I can put my anxiety on pause when I put myself in a really happy place.

- Finally, I remind myself that no one is perfect, that every soul has a purpose and every human has the right to be happy. I forgive myself for my mistakes and I pledge to enjoy the small things that make me smile, more and more every day.

Jennifer Cook O'Toole

Christmas Eve beats Christmas Day, hands down. Christmas Eve is exciting—sparkling, clear and glittery. Christmas Day, though, is a bit lackluster by comparison. The "merry" is kind of... smudged. No real surprise. Gearing up for something wonderful is often more exciting than the actual event, be it Christmas or birthdays, desserts or first kisses. When what we anticipate is good, the buildup is often more delicious than the thing itself.

On the other hand, when we are anxious or afraid, the longer we have to marinate in our worst-case scenarios, the more awful we feel—and suddenly we've inflated a raindrop-sized problem into a hurricane-sized worry.

Now, to be fair, Aspie anxiety makes sense. It serves a purpose. We are constantly scanning the horizon for problems because we're trying to protect ourselves from the chaos of daily life. Too often, just when we think we have our footing, unseen blunders knock us off of our feet (over and over again). And, logically, we look for something "fixed" to grip onto. We dig in our heels, clutching hold of rigid routines, worn-out relationships and unbending opinions because, amidst the unpredictability, familiar feels safe.

But familiar also keeps us caged in. Instead of seeing a need to adjust, we see a threat; an alternative is a challenge, a gauntlet thrown down rather than a variant possibility. Having been hurt before, we imagine the worst outcome of every bump in the road, venturing endlessly from one "what if" to another.

That, my friends, is our undoing, because life's most magical moments happen outside of our comfort zones. Nothing new happens where we've already been. If you want something you've never had, you have to do something you've never done. I know. In one year, I've gone from stay-at-home mom to world-traveling author. How? By taking a risk. By feeling the fear and doing it anyway. And if I can do it, so can you.

Our routines, our rituals, our "it has to be this way" rules aren't absolutes—they're facades. There is only one constant of which you can be sure: change. Friends move. Breakups happen. Loved ones pass on. And as Will Rogers said, "Even if you're on the right track, you'll get run over if you just sit there."

Like you, I worry every day. Sometimes they're small worries (did I pay that bill?), sometimes big (how will my kids manage after I'm gone?). Often they're irrational worries (I'm sure I'll slip up and this brilliant career will be snatched away in a moment). But grasp tighter onto routines, opinions, plans, and we will, without a doubt, find those fixed circumstances torn or worn away. What then? How do we stay steady on our feet if there's nothing to hold on to?

From one step to the next, our logic isn't always…logical. Consider what could happen instead. Breathe. Ask yourself, "When have I been in a situation like this before? What could I have done differently? How can I use that information now?"

Life's scenes will change. But the imprint of the experiences and patterns we have lived, seen, felt and known—those stay with us. They become a repository for observations, a well of data with which we should compare new situations, people and challenges, and apply the lessons we've learned.

And then remember Christmas Eve. Anticipate. Change will, indeed, happen in every part of your life. So with gratitude rather than fear, learn to appreciate the here and now. You are far too fabulous to be the only thing standing in your way. Move beyond the familiar…and embrace your every unwritten tomorrow.

Richard Maguire

I call anxiety the permanent emotional state for autistic people. A lot has been written about why this is, so I can recommend reading Deborah Lipsky's *From Anxiety to Meltdown*. The causes, effects and what to do about anxiety are explored; I can thoroughly recommend this book.

From my own life experience, I can say that anxiety is my constant companion. Much of my life and strength have been used up on anxiety. I used to worry about this, but strangely, it is *not* worrying about anxiety that has brought my anxiety levels down. I worked this out only a couple of years ago. I no longer seek to be rid of anxiety or to believe I can get to a life of peace and relaxation. That was one of the most helpful realizations in my life.

Instead, I must manage anxiety and seek relaxation where it may be found, when it may be found, and not expect it to be a long-term experience, so I avoid becoming overstressed when anxiety returns.

- I manage anxiety by listening to music. I do my most profound thinking and creativity to music. Music can get me into the right emotional place to overcome anxiety and be creative. I do all my writing to music and I am currently listening to *Lady in Red* by Chris De Burgh. Without music, I would not be able to get my head together enough to write.

- Exercise. I cycle and walk lots. Exercise burns up adrenaline and causes the release of endorphins, serotonin, estrogen, growth factors and dopamine. All of these are good for my body and good medicine. My body will repair itself better, recover better from infection, I will feel better, my head can clear and my intelligence can increase. Anxiety goes down.

- Our family has a dog. Walking him gives exercise. Both we and the dog share in the production of oxytocin, which helps with feeling calm and relating to people. Our dog is a good friend, he takes us as we are, he greets us, we are never lonely and he cares when we are ill. He gives and receives love. That trait is good in every way. Animal therapy can helps lots. If you like animals, check this out.

- I have learned that all bad situations come to an end. I have also learned that I can end bad situations, which is very empowering and liberating. Learning that was a real turning point in my life. I am not a victim of circumstance, instead I am a living, dynamic human who can make choices and influence life. You are too. We make our luck.

- Good times can be maximized and repeated. This takes energy, social skills and an ability to initiate things in life. Learn from a good mentor how to do this.

- Daylight is good. Seek it out, especially if you are in a country that has winters with short days.

- Attend to your sensory needs. This will bring comfort. Get enough sleep.

- Give yourself permission to rest, and practise resting when you feel good so you can do it when you feel overanxious.

Anxiety consumes energy, so the lower it gets, the more energy you will have for life; this in turn reduces anxiety. There is a positive feedback system here that you can construct when reducing anxiety. Take control of this—it is so liberating.

RECOMMENDED READING

Lipsky, D. (2011) *From Anxiety to Meltdown*. London: Jessica Kingsley Publishers.

Anita Lesko

Before learning I had Asperger's, I was puzzled about why I always felt anxious. Even if there was nothing to be anxious about, I'd find something. In my research of Asperger's, I discovered anxiety is an inherent aspect of the syndrome. It is a feeling like an animal in the wild—always on a heightened sense of awareness, looking out for predators.

I can dream up endless things to get anxious about. I wasn't quite so bad in my younger days. Heck, back then I was like Evel Knievel—jumping horses over six-foot-high obstacles and flying in fighter jets! Now I'm afraid of the most mundane things. Go figure. Maybe it's just plain old age. But maybe it's Asperger's. I'm putting my money on the Asperger's.

It is easy to identify this problem but not quite so easy to correct it. First, you need to identify the source. Why is it making you anxious? Then try and rationalize your worries. Dissect each negative anxiety-producing thought. Don't expect to change a lifetime of feeling anxious. Your goal is to lessen the level of anxiety; each little step you make in the positive direction is a big achievement.

Start a journal. Write down what makes you anxious. Sometimes you don't even know what it is. Trust me. I've been there. I still am at times. By putting it on paper you can "see" it better, and that's half the battle.

One thing I've got to say about anxiety. I've always had a sixth sense about certain things. I would have a bad feeling about a particular person. That feeling would come to pass to prove me correct. I have learned never to ignore that internal red flag. If it starts waving, I follow my gut instincts. They have never been wrong. Other Aspies have shared those exact words with me. We can see things others cannot.

Anxiety has controlled my life in so many ways. Driving is one of them. I did learn to drive in high school. It was too overwhelming at that time in my life. Driving a car is massive sensory overload to an Aspie. To other teenagers it is their ticket to freedom. To me, it was a nightmare. I was very happy to be taxied around by my mom. It was a normal way of life for us. It wasn't until I was 40 that I began driving everywhere on my own. I was ready for it then. I advise everyone the same. Don't be afraid to try it again when you are older. Just because you couldn't do it at age 17 doesn't mean you can't at age 40.

Anxiety can plague you in, oh, so many aspects of your life. In the Asperger's support group I organized, I saw it firsthand—people so anxiety-stricken, they simply couldn't function. Even the activities of daily living stressed them. They were simply paralyzed with fear. Seeking out others with whom to discuss your fears will help you begin your journey.

Another key piece of advice is to think positive. Believe in yourself. Don't focus on your shortcomings: focus on your strong points. Neurotypicals have a talent for focusing on your weak points—show them you've got a lot more strong ones! If they close a door on you, go find another one to open. Feeling positive about yourself will decrease your anxiety. If you feel positive, you will believe that you can succeed. If you believe you can succeed, you *will* succeed!

Dr. Know

Aspies can be quite good at many things. One of those things tends to be "worrying." Worrying isn't necessarily bad, as it may well lead you to be better prepared, but it can be detrimental in excess.

Whenever possible, plan and prepare in advance. Avoid being in a rush to leave the house so that you can do things with enough time and mentally register them. You can also prepare a checklist and go through it, so, for example, you will be sure that you *did* leave the door locked, even though you may not remember doing it.

Routines can help. One example is that you can keep all the stuff you ever need when leaving the house in a backpack, purse or jacket pockets, so that you only ever need to check that you have that "container" with you to know that you are good to go. Keep a moderate sum of money there (separate from your wallet) for any emergency.

Having access to your special interests is a good idea. If you like to read, have a book accessible; if you like video games, consider a handheld device. These can be kept in your "container."

Repetitive motions may help you release some stress. Choose something that you are comfortable with (depending on how self-conscious you are doing some of these in public). Tap your feet, fidget with a pen, or get something else to keep your hands occupied (something in your jacket pocket, an anti-stress ball or something similarly squeezable that you can keep handy, perhaps). You can improvise by twirling your hair, stroking your chin, licking or touching your lips (this is usually effective, as it is associated with positive experiences such as eating or kissing).

In some situations, there really is nothing that you can do, so try to convince yourself that it is not productive to keep thinking about it. Even though it is counterintuitive, remember that there are times you are able to come up with a solution when you are not worrying about a problem. So make the effort, try to relax, and give your subconscious a chance to provide a solution.

Many people (Aspie or not) have anxiety about the unknown. A good solution, then, is to make things as known as is feasible:

- Are you anxious about going somewhere and getting lost? Look up directions, have a map or GPS device with you.

- Are you concerned about your health? Find some information and consult the necessary professionals.

- Are you intimidated about talking to someone? Rehearse beforehand, so that you know what you would like to say (try not to overdo the rehearsing, though). You can also try communicating in writing.

- Are you scared about dying? That is one of few certainties of life (maybe the only one), so I recommend appreciating that certainty for what it is, and focus on worrying about living your life instead!

- Are you anxious about the future? There is not much to getting rid of this unknown. You can try planning in the long term, but keep in mind that, for certain things, planning too much in advance is not efficient, because there are way too many uncertainties. Don't forget about the present, because it is in the present that you make your future.

Dr. Tony Attwood's Advice on Overcoming Anxiety

When someone has an Autism Spectrum Disorder (ASD) such as Asperger's syndrome, they will experience far greater anxiety in their daily life than the vast majority of neurotypical people. Anxiety is perhaps the greatest source of stress for those with an ASD and worry can be an almost constant companion, with intermittent episodes of intense fear or panic. This was confirmed in the survey conducted prior to writing this book, with 98 per cent of respondents reporting that anxiety is their primary cause of stress.

We do not know exactly why those with an ASD are more anxious than neurotypicals. Explanations range from the neurology of the brain—for example, we know that those with an ASD are likely to have structural and functional changes to the amygdala (which processes emotions, especially anxiety)—to painful environmental experiences such as sensory sensitivity, as well as high levels of anxiety being created by being the frequent victim of "predators" (especially at school), fear of failure and ridicule, and not knowing what to do in a new or unanticipated situation. There can also be an extraordinary sensitivity to the negative emotional thoughts of others, with intense anxiety in such situations. Being highly anxious most of the time is emotionally and physically exhausting and leads to hyper-alertness, constant vigilance and racing thoughts, difficulty getting enough rest and falling asleep, and stress-related medical conditions.

How can a person with an ASD, living on a planet that creates so much anxiety, cope with feeling almost constantly nervous and fearful? There are many strategies that are known to alleviate anxiety that have been recommended by the authors in this chapter, and there are also some that are effective, but *not* recommended.

Potentially Destructive Strategies

The following are *not* recommended strategies, as they can be destructive for friendships and relationships.

BECOMING A CONTROL FREAK

When one is prone to anxiety, there is a tendency to develop strategies to control everyday experiences that have the potential to trigger greater anxiety, or even panic. Such strategies can include defiantly refusing to engage in a particular activity, or the use of emotional blackmail, such as threats to damage something or hurt someone, in order to escape having to comply with a request or expectation to participate in an activity that has previously been, or is anticipated to be, a cause of intense anxiety. Sometimes psychologists describe these anxiety management strategies as Oppositional Defiant Disorder (ODD) or Pathological Demand Avoidance (PDA). These strategies can be effective in avoiding anxiety for the person with an ASD, but are not appreciated by neurotypicals, who accuse the person with an ASD of being a control freak or a domestic terrorist. Being excessively controlling or threatening will have a detrimental effect on friendships and relationships and can lead to arguments, and punishments from parents and teachers. It is important that the person with an ASD communicates clearly why a particular situation is perceived as creating intense anxiety, and that neurotypicals work collaboratively with the person in using strategies other than avoidance to alleviate anxiety. The person should be encouraged to be brave, and should be supported in any situation associated with anxiety.

DEVELOPING ROUTINES AND RITUALS

Another effective strategy for managing high levels of anxiety that can be of concern is the use of excessive routines and rituals, which reduce anxiety by being soothing and relaxing. It is interesting that the new diagnostic criteria for ASD in the Diagnostic and Statistical Manual of Mental Disorders (DSM-5) (American Psychiatric Association 2013, p.50) includes the diagnostic criterion of inflexible adherence to routines and ritualized patterns of behaviour.

My clinical opinion is that these behaviours are simply means of alleviating chronic high levels of anxiety rather than a distinct and unique diagnostic characteristic of ASD. These strategies may be effective, but the routines and rituals can become excessively prolonged and interfere with being able to engage in other activities. There can also be extreme distress if the routines and rituals are interrupted or prevented. The person with ASD who engages in these behaviours may have few alternative measures to alleviate anxiety and the contributions of the authors of this chapter provide alternative strategies, such that the compulsive and prolonged nature of routines and rituals can be significantly reduced.

An Emotional Explosion

Another strategy that is not recommended is to have a quick, destructive release of anxious energy, to "cleanse the system." Anxiety is a valued emotion for survival. Anxiety alerts the body to potential danger and enables survival by responding with a release of energy for "fight" or "flight." But what should be done with that high level of emotional energy? When the response is fight (as in fighting the tiger that wants to eat you), clearly physically fighting—or arguing—with someone to absorb the energy is not a wise action for obvious reasons; high levels of anxiety release high levels of energy and strength, and unfortunately the cognitive control of actions (thinking before responding) seems to be switched off when experiencing such intense anxiety. If there is an irresistible urge to have an emotional explosion, the emotional energy may be released in a "controlled explosion" by "creative destruction," for example, crushing the contents of a recycling garbage container, such as cans or cardboard packaging.

Misuse of Alcohol and Drugs

At low levels of consumption, alcohol is a relaxant and is a tempting means of dissolving anxiety. However, consumption of alcohol below a permitted age is illegal. This is for sound reasons. Alcohol not only acts as a poison that temporarily affects brain functioning, but also as a disruption and inhibition to brain development during adolescence and the early adult years.

Alcohol impairs thinking, reasoning and judgement, hence laws that prohibit driving when under the influence of alcohol. People who are intoxicated are not smart, and those with an ASD need all their intellectual abilities at their peak to process social situations and cope with so many aspects of life. In the long term, excessive consumption of alcohol can cause a clinical depression and affect friendships, relationships and employment.

Marijuana can alleviate anxiety and create a feeling of isolation from the social world. It is a very tempting option for those with high levels of anxiety, such as young adults with an ASD. However, it is illegal in most states and countries, potentially addictive, and reduces motivation and intellectual capacity. For these reasons it is not recommended as a strategy to alleviate anxiety.

If drugs are to be used to manage anxiety, there are prescription medications that are effective, so long as they are used as prescribed. Those with an ASD are not unique in having high levels of anxiety and we now have a range of medications that have proved successful for both neurotypicals and those with an ASD. However, it is interesting to note that the authors of this chapter have successfully managed anxiety without recourse to medication.

Constructive Strategies

The Aspie mentors have provided wise advice on how to cope with, alleviate and manage anxiety. The strategies can be divided into specific groups that provide a range of anxiety repair mechanisms.

PHYSICAL ACTIVITY

Several mentors have stressed the value of regular exercise in reducing anxiety. It is a way of releasing emotional energy and clarifying thinking. Sometimes, being clumsy in sporting activities during the school years and being teased by peers regarding physical abilities and dexterity can lead to the belief that physical activity is to be avoided. However, we know that physical activity can be more effective than medication and even psychotherapy in alleviating anxiety. It may help to consult a personal trainer who can assess your body type and personality to determine what physical activity would be most effective. This does not have to be team sports, and can include solitary sports such as cycling, swimming, horse riding or going to a fitness centre. Regular exercise is excellent for mental and physical health and I know of several famous sports personalities who have Asperger's syndrome. Their Asperger qualities of perfectionism and determination have contributed to national and international success.

Relaxation

Anxiety results in tension, which can be relieved by relaxation activities, particularly meditation. In Western cultures, there is a growing awareness and appreciation of the value of activities such as yoga in encouraging a general sense of well-being and providing an antidote to anxiety. Low levels of relaxation can be achieved by being comfortable and engrossed in listening to music that is calming and relaxing, while deeper levels of relaxation can be achieved using the many different meditation techniques. Many clinical psychologists are now using meditation in their range of psychological treatments for anxiety.

Another relaxant for those with an ASD is solitude, in the sense of being alone, rather than lonely. Actually being away from people and some sensory experiences can be a means of reducing anxiety, but how easy is it to ever be alone at high school? It may be possible for a student with an ASD to talk to a teacher about being able to retreat to a safe, secluded sanctuary at school during break times or recess. Solitude can be emotionally refreshing and a means of true and deep relaxation.

A further source of relaxation can come from being in nature, walking or camping in a natural environment, with few social encounters and only natural sensory experiences. It can also be relaxing to engage in activities that enable one to appreciate the patterns and symmetry in mathematics or architecture, or immerse oneself in repetitive, soothing and creative pursuits such as knitting, embroidery, carpentry or the repair of watches and machinery.

Special Interests

There are many reasons why someone with an ASD might have a special interest, but one of the reasons is that time engaged in the interest may act as a "thought blocker" to anxious thoughts. Being so engrossed and hyper-focused on an activity creates a barrier to anxiety and provides time devoid of anxiety. Being engaged in the special interest can actually be a time of intense enjoyment and achievement. However, there needs to be an awareness that the engagement in and enjoyment of the interest can be almost addictive, in addition to which neurotypicals may not understand how valuable the special interest has become in preserving your mental health.

Sometimes, the origin of a special interest is as an attempt to overcome fear by acquiring knowledge; for example, fear of the sound of thunder may lead to a special interest in weather systems. The special interest can also be a means of escape from everyday worries. The person can create and enjoy living in the relatively safe imaginary world of fiction or internet games in which they are valued, socially successful and free from anxiety. This is a useful strategy, but needs to be one of many, so that the activity does not become irresistible and compulsive. Unfortunately, if the special interest has become the primary means of effectively alleviating anxiety, any thwarting of access to it will result in severe agitation.

There is another aspect to special interests relevant to emotion, and especially anxiety management and depression. Having high levels of anxiety is mentally and physically exhausting, which in the long term can contribute to feelings of being emotionally drained. Time engaged in the special interest, therefore, can be re-energizing time.

Neurotypicals may not always appreciate the many valuable aspects of the special interest for someone with an ASD, and it may be useful for this section of the book to be shared with parents or family members. They may then perceive the time engaged in the interest with more tolerance and understanding. However, it is important to have a compromise, such that the interest does not take up an excessive amount of time, or prevent you from engaging in some family activities.

Being with Animals or a Favourite Person

There are social strategies that can reduce anxiety, for example, spending time with adoring pets who make you feel safe, or being with someone who seems just like a sponge that soaks up your worries. On your mobile or cell phone you can have pictures of pets or significant calming and accepting people. An audio recording of a supportive friend saying positive and reassuring comments can help during anxious moments.

If you have difficulty expressing your anxiety to a friend or family member in a face-to-face conversation, you could perhaps send that person an email or text, as you may have a greater eloquence in describing and disclosing inner thoughts and feelings by typing rather than talking.

DIET AND NUTRITION

Several mentors have stressed the importance of having a good diet and nutritious food as a means of reducing a propensity for anxiety. While junk food may be tasty and easy to acquire and eat, and even provide some comfort in the short term, the problems outweigh the benefits. Not only does excessive consumption of fats and refined sugars lead to weight gain, it also has a role to play in increasing anxiety. On the other hand, a diet rich in whole foods, fruit, vegetables, nuts, complex carbohydrates and lean protein appears to have a beneficial effect on both sleep and mood. There is no doubt that healthy food does contribute to a healthy mind.

SLEEP

Sleep has many functions, one of which is to refresh mind and body. People who have an ASD are notorious for having a poor sleep pattern and not enough sleep. The sleep cycle associated with ASD can be unusual, for example, taking some time to actually fall asleep (especially if worried about events during the day or anticipated tomorrow), and a tendency for there to be a disturbance of the depth and quality of sleep subsequently. While attention to diet, and medications such as Melatonin, can help establish a reasonable sleep cycle, if problems persist, I recommend a referral to a sleep clinic at a local hospital to explore how your sleep could be improved. Having restful and deep sleep can lead to an improvement in the ability to manage emotions such as anxiety.

MATURITY

As you mature, you will have increasing ability to put an event into perspective, so as not to "catastrophize." You will become better able to cope with, and tolerate, situations associated with anxiety that previously would have been avidly avoided, or accepted very reluctantly and endured with great difficulty. With increasing maturity, there is a greater appreciation of your inner strengths and abilities, which renders you less vulnerable to anxiety. The mentors have not removed anxiety from their lives, but they have learned many strategies to cope with it and to prevent its extremes. The "power" in the maturing intellect means that instead of anxiety controlling you, you control anxiety.

REFERENCE

American Psychiatric Association (APA) (2013) *Diagnostic and Statistical Manual of Mental Disorders, 5th Edition*. Washington, DC: American Psychiatric Association.

Artwork (See Plate 1)

Painting: Anxieties

Artist: Charlotte Poe

Artist's Commentary: Anxiety is every word your brain whispers to you as it convinces you not to leave the house, not to talk to a friend, not to get up in the morning. Anxiety is the black cloud over your head that fills your head like a storm and doesn't leave room for you to think or breathe. Anxiety is the worst part of you, and that's the hardest part, that it's you and the battle is within yourself. It is all-encompassing and determined to make your world as small as possible until it has shrunk down and you're alone, helpless and completely without.

Painting: Paralyzed by the Fear

Artist: Michael Tolleson

Artist's Commentary: There is the hot burning feeling of anxiety swirling around her head and body. Her face is half hidden in the darkness and her body is curled to protect herself from everything that is attacking her. Her upper torso is laid bare, vulnerable to what may come. Her covered and clothed body appears to have turned to stone.

CHAPTER 2

Overcoming Poor Self-Esteem

Stress Ranking: 2

Ranking of issue by stress caused

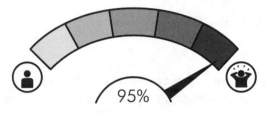

95%

Percent of respondents living with issue

80%

People with Asperger's/HFA may have issues with their self-esteem and self-identity. Some examples of self-esteem/self-identity issues include: not knowing and/or liking who you are, believing the criticism of peers, feeling "I'm different/not normal, so I'm defective," feeling like you don't fit in, feeling like being "different" is bad or unworthy, feeling like you're really from "another planet," and focusing on your own personal mistakes (perfectionism)—which may also make you feel stupid. Do you have concerns about your self-esteem and self-identity?

Alexis Wineman

Growing up at times was hard for me. I looked at myself as nothing more than a burden to my family and I never understood why. I never really spoke to anyone outside my family unless I had to and rarely played with other children. I was afraid to be myself because I thought I wasn't good enough. I always tried to go unnoticed so I could avoid those judging eyes of my peers. In class, I often "flew below the radar" of my teachers to avoid being called upon. The shadows were where I belonged and no matter how much I would reach out to the light, my hand would always get smacked away, telling me that I was only allowed to be invisible. So that's what I did. I would always look out and see my classmates playing with friends, having fun, while I walked aimlessly by myself. I remained a nobody until high school.

Even after my diagnosis nothing changed, not until I realized that being different isn't something to hide. I came out of the shadows, but very slowly, and for once no one pushed me back. I stretched my legs and I started to run. I wanted to make up for all the time I had lost, but I also did not want to be crushed. I got involved in after school programs, like cross-country, speech and drama, cheerleading, student council, art club, and so much more! Some of these efforts were more successful than others, I might say, but I learned from all of them. I was able to show off who I was, instead of hiding it like I had in the past.

Being true to myself was the greatest thing I could have ever done. I guess what I'm trying to say is, like what you choose to like, do what you want to do, and accept everyone for who they are, because once you accept them, the more likely it will be that they will accept you.

The most important lesson is that you first have to accept yourself. The moment I did accept who I was, warts and all, people realized that maybe I was strange, but I was also a lot of fun. I started making friends and they began to accept me for who I was, even if they did not really understand why I was that way. By the time I graduated from high school, I not only had accepted who I was, I was also proud of who I was and what I had accomplished. This was something I never thought would be attainable.

Liane Holliday Willey

Oftentimes I feel distraught and ashamed when I think about the big and small mistakes I've made while simply trying to live my life in a productive and decent manner. I'm especially upset when I think what I've done has hurt or embarrassed someone I care about. I'm angry when I realize I've done something to cause my bank account to lose money. And I'm never thrilled to realize I probably looked like a fool or nasty person to whomever I was involved with when I didn't behave in a way that made good sense to my situation. Then I get angry realizing if society would just be more tolerant and caring toward people with differences, invisible differences included, I wouldn't feel the need to beat myself up for being odd, for being me! I've had more than my share of bangs and bruises given to me by people and situations that seem to live to prey upon innocent people, like those of us who have Asperger's syndrome. I had a person who I thought was my very best friend virtually ruin my reputation and my place of business by telling all our clients I was crazy and convincing them to leave and take their business with her to a competitor. If that weren't enough, this so-called best friend then broke our business agreement and claimed bankruptcy, leaving me with an extremely large bank note, one it will take me decades to pay off.

My father used to ask me when I was going to learn no one could be trusted, and while I have spent my entire life believing there are plenty of people to trust, I've come to the point where "plenty" must be changed to "few." In order to save my self-esteem and self-worth, I have had to surround myself with a very small group of people and pets that will give me the respect and understanding I need. Before I trust anyone or accept any invitation to any place, I give myself a week to vet that person or experience to do what I can to be certain I'm not about to engage with something dangerous. I now know it isn't I who is the mean, bad, evil, predator. I'm the goofy, often misguided, often clueless, typically uncoordinated, accidentally rude and obnoxious Aspie. True. But I'm not part of the human machine that consciously does harm to others. Therefore, I remind myself, I am not the bad guy in this story. I'm not saying I'm the consummate victim, but I'm certainly not the bad guy. I'm just me doing the best I can to help others, live honestly and create a legacy with which I will resonate proudly.

Lisa Morgan

I'd like to address the self-esteem/self-identity issue. Throughout my whole life, I've been able to "see" problems in such a way that creative solutions come easy to me. There have been many, many times I have not shared my ideas because I felt like no one wanted to listen to me, or others would think my idea was stupid, or because no one expected me to be able to contribute anything to solving problems. This negativity was a direct result of being teased unmercifully in grade school because the other students just didn't understand my way of thinking.

I have sat in countless meetings, classrooms, living rooms, and so on, not saying a word, only to have someone else eventually come up with the exact idea (or a very similar idea) that I secretly had, which everyone then loves and adopts as the solution. Or, I will mention my idea to a person near me, who will like it and share it with the group, but never give me credit as having come up with the idea in the first place.

However, what I have come to recognize over the years is that my ideas are great! They are creative and wonderful. I have learned to trust my judgment, to accept that I do think creatively, and be brave enough to share my ideas. When I help solve problems in ways no one else thinks of, it helps to give me the credibility with my peers that I crave.

Over time, my peers learn I am a creative thinker who can help to problem solve. I have learned to take the risk to speak up and share my thoughts, to accept the possibility that others in the group might fine-tune my ideas to optimize them for the greatest potential, and even to accept that my ideas may be turned down for better ones.

When my ideas are accepted, appreciated and implemented, my self-esteem gets a bit higher, problems are solved, and my peers get to know me a little bit more.

Anita Lesko

I shall dare to say that everyone with Asperger's has had feelings of low self-esteem at some point in their life, if not most of their life. It doesn't take a rocket scientist to figure out why. Because we are different, we get bullied, harassed, treated differently, ostracized, shunned… It all adds up to a person having low self-esteem.

Being the "take the bull by the horns" person that I am, I've taken this one by the horns long ago, and put a new twist on it. Think back to all those individuals who have bullied you, shunned you, treated you like a second-class citizen—yes, all those people. Now just stop and look at the whole picture: who *really* is the lesser person? You, the victim? Or the predator? The predator is the bad guy, certainly not you. Why, then, should you feel badly about yourself? You shouldn't. Ask yourself: would you do mean things to another person who has done no harm to you, just because they're different? I'm betting your answer is "No!"

I am urging all Aspies out there, and anyone else who's different for whatever reason, to stop having low self-esteem, and start appreciating yourself. You have the right to feel good about yourself just like everyone else does. Even more so, because you're the one riding high on a white horse, being the good guy. Those bullies are the bad guys on the black horses. Just like in the movies!

While I was talking to Temple Grandin one day, she stated that she lives her life by "Roy Rogers' Rules for Living." Immediately after the conversation, I flicked on my computer and Googled the rules. Here they are:

1. Be neat and clean.

2. Be courteous and polite.

3. Always obey your parents.

4. Protect the weak and help them.

5. Be brave but never take chances.

6. Study hard and learn all you can.

7. Be kind to animals and take care of them.

8. Eat all your food and never waste any.

9. Love God.

10. Always respect our flag and our country.

All these years, I have been abiding by Roy Rogers' Rules and didn't even know it. Temple said she figured people would think she's an "old fogy" for talking about Roy Rogers and his rules. The reality is, if people chose to even consider these rules, this world would be a much nicer place to live in. However, we all know that sometimes there are exceptions (e.g. maybe your parents weren't the best role models, or eating all your food wasn't physically possible). Just know that a person who lives by fair values is a good, kind-hearted soul who can feel proud of who they are and what they stand for.

The bullies of the world, and those who have abused us, harassed us and shunned us *do not* fit into the above category. *They* are the ones who should have the low self-esteem, for *they* are lesser people, the ill-bred ones, the ones who should be ashamed of themselves and hang their heads low. *They* are the ones with the mental problem, that they have a need to put down another person to make themselves feel good.

My Aspie friends, hold your heads up high, feel proud of who you are, and stop letting these lesser people affect you. Feel in your heart, in your soul, that *you* are superior to those people, because you are.

The next time someone does something nasty to you, just look at him or her, smile to yourself, and think just how pathetic that person truly is. Never allow anyone to drag you down to his or her low level. Always stay high on your white horse!

Happy trails!

Mary Robison

I have mild prosopagnosia as a part of my ASD, so I often do not recognize people. Yet, my parents expected me to know the difference, not just between my siblings, but also between adults that I did not see daily. It was (and continues to be) impossible! I felt defective and retreated into severe shyness as a way of not having to deal with those whom I didn't recognize. I was terrified much of the time as I never knew who people were. I rarely smiled at anyone. I didn't know that people smiled for reasons other than happiness. In my late teens, I saw that shyness was no longer a viable coping mechanism—I was passed over for recognition of my accomplishments and others took credit for what I did. I decided that I couldn't be scared and shy any longer.

I decided that dealing with other people had been difficult but was now going to be terrific. I convinced myself of this as an ASD special interest. I pretended that I recognized everyone. But I needed to find a way to show people that I was glad to see them, as I couldn't greet them by name if I didn't really recognize them. I practiced in a mirror to find an expression that looked cheerful—I found an open smile that included my whole face, not just the baring of teeth. I then practiced it as my default expression until my cheeks, eyes and forehead muscles hurt! Then, I practiced it some more. I started to use it in public.

Much to my surprise, when I smiled at other people, they smiled back at me. I was no longer invisible (or worse, considered to be stuck up—something that I never knew until someone told me that that had been their earlier impression). People talked to me spontaneously. They asked me for directions and for my opinions. I had also practiced talking to a tape recorder as a child; I decided that I was like a reporter for these strangers. Gradually,

I got more and more confident in responding in public venues. And I had things to say.

Better still, I found that smiling with my whole face actually changed my mood. And when other people smiled at me, it changed my emotions. I felt better—not depressed. As my confidence grew from my ability to convey information to strangers, I started to speak first, to both friends and total strangers. Of course, there were occasional problems; when walking down the sidewalk, smiling, while visiting New York City, I was accosted by a dirty old man who was looking for things that I wasn't offering. My visible recoil made him retreat in confusion. I decided that one jerk wasn't going to affect how I interacted with everyone else. I liked having people smile at me. Getting those smiles made me feel like I was worthy of them—that I was *not* the freak I'd always thought I was, deep down inside. There is research indicating that the act of smiling with a full face (not just with the mouth) releases endorphins that really do make you feel better.

Smiling has other positive effects, too. There is additional research that indicates that other people are more likely to respond to you positively when you smile—and that is my point. If there is something that you can learn, that will make other people less likely to take offense at your ASD idiosyncrasies, you should learn it! All it takes is practice. As Aspies, we spend thousands of hours becoming highly proficient in our special interests; learning to smile convincingly is something that takes far less time, yet makes your life a lot easier. Smile! Aliens from another planet do not smile; humans do, and humans respond positively to those who smile at them. It really will make you feel better about yourself.

Richard Maguire

Ugh! Growing up with undiagnosed autism was horrid most of the time. My life was a matter of missed opportunities, social disasters and misunderstandings; being told I was lazy/stupid/slow/silly/difficult and worse. People wanted to know what was wrong with me. I wanted to know too—I felt like I was going mad. There was no other explanation available.

Is this your experience too? What is your self-image? Is it based on people's criticisms of you? Is it based on beating yourself up and being convinced you can't do right for doing wrong? This was my life until the last decade, when things made sense and I began reloading with a new self-understanding and esteem.

When I was in junior school I wrote a piece about what I would like to be when I grow up. I said I wanted to be an eccentric. My teacher and parents took note of this. Now I know that was the most authentic expression of ambition I ever made. I knew I was different and I was trying to find an expression of this and a place in life where I could be different, happy and have friends.

It takes us a long time to tie together all the things that we are, and then to be able to link them to ourselves and have a self-image leading on to self-esteem. For so much of our lives we are judged as wanting because we did not meet developmental targets or act normal. I reckon the most fun thing about being autistic is having fun with being different, being so obviously a mark one original. Everyone is unique, and we have an ability to show this in the raw through our autism from birth onwards.

What is needed is an exploration of who we are in a way we can make sense of. We need to build up a new understanding of who we are based on the normal autistic ways of developing and living. Autism is a natural occurrence, and our job is to feel and know this in spite of what we are told by our educators, families, peers and medical people. To do this can require all of our autistic determination and focus.

It is helpful to get positive feedback and spend time with people who like us for who we are in order to get a picture of who we are and how we operate. It is said that autism is like having a different operating system from other people. I think that is a good way of seeing ourselves and how we operate. Most people are Windows PCs, the arty people are Macs, and we run on Linux. We will need programs to help us interact with the majority of Windows people. And at our heart is a different, not inferior, operating system.

Our coding is written differently and works just fine if we can get a handle on it, and understand and feel good about this. I have mentored many autistic people who love knowing how they operate—that they are normal in the world of autism. That is such a relief and a basis for building a self-image, identity and self-esteem that makes sense and values them for who they are.

Eventually it becomes good to be different and to complement the normality we live next to. When we get to this point, people will relax with us, and life gets better.

After 46 years of learning, I am an eccentric now and loving it. Go on! Try it! You will love the person you are, then other people will, too.

Larry Moody
BECOMING ONE WITH ASPERGER'S

Asperger's syndrome is my friend, not my enemy. As it turns out, I succeeded in this world not in spite of my Asperger's, but because of my Asperger's. The Universe, God, our Creator, or whatever term you prefer to use, doesn't create trash. When one side of life's balance scale tips downward, the other side tips upward. When we are presented with life's challenges, we are also presented with opportunities. My life has, in some respects, been very difficult, and in other respects, very easy. It's a reflection of my "splinter skills," or being exceptionally good at some things and equally poor at others. And all for reasons different than I thought for most of my life. Legally blind in one eye since birth, and with tinnitus and partial hearing loss from working around very large engines before the Occupational Safety and Health Administration (OSHA) required hearing protection for my job, I created plenty of excuses for my problems.

I lived most of my life feeling like I was always struggling on the fringe of society, never quite fitting in, and never quite understanding why I didn't. I was shy. I was gifted. I was a slow learner. I was brilliant. I was irritating. I was odd. I was creative. I was a loner, a misfit. What I really was—an Aspie—went undiagnosed.

At age 53, after repeated failures at conventional marriage counseling (which is generally counter-productive for those of us with an ASD), a third and very perceptive psychologist recognized that there was something organically wrong with me and we set out to discover what it was. Through a series of referrals and testing, they initially determined that I have ADHD (attention deficit hyperactivity disorder) (inattentive subtype) and a weighted Wechsler Adult Intelligence Score IQ in the 99th percentile. I went through a series of drug trials and found one that noticeably helped me focus. But over time, it became apparent that I wasn't making the progress expected in dealing with my ADHD—that something else was going on with me. About a year or so after my ADHD diagnosis, more and deeper questioning uncovered my Asperger's syndrome. Additional testing also uncovered an extraordinarily good long-term memory, and an extraordinarily poor short-term memory. I have very limited ability to appropriately interpret facial expressions. It also appears that I may be what is called a "visual-spatial-mechanical savant" (which could also explain why I succeeded as an engineer). I have auditory distortion issues, and an unusual sensitivity to flickering lights. I am a virtual poster child of splinter skills.

Even with my learning difficulties obvious early in life, my parents instilled in me a belief that I could learn to do anything I set my mind to do, as long as I was persistent and didn't give up. "If at first you don't succeed, try, try again." I've had many opportunities to quit trying. Sometimes I did give up, but not for long, and never forever. It took me 11 years to earn my Bachelor of Science degree in engineering. I gave up and dropped out of college twice, briefly. I flunked one of my required math courses *four times*, getting a passing grade on my fifth try. That's persistence! Persistence has served me well.

One of the, if not the, most pivotal events in my life was my decision to study the martial arts. Having been pervasively bullied for most of my life, I decided at the ripe old age of 22 that I wanted to be able to beat the sh*t out of the next bully that tried to pound on me. Yes, I know, that's the *wrong* reason, but that was my reason. That was in 1972, 12 years before the *Karate Kid* movie came out. The instructor I found (O'Sensei Ngo Dong, Cuong Nhu Oriental Martial Arts) became in effect my "Mr. Miyagi," who focused as much attention on teaching ethics as on technique, and he also became a lifelong friend. Along the way, I learned self-respect and self-control and gained a great deal of self-esteem. Something in my "aura," my "self," changed at that time and the bullies of the world no longer perceive me as a target.

Since shortly after beginning my study of the martial arts, I have never again been physically attacked. However, I have encountered my share of psychological bullies in the business world, and the self-confidence I gained from my martial arts studies has been invaluable while standing up to them. Just learning how to fall to the ground has protected my clumsy self from serious injury on many occasions.

I now have a fresh perspective on my world. I determine my destiny! I create my reality. Some would say that I was given a lemon of a life because of my AS. If that is so, then through my struggles I've learned how to make lemonade! And my lemonade turned out to be quite exceptionally good.

John Makin

In several ways this was always a problem for me, yet in other ways I was blessed by circumstances that enabled me to be myself.

I grew up in a small market town in the English Midlands. The town was so small; everyone knew that my father was a dentist. This placed me in a different social class to most of my peers, yet at the same time, both he and my mother were from the lower working class. So we did not mix socially with the professionals' families or with those from our family's roots.

At the grammar school (11–18, academic streaming) I didn't fit in any social group and, being a single sex school, I had no contact at all with girls. Add to this mixture the fact that I have Asperger's, and one may imagine how isolated I was and how hard it could have been to forge an identity. Not being accepted within any social grouping, I had to choose what sort of attributes would define me. Hanging about on the fringes of other groups, craving some scrapings of acceptance was not something I could do.

So I became "my own man"; I rejected the peer values that seem to be common amongst teenagers. I didn't listen to pop music, I chose folk or classical; I didn't smoke, nor chase girls (which was very easy, as my circumstances were such that I never met any); I didn't follow the current fashion trends but dressed in a rather conservative fashion; I was courteous and polite to my elders; I diligently followed school rules. I was a moral, well-behaved, polite young man. This also meant that I was never much of a target for bullying, since I did not seek peer approval.

We are not like other people.

So what are we like? How do we fit into the world around us? For, in the end, that is what self-identity is all about. Let me say that I do not hold with seeing ourselves, "Aspies," as some separate part of society. Society is made up of all sorts, different shapes, sizes, colors, sexes, races, religions and abilities; and we are a part of that mix: a part *of* and not apart *from* it.

You have your own story to tell, your own truth that you must accept and make your own. You are not less than anyone. You are not deficient in some way. You are complete in your own way.

Be proud of who and what you are, not apologetic for who and what you are not. Nor should you feel a failure because you need help in some areas. Everyone needs help at some time in life, even if it is just someone to talk to.

In summary, do not be defined by your autism/Asperger's, it is but a part of who you are. Be yourself, you are unique with your own skills, interests and abilities. If you are a square peg, there is no advantage in looking for a round hole!

Dr. Tony Attwood's Advice on Overcoming Poor Self-Esteem

Sometimes journalists will write an article on ASD and refer to "those who suffer from autism and Asperger's syndrome." This statement causes me to become very annoyed, as I feel there is both a misunderstanding and a misinterpretation on the part of the writer. You do not "suffer" from Asperger's syndrome in the sense of it being a recognized medical cause of acute or chronic physical pain and discomfort, which is usually the implication in these articles. However, there is a degree of suffering for those who have Asperger's syndrome, and that is from low self-esteem. The primary causes for low self-esteem are rejection, being ridiculed and tormented by peers, and a belief that being different means being defective. This can lead to feelings of depression, irritability and an active avoidance of social interactions. The problem is not Asperger's syndrome itself, but the attitude of others towards someone who is different, and the compensation and adjustment strategies the person has to make to feelings of low self-worth and lack of self-acceptance.

Peer Rejection

During adolescence, a teenager's peer group has an extremely powerful effect on self-esteem. A compliment from a parent may be worth one point towards happiness and self-acceptance, but a compliment from a peer is worth one hundred points. Unfortunately, teenagers who have Asperger's syndrome are rarely complimented by peers and actually experience daily rejection and many derogatory comments. Those comments, such as being a loser, weird or stupid, can become the foundation for low self-esteem in adolescence and a gradual belief that these characteristics must be true. This is especially so when you do not have a friend to contradict the comments, and they are repeated so often and by so many people. No wonder that the vast majority of those who have an ASD have low-self-esteem.

Coping Strategies

The authors of this chapter have described coping and adjustment strategies they originally used that are understandable, but that they eventually recognized as not conducive to improving self-esteem. They subsequently acquired strategies that are much more constructive and successful. You have a choice.

BECOME A RECLUSE

One strategy is to avoid the toxic effects of rejection and ridicule by becoming a recluse, at school and at home. The coping mechanism is to retreat into isolation, feeling depressed, lacking respect and feeling you are of no value to peers. You simply provide them with someone to tease and feel superior to. It is understandably psychologically safer to become "invisible" and to try to blend into the background at school, suffering in inconspicuous silence, and retreating to a bedroom, a safe, high tower in the secure castle that is home.

Escape into Imagination or a Special Interest

Another strategy is to escape into imagination, a fantasy world where you do have value, respect and control, and thus high self-esteem. This can be by reading, and especially writing, fiction, where you imagine you are a hero (such as Harry Potter or Dr Who) who is brave in conquering adversity and is eventually valued by peers. Alternatively, you may spend time engaged in a special interest as a thought blocker to prevent negative self-thoughts and to avoid mentally replaying the derogatory comments of peers that echo in your mind.

Learn to Imitate

One way of coping with low self-esteem is to artificially become a person that would be included and accepted by peers. This is achieved by avidly observing and learning to imitate others, that is, to act an alternative persona in social situations and create a mask or false self. This may succeed temporarily, but the intellectual and emotional exhaustion from "faking it till you make it" can be enormous. Adding to the exhaustion may be the belief that your true self must always be hidden from others.

Arrogance

For some adolescents and adults with an ASD, if there is no self-affirmation from peers, a coping strategy that is self-soothing and boosts self-esteem is to become arrogant and develop a feeling of superiority to others. Unfortunately, when this strategy is taken to an extreme, there is a risk of being diagnosed with the characteristics of Narcissistic Personality Disorder, only adding to existing complications. The arrogance is a form of over-compensation, which in the end alienates family members and potential friends.

Accept that Different is Not Defective

Thus, the strategies of isolation and depression, escape into imagination, imitation and arrogance can be effective coping mechanisms to feeling and being perceived as different, defective and rejected. However, different is *not* defective. The authors in this chapter have been adamant that higher self-esteem can be achieved by alternative, more constructive strategies.

A central element of a more constructive approach is to be true to your real self. It is to accept being different and to focus on appreciating qualities in personality and abilities rather than difficulties and derogatory comments from peers. This requires a major paradigm shift.

There is an activity that can help you focus on your qualities. Start by creating two lists, one headed "Qualities in personality," the other "Qualities in abilities." Think of those aspects of yourself that you are proud of, have received compliments for, or you know are valued by others. You may have personality characteristics such as being kind, having a strong sense of social justice or being a loyal friend. Your abilities list could include having a great memory for facts and information, a sensitive sensory system, or being talented in mathematical abilities, information technology, creative writing or singing. The next stage is to ask family members and friends for additional qualities you could add to the list; then create a file on your computer with a separate page for each quality. The file can then be used as a diary to regularly record instances where you demonstrate each quality. You will then be able to read and be comforted and reassured by examples and illustrations of your unique qualities. Over time, new qualities and achievements will be identified, many of which will be due to the characteristics of ASD. This file becomes a visual, tangible and evolving and expanding record of qualities in personality and abilities that creates a strong and accurate self-esteem. This will also create greater resilience to the torments of peers and act as an antidote to low self-esteem and feelings of self-loathing and depression.

Find Others with Similar Interests

There are other ways to boost self-esteem. One is to find a like-minded peer group, some of whom may well have similar characteristics and experiences as yourself. For example, you could join a hobby or interest group: some examples might be a highly specialized group, such as young adults who appreciate Japanese manga and anime; or a group that works together to design computer games; or a music ensemble or choir. This can be a relatively safer environment where your qualities are recognized and appreciated, thereby boosting self-esteem.

Nature and Animals

Another strategy is to spend time in nature or with animals. Pets are great for improving self-esteem in terms of being pleased to see you and needing you. You can also talk to them about your problems and they have amazing non-judgmental listening skills and accept and value you for who you are.

The Impact of ASD on Self-Reflection

Adolescence, for all teenagers, is a time of considerable introspection, determining who you are, and who you want to be as an adult, and also a time of deep self-reflection on aspects of one's character and feelings. Those who have an ASD have considerable difficulty with introspection and self-reflection for several reasons. Research suggests a genuine difficulty conceptualizing one's thoughts as a part of impaired Theory of Mind abilities, and clinical experience suggests a limited vocabulary to accurately express emotions and describe personality characteristics. Someone may ask the person with an ASD, "What are you thinking and feeling now?" and the reply may be, "I don't know." This is not being obtuse. The full answer could be, "I don't have the ability to conceptualize my thoughts and feelings in a coherent way that you would understand, and I do not have the words and language to precisely express my thoughts and emotions."

In my own clinical practice, I focus on developing an adolescent's self-reflection and disclosure of inner thoughts and feelings, sometimes by typing rather than talking; and developing a vocabulary to precisely describe different emotions, as well as the depth or intensity of emotion using a scale or "thermometer" from zero to ten. There are also activities that can be used to increase the vocabulary of words that describe specific personality characteristics. An adult with an ASD said, "I need a language to describe myself." The self can also be expressed in art—for example, creating a collage to describe aspects of self and inner thoughts and feelings; in music, in lyrics or composition, to express emotions; and in writing poetry or short stories to express inner thoughts and experiences.

In psychological terms, there can be a fragmented self, a form of identity failure and a genuine difficulty describing the psychological self in conversational speech. For those with an

ASD, descriptions of self can be in terms of actions (what I do) and accomplishments (what I achieve), rather than a social network (defining self by friends and social circle), belief systems (such as religious or political beliefs), or a personal philosophy (such as "I like to..." or "life is..."). Some adults with an ASD can actually be overly self-reflective and dwell excessively and pessimistically on their inner thoughts and feelings. There may need to be guidance from a psychologist or counselor on constructive means of self-evaluation and acquiring realistic and positive self-reflection and self-esteem. This is particularly important when the person may have been psychologically traumatized by bullying and teasing and internalized and believed the torments and accusations.

The Value of Being Different

Society clearly needs people who have an ASD such as Asperger's syndrome, and some of the greatest advances in the sciences and arts have been achieved by those who have the characteristics of an ASD. I recommend reading some of the books published by Jessica Kingsley Publishers that have explored creativity and achievement and ASD (Fitzgerald 2005; James 2006). Reading about "Aspie" achievers is an antidote to believing that those who have Asperger's syndrome are losers. Indeed, the next stage of human evolution may be Asperger's syndrome.

I have been a great fan of Brian Wilson, the founder member of the Beach Boys. He wrote a song entitled *Heroes and Villains*. Those with an ASD may feel they are villains, but actually they are heroes. You are not mad, bad or defective, just different. You have much to be proud of. Gradually build your self-confidence and self-belief and know that ASD is only a small part of who you are. It is important to accept and love who you are. ASD gives you qualities as well as difficulties: learn to admire those qualities, accept yourself for who you really are, and be a first rate Aspie, not a second rate neurotypical.

RECOMMENDED READING

Fitzgerald, M. (2005) *The Genesis of Artistic Creativity: Asperger's Syndrome and the Arts*. London: Jessica Kingsley Publishers.

James, I. (2006) *Asperger's Syndrome and High Achievement: Some Very Remarkable People*. London: Jessica Kingsley Publishers.

Artwork (See Plate 2)

Painting: Mirror Image 2

Artist: Kimberly Gerry Tucker

Artist's Commentary: Because I'm soft spoken, I get overlooked. Words come late or not at all; so many thoughts, ideas and opinions go unexpressed. That's a vulnerable, frustrating, sensation, especially when it's a lifelong thing. As a result, I have visited ugly screaming, "bang-your-head" places. Unexpressed wants build up and unexpressed words are fractured unspoken pieces in me. Even though my spoken words are sometimes nonexistent, and my expressions do not portray my emotional state in a meaningful "real-world" way, I believe I'm still wholly there amongst the pieces. *Mirror Image* is a self-portrait with the literal meaning of feeling fractured. There's personal satisfaction, self-worth and pride that accompanies the act of depicting strong emotion with paint. That's what self-esteem is. I can't allow it to disintegrate. I enjoy working with broken pottery too, and putting the pieces back together by way of mosaics. I've always been fascinated by broken pieces.

Painting: Wrong Planet

Artist: Michael Tolleson

Artist's Commentary: As with most people with Asperger's, this isolated person is elevated. She is more than her surroundings. She appears to be dressed the same as everyone else, but she is more than they could ever be. Because she is elevated and different in obvious ways, she is alone and so very cut off from humanity.

CHAPTER 3

Accepting and Working with Change

Stress Ranking: 3

Ranking of issue by stress caused

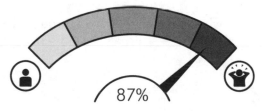

Percent of respondents living with issue

87%

Many people with Asperger's/HFA get upset (stressed) when change happens. Some examples of change are "simple change": your bus is late, your pencil broke at a very bad time, or the mail didn't arrive; and "complex change": your family moves to another house or city, your parents get a divorce, or your pet dies. Do you have difficulty with the stress that comes from change?

Temple Grandin

Change was hard for me. It is best to have a warning. Tell your employer or supervisor that if your schedule is going to get changed, to warn you a few days in advance. I found that surprise changes were very stressful.

In 2012, the entire faculty in our building at CSU (Colorado State University) had to move out so the building could be remodeled. Fortunately, I had several months warning so I could throw out lots of stuff and pack up. I handled this well because it was not sudden.

Find a person who can help guide you through these stressful times.

Anita Lesko

Dealing with change is extremely difficult for someone with Asperger's. We thrive on routine. The slightest deviation from that can have extreme impact. We like to be able to predict what is coming next. That provides a comfort zone. When that comfort is removed we get unhinged. Simply put, we feel like we're going to unravel at the seams. Everything becomes magnified. Anxiety then skyrockets. This can manifest itself in numerous ways such as withdrawing, getting flustered, decompensating. Only another Aspie knows the feeling of inner turmoil that results from change.

The stress response is directly proportional to the degree of change. My cortisol levels are regularly raging in response to changes.

I absolutely do not do well with immediate change. If something is due to change in several months I can slowly adapt to it. Sometimes after the change occurs, I realize it was for the better. But just forget the instant change. It isn't pretty. Those in my workplace can verify that!

At work, my comfort zone is the main operating room. I work with the same surgeons doing the same types of cases. The OR staff is consistent as well. We all work together like a finely tuned watch. I've been an anesthetist for over 25 years and have done over 40,000 cases to date. I've specialized in the most complex of cases, such as transplants and neurosurgery. I am a very highly experienced anesthesia provider. But if I'm asked to go to another area of the hospital, such as MRI or Ambulatory Surgical Center, I become very distressed. I instantly think of all the new people, equipment, and routine I'll have to instantly accommodate to. I go into a tailspin. I cannot help my reaction to this request for change. I would not expect others to understand it. They don't have Asperger's. I know that I can get very unpleasant when asked to leave my comfort zone. Much as I try not to, it's the best I can do.

My supervisors have finally figured out how to operate the Aspie! They make a wholehearted effort to keep me in the main operating room working with the same several surgeons. I am very content and pleasant and simply do my job. All goes very smoothly. I feel like a new person.

Coping with change remains very difficult for me. If you can arrange a change to take place over a period of time you will be better able to accept it. That time allows you to internalize the change and, all being well, figure out ways to compensate for it. Try to look at *any* positive outcomes of the upcoming change. I am often surprised that there is something better as a result of the change. Try to look with an optimistic eye at the event.

Advice on dealing with immediate change is more difficult. I am nowhere near mastering that. I have, however, learned to do several things that do help. I have learned not to allow myself to get extremely upset. I focus on regular breathing and staying calm. I focus on the task at hand. Try to tune out extraneous stimuli; trust your inner self to guide you through the change; talk to others to learn how they feel about the change—often you will see that others are just as upset, or even more so than you are: they simply don't show it. Remember that you are not alone in your feelings of discontent. That should bring comfort.

Approach each new change with the experience you have gained from past changes. Always look for the positive side!

Ruth Elaine Joyner Hane

A counselor for students at the University of Minnesota called me to ask the possible reason that someone diagnosed with autism would drop out of college after her chemistry professor gave the class a surprise quiz. She was perplexed, since it was only a quiz and would more than likely have helped the entire class gauge their progress in understanding the course content. If the student had failed the test, then there were several options for accommodations that the university could have offered her. Dropping out was the last possibility.

I had met the counselor after I gave a speech, "Autism and Sensory Overload." I explained that most of us on the Autism Spectrum do not like a surprise, since it will cause us to panic, as if our house were on fire and we had to get out. Many people do not like surprises. I believe that the emotions of surprise and terror are closely linked in the brain, especially for a person with autism.

To a lesser degree perhaps than a pop quiz, are daily changes. The toothpaste cap rolls underneath the sink and our programming is to replace the cap on the tube as the final step in our mouth hygiene schedule, and we cannot reach the cap. Or, someone drank all of our favorite fruit juice and we have to go without, or substitute another choice on a morning when every decision is painful.

Perfectionism may contribute to a person's aversion to or resistance to change. For some of us, making a mistake is considered fatal. Every misstep is viewed as a failure, proof that we are stupid, a worthless fool, or worse. We are our own unkind critics, telling ourselves the things we expect to hear from an adversarial, often imaginary audience. If we concentrate, we may recognize the cadence and word choices of someone we know, our mother, father, a teacher or a peer.

The truth is, most accomplishments are from years of concerted effort. Most "overnight" successes usually result from seasons of work. Earned acclaim usually comes from years of trials and failures.

Becoming a successful clothing designer does not happen overnight. I began sewing when I was nine years old while staying with my Aunt Mary. My grandparents shared the large farmhouse and the communal dining room with Aunt Mary's family. I discovered a mysterious black treadle sewing machine near the window of that dining room, a cut-lace doily resting on top. I asked my grandmother, "Can I sew on the machine?" She said, "Yes, maybe the rhythm of pressing the foot plate back and forth might get rid of some of your excess energy!"

Each day, after I finished my chores, I sat upon the stool at the sewing machine, and then lifted the white cloth covering the lovely gold gilding. To assure my safety, grandmother removed the sewing machine needle, dropping it in the wooden drawer underneath the machine. When I became skilled at starting and stopping, I practiced fast and slow. Grandmother was an excellent teacher. After weeks of practice, she said I was ready to sew, placed the needle in the sewing machine and taught me how to thread it. I continued sewing, making mistakes and learning from them. I found the repetition of sewing to be calming, and chose clothing design for a career, eventually designing dresses and hats in a New York workroom.

Becoming aware of your sensory needs and advocating for accommodations will help when a change happens, like a lost toothpaste cap or a surprise quiz.

Charli Devnet

I am an extremely change-aversive person. My inability to cope with change has been my downfall. If I were Clark Kent, I would have spent my life searching for a flight back to Krypton rather than fighting for truth and justice.

Even a minor deviation in the ordinary course of things presents me with a problem, but there was one major life change that nearly destroyed me: the summer I turned 13, my parents sold our house in my home town and moved to a remote, rustic area in upstate New York that I called the Kingdom of Frost.

I was a mischievous, spunky, bright and brave tomboy. I was different from the others. Bullies chased me. And classmates mocked me for the funny way I talked and walked. I had difficulty controlling my emotions. There was no diagnosis of Asperger's in those days. My teachers considered me a gifted child with behavioral problems, and I was subject to regular disciplinary actions.

Despite this, I enjoyed school and life. The village where I lived was small and tight knit. It could easily be traversed by bike in an hour or two. I had two sets of grandparents and numerous aunts and uncles almost next door. I had playmates of my own and a best friend for whom my heart still aches. On this soil, I thrived and grew strong. By junior high, I had surmounted many of my early difficulties. I tamped down my inappropriate behaviors so that my teachers treated me with more respect. I had fought off the bullies and learned to act more like my classmates. My grades were excellent. I played sports and, by dint of hard work, succeeded in masking many of my motor skills deficits. In short, I had almost achieved my childhood goal of becoming "just one of the kids." Then came the move. And life as I knew it came to a screeching halt.

How did I handle this transition? The worst way possible, short of suicide!

I did what many young Aspies do, given unbearable circumstances: I disassociated myself from the world. I made no new friends to replace the ones I had left behind. I no longer took part in sports. My grades tumbled. I immersed myself in fantasies and tuned out the world. In an effort to protect myself from the pain, loneliness and homesickness that engulfed me, I went into hibernation.

Five years passed. Suddenly, I was free to leave the Kingdom of Frost! I popped my head out of my burrow like a groundhog on February 2nd. Is it spring yet? Am I grown up yet? The answer was a resounding "no." During my hibernation, I had not only failed to mature, I had actually regressed. I was less able to cope at 18 than I had been at 12. All the social skills I had painstakingly acquired as a child had evaporated. I may have looked like an adult but I was as clueless as a kid in kindergarten.

Clearly, building myself a shell proved a bad strategy. I should have sought an adult mentor. There were adults who might have reached out to me—neighbors, teachers, the local librarian—had I only been willing to ask. And therein lies my wisdom. If you ever find yourself stranded in the Kingdom of Frost, do not try to go it alone and do not crawl into a hole like I did. There are people who care and will help. I finally did find an adult mentor (my aunt). She brought me slowly out of the abyss.

Liane Holliday Willey

Change will happen. There is no way around that fact. However, accepting change that is unavoidable is far easier than dealing with the ramifications that follow. The truth is, no matter how I prepare myself for inevitable change, I am typically ill prepared for it. I used to tell myself to buck up and do what needs to be done. I'd try to "gut it out" and force myself into the new situation. I'd tell myself I'd get used to the change eventually, but until that time came, I should just accept the fact I'd be stressed and unhappy. Eventually, I found out this was nonsense. When I try to convince myself unhappiness is something I should suffer through, I end up even less productive and even more resentful of the change. Now, I lean toward a pragmatic response to change.

The best I can do when life goes away from my plan is stay in the moment. By literally paying attention to my feelings and particularly my apprehension, I can try to re-direct them toward something that will calm me down. I might send my thoughts to my horses playing in a field, or to a favorite book. In other words, I calm myself down by replacing the nervousness with something soothing. It's like meditating, but my meditation is around good memories.

While I stay in the moment, I remain mindful of the facts surrounding the change. By analyzing the change, I can typically find both positive and negative reasons behind the new situation. Putting myself in this thinking process helps me think more objectively. The change now becomes an academic challenge I can look at like a puzzle. I can face the negatives and try to turn them into positives either in my mind, in actuality, or both. For example,

I have a very hard time getting rid of my cars, even though I know the time will come when I must. When that time comes, I make a list of all the old car's negative aspects and a list of a new car's positive things. Things like gas, mileage, cost of needed repairs, dents and scratches, and wear and tear noises for the old car; and things like improved safety features and no more noises for the new car. I come up with anything I can that will speak on behalf of both vehicles. When the negatives start overwhelming the positives, I can usually start to accept. I'm not tricking my mind, but re-teaching it to understand the change is better for practical reasons. I can't usually argue with pragmatism.

I don't expect myself to find resignation easily or seamlessly, and so I am careful to set small behavior goals when I have to face a change. I tell myself to get used to new things slowly, in bits. If it were a new car, I'd try to focus on something that I like about it, say, the color. I'll keep looking at that color and let it float my nerves a bit. I'll talk about the color, think about it, and eventually it becomes a base on which I can put something else to be positive about. I keep building small things to like about the new element(s) and before long, my like list starts to wear down my dislike feelings. I grow less anxious, and oftentimes start to feel a sense of bliss in the new situation.

Of course, the reality is there are times I can do nothing to feel better about a change. Losing a loved one, being let go from a job, having to move…these seemingly bigger-than-life changes are mind bogglers for most of us with ASD. When these biggies come around, I immediately seek help from an expert, online support group, or a book like this one to help me through the worst of it. Realizing that no one is capable of getting through major life changes without some sort of negative reaction helps me to keep my self-esteem level, even if everything else about me starts to crack. Sometimes I am Humpty Dumpty, but thankfully, there are people in this day and age who can put me back together again. My advice: reach out if self-help measures aren't enough to move you along from resistance to acceptance to resignation and successful, healthy living.

Dr. Patrick Suglia

Change is inevitable. That's just a fact of life, and eventually you're going to face it at some point. What will you do about it in order to avoid a meltdown or an anxiety attack? First and foremost is to take a deep breath. Seriously! Just do it. When you start to feel the pressure building inside, it's time to go to work on tweaking your rules. Everything you do currently is done the way you do it because you made a certain set of rules by which you can handle it. Let's say your work routine follows a certain pattern. When the boss says it's time to do something differently, after you get thrown for a loop you simply take the rules that you already made for yourself and see how you can rearrange them to fit the new criteria. This is how I manage to be "flexible," and I use this same process no matter what the change is.

Whether you are a person with an Autism Spectrum Disorder or not, it is important to remember that everyone is affected by change, usually negatively so. Those of us with an Autism Spectrum Disorder are particularly affected because of how sensitive we are. Our sensitivities can make us feel helpless, and at the same time make us appear helpless in the eyes of the neurotypical. Nonetheless, as long as we go through the rulemaking process in our head, not only can we get through it, but we can take charge of the way we react and respond through our "flexibility," which in reality is the way we craftily tweak our rules. This same process needs to take place whether you are in school trying to follow a teacher, at home doing household chores, or when difficult situations arise such as getting a flat tire or being late for work. Remember, things happen!

What helps is to have a backup plan in place. For example, I always carry some cash on me just in case my credit card doesn't work. I make it a point to keep extra pens on hand in case I lose one or one stops working. I always keep emergency phone numbers with me in case something happens to my car as I'm driving. Even though these things may seem small, they become very big lifesavers if something does go wrong. In this way, I am always prepared for when that change, that eventual change, does happen. When it does, the first and foremost thing you must do, as I said before, is to take a deep breath. That is the crucial first step to gaining the upper hand.

But what if the change is big, such as moving to a different area or losing a loved one? Again, remember that this affects the neurotypical as it does you. Yet there is a strength that you have in order to adapt to the situation better, and that is your ability to make your rules. In the end, there should never be such a strong attachment to the rules you've made for yourself, because change will eventually happen anyway. Look at it this way: your rules determine how you will function in the situation you are in the way it is now, and it may all change again tomorrow. Do not define yourself by your situation and your rules. Change is your test of strength and character, and this is a test you can't fail because of the strengths you possess. Sure, it will be very uncomfortable to have to change. But it really is possible.

Richard Maguire

I want to start by saying I do not think I or any other autistic person is averse to change per se. People often comment negatively on us, saying we do not like to make changes. I would maintain that every day we must radically change and pretend to be what we are not neurologically designed to be. We need to be chameleons every day, and this is exhausting. I maintain that we make changes very well, mostly by necessity, more changes than most people manage every day.

What is significantly different with us is how we make short-term or sudden changes. As autistic people, we are monotropic thinkers; read Wendy Lawson's *The Passionate Mind* for an in-depth exploration of monotropism. We are concentrated, deep and passionate thinkers. To ask one of us to make sudden quick changes puts us in a painful situation. Making quick changes looks like a non-autistic way of thinking; we are deep thinkers and need processing time to make changes.

When I am running autism training, I have an exercise, using Jenga blocks, that illustrates how we change our minds, how long it can take and how precise the process is. I use two plates: one has a mug on it, the other a margarine tub. The Jenga tower is assembled on one plate alongside the mug or the tub. The plates are fairly small. This makes the task tricky and replicates the adjustments we need to make in life. Nothing is perfect. I ask people to reassemble the Jenga tower on the other plate next to the other item, one brick at a time. The items represent two kitchen activities, getting a drink and getting margarine for toast. The tower represents a gestalt made by an autistic person for each activity and the changeover is not complete until the tower is fully assembled on the other plate—not easy, as the plate is too small. This usually takes a minimum of two minutes 45 seconds. I ask people to think about how they would feel if every change took this long. They say they would get tired, annoyed, and not want to make as many changes in a day as they do now. Then they get the idea of how autistic people manage changes from one concentrated position to another, and how difficult this is. We need time to process, consider, plan and execute changes, even seemingly simple ones like going from one thing to another in a kitchen at breakfast time.

When I train people to work with autism, I impress on them the need to give time and quiet so autistic people can manage changes. They soon see the importance of this, and report that people they saw as uncooperative are really overloaded and anxious about changes, not averse to them.

In your life, practise feeling relaxed about how you manage change; you are autistic and your thought processes are detailed and linear. It is okay to make and ask for time to process changes. This can relieve a lot of pressure and anxiety. I have found most people respect what I say and ask for when managing changes. And what about the people that don't accommodate my autism? I move on.

Sometimes, quick changes are needed, and I deal with these by having pre-prepared scripts for them so I can change quickly when there is a need. That is a lot more comfortable than trying to work out the change from scratch every time.

RECOMMENDED READING

Lawson, W. (2010) *The Passionate Mind: How People with Autism Learn*. London: Jessica Kingsley Publishers.

Lars Perner

Even before I was diagnosed with Asperger's syndrome at age 31, I was keenly aware that I intensely disliked change. I knew that I was different from most others in this regard—at least in the way that rather modest changes would bother me. There are a variety of reasons why change can be upsetting. It often means that there is a need to adjust carefully developed coping mechanisms. In addition, even when change is announced, that announcement often happens uncomfortably close to the time that the change takes effect. And the change often comes as a surprise. Ugh!

Those of us on the spectrum often have a very difficult time understanding a rather perplexing and unsavory world. To avoid being overwhelmed, we much prefer to be able to control our circumstances. Change, and the way it is implemented, can be especially frustrating when one is growing up and has little control over one's environment. Well-meaning others might unwittingly exacerbate the problem with unfounded and completely unrealistic assurances, such as, "Everything's going to be all right!" I had little confidence that people who said that actually knew what they were talking about. I seriously doubted that it would. To me, it actually came across as though they were grossly insensitive—or at best, reckless—in not comprehending the anxiety and frustration I was experiencing. Adults were supposed to be responsible and not let the situation get dangerously out of hand!

Many people are frustrated by rules, and there have certainly been rules that I felt were unjust or just stupid. For the most part, however, rules have been a source of comfort to me. They seemed to foster a certain kind of civilization and imposed limitations on the range of unreasonable things people could do to me. Therefore, changes in rules—or simply seeing these ignored—were a source of major distress to me. At the same time, it was also very difficult for me to grapple with "new" rules that were suddenly pointed out to me. My belief that I had a complete overview of my obligations and of the restrictions on what others could do to me would be shattered.

Preparation for change is important to me. I need time to think through the ramifications of the change and its impact. I may also need to prepare for new demands. It is not easy for me, for example, to see other people perform an activity and copy it. I do not have a good way to "take in" and replicate a series of continuous actions. I need specific steps to take and preferably written instructions. Being expected to simply follow others immediately is not workable.

It is a reality of life that as one grows up, family and society in general will have more demanding expectations as one's ability to function and take responsibility increases. Often, such increasing demands come about rather suddenly, and may emerge not as an explicit announcement, but rather as criticism of behavior that was previously accepted. Having always been rather sensitive to criticism, I found that such feedback compounded the problem of a sudden and unanticipated change.

No, I think that Sheryl Crow is way off target in her ridiculous belief that "A change would do [me] good!"

Dr. Tony Attwood's Advice on Accepting and Working with Change

Neurotypicals have a strong drive for, and enjoyment of, change, variety and spontaneity. They are bored by predictability and routine. However, for those who have an ASD, change is associated with uncertainty. Variety is not necessarily the spice of life and surprises and change can be perceived as aversive. There are two main reasons why those with an ASD have problems accepting and coping with change, the first being cognitive—having to be flexible in thinking and planning—while the second is the emotional rather than cognitive reaction to change.

One of the characteristics of the cognitive profile of those who have an ASD is having a "one track mind," a singular way of achieving success. Like a train on a single track, this is a convenient and efficient way of travel, as long as there are no blockages on the track or diversions that require switching to an alternative track. Psychologists refer to this flexibility (or inflexibility) in thinking and problem solving as an example of impaired executive function (see Chapter 8). Neurotypicals are more like a four wheel drive, all-terrain vehicle that can easily find an alternative way to a destination. They quickly identify an alternative route or plan.

Sometimes the person with Asperger's syndrome wakes up in the morning and has a "single track" approach to the day ahead, having a mental, and very detailed, "video" of exactly how the day will proceed. There may be no "plan B" or visualization or conceptualization of alternative options should there be a change in events or expectations.

When a change occurs, there can be a tendency to view the new and unanticipated situation with a mind that looks for differences, not similarities. Neurotypicals will consider what situations in the past have been similar to the current one, and use information from those memories as a starting point to determine what to do to cope with the change in expectations. Those with an ASD may mentally "freeze," seeing the situation as without precedent, and therefore have great difficulty conceptualizing an alternative strategy.

There can be another cognitive factor, in that the person with an ASD uses so much intellectual capacity coping with daily life, there is very little cognitive capacity in reserve to mentally plan what to do when the unexpected occurs.

When change is anticipated or experienced, there can be an increase in anxiety, especially performance anxiety and fear of making a mistake, as well as feelings of being overwhelmed, confused, insecure and vulnerable. The subsequent increase in anxiety and agitation actually increases cognitive rigidity and makes constructive adaption to change even more elusive. Change is also a trigger to release intense anxiety that may have been building up for some time, and thus it is quite understandable that those with an ASD have difficulty accepting, coping and working with change.

I suspect that in medieval history, adults with Asperger's syndrome were to be found in monasteries, enjoying the routines and rituals of the monastery with a clear predictable schedule for the day and an emphasis on solitude and tranquility. Modern life is extremely challenging for those with an ASD. This book is a guide to life on earth by fellow "aliens," the Aspie mentors; there are some adults who have Asperger's syndrome who would like to change the name of the syndrome to "Wrong Planet Syndrome." I would suggest that an alternative is "Wrong Century Syndrome."

Coping with Change

The first recommendation when change occurs is to remain calm, reciting the mantra, "If I am calm, I can cope." Being calm encourages flexible and adaptive thinking, making wise decisions and putting the event in perspective. The worst response is panic.

Family members, teachers, friends, colleagues and especially line managers will need to recognize the psychological and emotional advantages of giving prior warning of change to allow the person with an ASD sufficient time to prepare a new mental script for the situation—to create a new mental "video" that provides an alternative script and sequence of events. That script and sequence can be enhanced by drawing a flow diagram of possible strategies and outcomes, and mentally being positive and optimistic when change occurs and recognizing the value of serendipity.

It is important when coping with change to recognize when someone could provide reassurance and guidance in what to do. Asking for help in such situations is not an indication of incompetence or stupidity, but actually a wise strategy.

Once a new strategy has been identified and visualized, the alternative "script" can be written to provide a clear visual strategy that is easier to remember. When emotional stability has returned and the change successfully accommodated, it is important to give yourself some positive feedback which will encourage you to cope with future changes. You can cope. The Aspie mentors in this book prove it.

Artwork (See Plate 3)

Painting: The Visitation

Artist: Stephanie Tihanyi

Artist's Commentary: In this painting, the past and the future meet at the crossroads of a house (symbolizing self). Part of the self is imbedded, frozen and trapped in the (painful) past, but another part is beginning to sense freedom and possibility of transformation. Friends await (cat) and the birds show the way.

CHAPTER 4

Living with Meltdowns

Stress Ranking: 4

Ranking of issue by stress caused

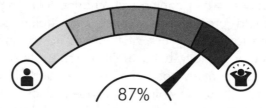

87%

Percent of respondents living with issue

83%

Many people with Asperger's/HFA have difficulty with meltdowns. Some examples of meltdowns include: getting angry, being unable to process information, running away and shutting down. Do you have difficulty functioning with your meltdowns?

Mitch Christian

My frustration issues can often result from a buildup of little things over the day that lead to becoming upset over what seems to be something trivial. For me, this can be the result of sensory issues, interactions with other people, or anxieties about traveling and being away from home. To lessen this buildup, I make sure I give myself plenty of down time during the week to get away from the stress-building situations. That includes having an area in my house where the lighting and sound are at a low level, and where I can escape the need for constant interaction with other people. For vacations, I take periodic extended weekends instead of several days in a row, so the change to my routine is kept at a minimum.

Staying involved in activities that I enjoy on a regular basis is a good way to keep tension from growing inside of me. The trick is to limit myself to certain hours during the day for the fun stuff so I don't get too stuck on it, and to balance that with chores that break me out of the rut caused by focusing too much on one thing. So, for instance, movies and television viewing are kept to the evening hours, and video games on weekends only. I listen to a lot of music, but make sure I take a break from it periodically throughout the day. Internet browsing and general reading also have their time and place, but getting away from the computer or portable electronic device reminds me that there is a real world out there.

Proper diet, exercise, and getting enough sleep play a large role in stress management as well. I eat organic food to limit unknown effects from added ingredients, and I've found that caffeine has been a big source of my tensions in the past. After drastically reducing my intake, I discovered that I'm much less prone to fits and my overall anxiety level is much lower. I exercise regularly, with 15-minute walks several times a day. And taking a quick nap during the day can make a lot of things better. I also think that exposure to sunlight on a regular basis helps my overall mood.

When I have felt the need to release my frustration, I've always kept it away from others, and generally try to let it out in a harmless way, like throwing pillows at the floor so nothing gets damaged. I often curse to myself, but I realize that it's another method of release and try not to feel guilty about it since no one is injured. Sometimes, I used to scream when I was driving alone in my car because traffic frustrations would get the better of me. Now I give myself plenty of time to get to my destination and I've become less nervous about being late. By managing the causes of meltdowns, I've been able to reduce their frequency and severity a great deal.

Alexis Wineman

Screams…lots and lots of screams. But to me, these screams were explosions of emotions that would happen so often that I just wanted to disappear so they wouldn't happen again. I would always ask myself why I was the only one who went through these explosions, but answers didn't come until later, with my diagnosis. No matter what was happening at the time, next thing you know there would be crying and screaming, and oftentimes I would hurt myself. It got to the point where I was just living from one meltdown to the next. I felt so guilty that I was putting my family through all of this stress, but no matter how hard I tried to stop this madness, the meltdowns kept coming.

As I got older, I was able to find ways to cope with most of the stresses of each day and I started communicating more with my family about when I needed some time to myself. I know that meltdowns are always going to happen, but the older and more mature I get, the less frequent and less intense they will be.

I know that everyone with autism is different, so finding a way to cope will be something that each person will have to figure out on his or her own. For me, every morning before I start the day, I walk in circles while listening to my iPod for about half an hour to get focused on the day ahead. If I am able to get this time to myself, the day really does seem to go better, because I approach the day calmer than if I was rushed out the door. Some days when unexpected things happen, I find myself needing that pacing time again to get me refocused. Given that everyone seems to have different triggers for meltdowns, it is important to try lots of different ways to help yourself regroup.

Once you find something that helps you to refocus, life will get better.

Richard Maguire

Meltdowns happen and everybody has them. Whenever I do autism training with non-autistic people, they recognize the meltdown and can relate their own experiences of totally losing it through an excess of adrenaline. As far as I can make out, the difference between autistic and non-autistic people is that, most of the time, we live with higher levels of adrenaline and heightened sensitivity. Our senses are more easily shocked, and working out life is harder for us because we are a minority population that runs on a different operating system. As a result, we experience more stress, anxiety and meltdowns.

I have found that meltdowns are inevitable in my life. I'm learning that the key to dealing with them is to be more emotionally aware, and more aware of my sensory input, to learn more effective and timely communication, to be happy with being autistic, and to know the meltdown process and ways to deal with it. These things have helped reduce the occurrence of meltdowns and the play dead meltdowns I have.

As a child and teenager, I felt helpless against meltdowns; they had me in a destructive cycle. I hurt people, lost friends and got into all sorts of trouble. My meltdowns were either the explosive sort, or I would run for miles. A meltdown is the result of anxiety and the resulting excess of adrenaline. There are three ways a meltdown can manifest: as an explosion of violence (the fight response), running away (the flight response), or becoming totally passive and playing dead (the play dead response). I think all three responses are equally serious and indicate that someone is terrified beyond coping, even if only the fight or flight responses seem serious to onlookers.

I developed play dead meltdowns in later teens as they attracted kinder responses. I have hit out at people, trashed my room, self-harmed and lots of other things in meltdown. These all scared me, as did the inevitability of the next meltdown, which then made a meltdown come sooner. I had play dead meltdowns several times daily, and explosive meltdowns at about 18-month intervals in early adulthood. Today, I play dead a couple of times a day and explosive meltdowns have not happened for a decade now.

The key to this change has been to get better at managing anxiety. Lower the anxiety, and the incidence of meltdowns will reduce. I have learned to get some control of meltdowns and moved away from passively accepting that they will control my life. That has been a liberating change in the last decade. I don't need to be as scared of meltdowns as I used to be.

I have also learned to regulate my life to control my anxiety and energy levels. These days I work freelance so I do not have to work in a pattern that takes no account of anxiety and energy levels. I went part time in later years of having a job. I also negotiated coping strategies with my employer, the main one being to be able to go to the toilet to meditate and calm down to control anxiety levels. That helped me work more consistently and productively. I would recommend part-time and flexible working for many autistic people.

Having some control over meltdowns has been liberating and enabled me to have more control. Basically, the happier I can be, the fewer meltdowns I have. Lots of things cause happiness and I help other autistic people find more happiness.

Meltdowns still happen and they hurt a lot, but crucially they do not need to be inevitable and their incidence can be controlled and reduced, and that reduces meltdowns.

Henny Kupferstein

I don't have a gauge to filter how much stress I am piling on. As a result, I crash in a giant, ugly way. Typically, my physical body starts showing signs of distress, such as altered vision, near-zero perception on reading and visual details, seeing dark spots, and feeling like my head is floating or bobbing, and my speech begins to slow to a final halt. I finally had a day where I shut down like that in public and couldn't find my way home. That's when I knew I had to get to the bottom of this. It was so terrifying that I vowed never again to allow myself to sink that low.

Sitting on psychotherapists' couches and talking is not going to help me uncover the issues, because I don't do that whole emotion/talking thing very well. Then I discovered CBT—cognitive behavior therapy. The method is simple, systematic, and easy to learn and reproduce in future situations on your own. It takes a while to be able to carry over from clinical sessions to daily living, but even from the first session, this changed my life forever. I was able to narrow down my reactionary behaviors to their source. I was never able to pin a reaction to an issue before. Now I could. And I can even attempt at times to do it myself, without a clinician. With CBT, I have learned to identify a stressor before it builds up and turns me into a useless puddle of brain-melt on the floor. I am a big believer in CBT. Stephen M. Shore jokingly said to me, "CCT is the oldest and fastest acting approach for treating autism...average latency between application and compliance is 15.4 milliseconds. Equipment needed: baseball bat. CCT stands for cranial concussive therapy." I say if you can't kill 'em, join 'em.

Seriously, another interim coping method was to recognize when I was going to crash, and quickly reach out to a neurotypical (NT). I began seeing these NT friends as translators. When an issue makes me feel like every lobe in my brain is shooting out multiple arguments, each one trying to convince the other why their position is the only one, my brain goes for a spin. I don't have the ability to sort through all the options by myself. Writing them all down intensifies my anxiety, since it puts it into my line of vision, making it tangible. I learned to recognize the signs of myself shutting down. Blurting out my issues in random order to an NT allows them to sort through it all for me, and hand the information back to me on a silver platter, all neatly categorized and compiled into black and white no's and yes's. I encourage you to seek out an NT who can be your translator. Know that you are not burdening them as much as you think, and that they take a personal pleasure in watching the change come over you. They assist by doing something that feels so easy and natural to them, but seems to have a powerful effect on you. Until we come up with an NT Emulator App[1] for that purpose, for now, use your NT translator for every ounce that he or she is worth. Stop beating yourself for not being able to work through these issues on your own. Just keep telling yourself, "I am great at so many other things."

Anita Lesko

Everyone who has Asperger's is familiar with meltdowns. I've had my fair share of them, and still do. Now they occur to a much lesser degree. I've also learned to recognize when one is coming and how to avoid it.

When I was younger, I really didn't have too many meltdowns. If I did, they were nowhere near what the Aspie kids of today experience. My personal opinion as to why kids today have more intense meltdowns is that our present-day society is composed of non-stop sensory overload. This takes a toll on a child with Asperger's. With such a massive amount of stimuli, the reaction will obviously be proportionately larger. Another factor is the parents who routinely over-schedule their Asperger kid. That totally overwhelms the child, which results in a meltdown. Then the parent believes their child has behavior problems, while in reality the problem lies with the parent who cannot recognize the child simply needs down time. It saddens me to see the great number of therapists who prescribe medications to end the meltdowns—they also end a clearly thinking mind. I think of all the genius minds of our times who are now believed to have had Asperger's: Steve Jobs, Albert Einstein, Thomas Edison. If they had been placed on mind-altering drugs, I truly believe they would not have created what they did.

Meltdowns occur as a result of sensory overload. Sometimes you have control over your environment, sometimes you don't. I have learned over the years which situations to avoid in order to avoid sensory overload. If I walk into a restaurant and it's really loud, I turn right around and leave. I don't attend parties or places with lots of people. Avoidance is a simple solution. I do enjoy

---

1 NT Emulator App: from a conversation with Dr. Stephen M. Shore.

lunch with one or two people in a quiet restaurant, when I can focus on the conversation.

Meltdowns can occur at any time of the day, but are more likely at night. The more tired I become, the more likely a meltdown will occur. If I do succumb to melting down, it means I'm going to get *really* cranky and irritating. A meltdown can also occur from a change in routine. If I'm suddenly confronted by a change in assignment at work, it isn't pretty. I will get loud, asking if there's any way I can maintain what I was prepared to do. I know I get visibly upset. As much as I try, I cannot conceal it, nor stop my anxiety. This is an unfortunate part of Asperger's. Over the years I have been able to lessen it, but this part of me will never go away.

Sensory overload can be caused by seemingly simple things; for example, if I'm on the phone and someone near me starts talking to me at the same time, my hearing shuts down and I won't hear either one. Now I simply focus on whom I was originally talking to. I don't intend to be rude, but I have to tune out the other person.

Make a list of what generally pushes you to the meltdown phase. Think out a plan to help alleviate the problem or minimize it. There are many instances where pre-planning could help alleviate a meltdown. Keeping track of your need for rest is critical. Dr. Tony Attwood has said, in *The Complete Guide to Asperger's Syndrome*, "For each hour spent socializing, you need two hours downtime." This holds 100 percent true for me. It is exhausting to socialize, even with people I truly enjoy. Afterwards, I need to be in a totally quiet environment.

You have to watch out for yourself. Only you know what can precipitate a meltdown. Make rest a priority.

REFERENCE

Attwood, T. (2007) *The Complete Guide to Asperger's Syndrome*. London: Jessica Kingsley Publishers.

Charli Devnet

As a child, I threw tantrums at the least provocation. While irksome to my parents and teachers, these storms blew over quickly. As an adolescent and adult, I am, and have been, subject to more intense and longer lasting, albeit less frequent, emotional eruptions.

A child is a prisoner of her environment, but an adult learns to manage and guard against everyday stressors. For example, when I go out into the bright sun, I arm myself with sunglasses and a wide-brimmed hat. I avoid shopping malls on the weekends. If I must drive at rush hour, I take the back roads. If I see a new toy *that I just have to have*, I'll put aside money to buy it, or decide, after due deliberation, that it is not worth the cost. Minor inconveniences, which may have dominated your early life, are put in their place. That is the good news.

Unfortunately, as life unwinds, one is more and more subjected to major stressors, which undermine one's sense of the security of life and foretell loss and change: the loss of a job, the end of a relationship, serious illness for yourself or a family member, financial problems which may threaten eviction or foreclosure. Often these crises come suddenly, out of the blue, when you are not prepared for them and it seems as if the earth is slipping away beneath your feet. Being extremely change-averse, as are many Aspies, I can be sent into meltdown mode by these events.

For me, meltdowns come in two variations. There is the inward-directed meltdown, where one becomes weepy and despondent, feels helpless and hopeless, shuts down and may become immobilized or catatonic. In these cases, your misfortune seems to have come out of the blue. There is no one to blame but fate—or yourself.

Then there is the outward-directed meltdown, where one has a grievance against another. You may be overcome with a blind rage, feel like a wounded animal, cannot sleep or sit still, and try to strike out at the one who has done you wrong.

Sometimes both these moods alternate within the same episode. Having worked in law offices, I've witnessed even neurotypicals displaying such reactions to a divorce, or death of a parent. One moment they will be sorrow and woe, teary-eyed and subdued. An hour later they will be consumed with anger and making threats against their ex or the sibling who is robbing them blind. The emotions are natural, part of the human condition.

How you deal with them, however, is a measure of your maturity. My suggestions:

- *Breathe deeply and count to ten:* Your first-grade teacher was right. It helps.

- *Engage in physical activity:* Work out in a gym, hike a mile, run a sprint, or ride a bike or a horse.

- *Commune with nature:* This has a calming effect. Contemplating the awe and sweep of the natural world with its rivers, mountains and skies puts things into perspective.

- *Avoid the proximity of weapons:* No, you would never do *that*, but why court danger? If you have guns, or even sharp knives, lying about your house, put them under lock and key in times of great stress.

- *Talk to someone:* Call your therapist, caregiver, trusted friend, colleague or clergyperson. If necessary, call a hotline, talk to a bartender or the neighbor up the street. Keeping your emotions bottled up inside is the gravest mistake of all.

Dr. Patrick Suglia

Although I never felt that I had a problem with meltdowns, people who know me well will say that I surely did and that I still can if I let myself. When I read the description of what a "meltdown" really is, I just have to laugh and say, "Heck, I know a lot of neurotypicals that do that!" What makes it so unique to those of us with Autism Spectrum Disorders is the fact that we do it more often and we feel things more deeply. Because of this, we often can be inappropriate in the ways we express ourselves. The one thing that has helped me over the years is something I learned primarily because of the more "spiritual" way I look at things, and this can be summed up in two words: objective thinking.

Objective thinking is a matter of looking at whatever is affecting you from a different angle. Stand outside of yourself just for a moment and watch yourself from a distance. This works better if you take a few deep breaths first. The better you can see yourself from a distance, the greater chance you have of detaching from the situation just enough to prevent "emotional buildup." The sensory overload is really what causes the meltdown. When you come back to your "self," rational thinking follows, even though the feelings of anger, sadness or confusion may still be there. Neurotypicals experience these things too. But having that moment to "step away" before reacting makes it all work more smoothly.

So, what is so "spiritual" about objective thinking? Without going into any theological ideas, the original meaning of the word "spirit" meant "breath." Only by being able to breathe easily can we work our way through that which we feel choked by. We have to take that step outside of ourselves, just for a moment, before we can find the strength to carry on without much ado. This gives us just enough "breathing room," so to speak, to take away that debilitating strangling sensation. When we have that extra room, we can realize yet another advantage to objective thinking, and that is the gift of detached disclosure; you can express yourself quite readily and quite maturely so that the people around you can know exactly how you feel. This does wonders for fending off any pressure that people may actually be imposing on you. This in turn leads to rational discussion and negotiation over the troubling situation at hand.

Sometimes, when all else fails, all you can really do is go someplace for a while to be alone. This doesn't mean running away to where nobody can find you. It means having a predetermined space where you can be alone, a place where others know that they can find you if need be, and just letting it all out or taking all the time you need to sort things through in your own mind. In my younger years, this worked wonders in helping me regain my composure when I felt the weight of the world come crashing down on me. Over time, it helped me to discover that having such a space actually helped me with my creativity. Even as I wrote this very essay, I needed to separate myself from the busy surroundings of the restaurant I am sitting in and walk out into the nearby desert to collect my thoughts and listen to my intuition. It certainly helped a whole lot better than just sitting here feeling the pressure build up to the point where I was about to lose it. It's wonderful to breathe!

Dr. Know

I suggest trying to avoid or prevent meltdowns entirely. Sensory issues and anxiety can trigger or facilitate a meltdown, so keep them managed. Being well rested also helps.

Noticing you are heading towards a meltdown is very valuable, as you can then attempt to defuse the environment that is contributing to it. This is particularly important if you are prone to meltdowns where you become very angry. Make an effort to maintain awareness of your emotional state: this is probably not easy, but you should try to get progressively better at it (I never tried one, but wearing a heart rate monitor might provide a clear cue to help with this).

If possible, enlist the help of people you trust (a good example could be your parents) who could calm you down in situations they are involved in. Note that this could possibly even be a person who somehow contributed (in principle unintentionally) to your meltdown with some comment or action—they may be able to calm you down very effectively by clearing up some misunderstanding, or by comforting you. These helpers will ideally be informed about the topic and possibly be able to recognize that you are heading to a meltdown before you realize it. The responsibility is still yours: enlisting help is a good idea but don't depend exclusively on assistance, as there will be occasions where you won't have anyone you trust with you, or they are too wrapped up in the situation to be able (or willing) to help—so even when they are there, make your own effort to keep control and progressively improve yourself. It may be hard, but it is not impossible and can really improve your quality of life.

Dr. Tony Attwood's Advice on Living with Meltdowns

A meltdown occurs as a response to stress, especially being stressed and overwhelmed by social and sensory experiences. There can be a buildup of tension due to experiencing an overload of minor irritations, disappointments, exhausting social occasions and unpleasant sensory experiences. The release of the tension and stress occurs through an explosion of emotions and energy, almost like popping a balloon. The meltdown "cleanses" the system, re-booting the brain's stress and emotion management program that has "crashed" due to too many programs operating at the same time.

Prior to the meltdown, there will have been an accumulation of stress, so it is essential to monitor the psychological and physiological signs of increasing stress. The psychological warning signs can be in terms of the type and quality of actions and thoughts. As the tension increases, there can be a restlessness, lack of fluency in movements and an inability to control negative thoughts, as well as increasing intolerance, irritation and a desire to escape the situation. The physiological signs can be an increase in the rate of breathing, heart and pulse rate, and perspiration. These are the classic physiological indicators of an imminent fight or flight response.

Strategies to Reduce the Chance of Having a Meltdown
A Stress Thermometer

Each person with an ASD will have a unique series of warning signs that a meltdown is imminent. It is extremely important to make a note of, and record, those signs, perhaps as degrees on an emotional "thermometer" that measures stress and can therefore indicate that a meltdown is imminent. The signs at each level on the thermometer can be behavioural, physical or cognitive (a particular thought), such as saying obscenities, pacing, looking panic-stricken or "thunderous," or thinking, "I am about to explode" (or implode). Specific situations are added to the thermometer, such that if the thermometer ranges from zero to one hundred degrees, going to a shopping mall or fast food restaurant might create, for example, a resting point of stress of 60, and additional experiences, such as having to wait in line, add a further ten stress points or degrees. Eventually the stressors may go beyond 100, a "fuse is blown" and a meltdown occurs. Those you know well may be able to add their own observations of situations and behaviours that indicate to them your increasing stress. Many people who have an ASD have difficulty monitoring their own internal moods and stress levels, and may only be conscious of signs in the 80–100-degree range on their thermometer, while others may recognize the signs from 40 to 80.

A valuable means of monitoring stress levels is to use modern technology designed for sports activities that monitors pulse rate. These devices are now part of sports watches and wrist bands and enable the person with an ASD to intermittently check his or her pulse to indicate mounting stress. Another strategy is to listen to, and take notice of, other people pointing out to you your increasing signs of stress. Their observations may be more accurate than your self-reflection, particularly since you may have a tendency for denial.

A Stress Level Repair Kit

The Aspie mentors have identified a range of activities that can reduce stress levels, and significantly reduce the risk of having a meltdown. The repair mechanisms of first choice are *physical exercise* to quickly discharge the buildup of tension for the range from 80 to 100, and *relaxation activities* such as solitude, reconnecting with nature, listening to music and meditation to slowly release the stress for the range from 40 to 80. These activities need to be factored into your daily life and available to be used at all times of increasing stress.

Other options are interesting and effective, for example, *creative destruction*, such as crushing cans and packaging in the re-cycling garbage bin. Another is *"letting it all out"* and de-stressing by screaming obscenities. The act of screaming can actually be silent, for example retreating to a toilet and silently mouthing obscenities. There are also long-term strategies recommended by the Aspie mentors, such a having a *nutritious diet*, a *good sleep pattern* and what may be described as *mental health holidays*, that is, time off work or study to restore psychological rather than physical health.

Strategies that are Not Recommended

Strategies that are not recommended include suppressing the stress and repressing the agitation, which is then internalized as self-loathing and subsequently expressed as self-mutilation; or externalizing the stress by damaging valuable property, or being violent towards someone. These can be quick emotional repair "fixes" for intolerable levels of stress, but are not recommended because of the long-term consequences. It is also important to stay away from dangerous implements such as knives and other actual or potential weapons.

EFFECT ON OTHER PEOPLE

A meltdown is an extremely unpleasant experience for the person with an ASD, but it can also be a very frightening experience for neurotypicals. They can feel confused as to why the person with an ASD is experiencing and expressing such extreme agitation that may seem excessive for the situation. They may not know what to do to help and will need their own recovery strategies. It is very important to communicate with others the early warning signs of an imminent meltdown, to make sure they are aware of the signs on the stress thermometer, and to decide together what each of you can do to help at various levels of stress.

Should a meltdown occur, neurotypicals will need to know what could actually make the situation worse, such as asking you to explain why you are upset. They may not realize that in such a state of stress, a clear and coherent explanation is unlikely, and trying to give one may cause even more stress. They may need to check with you whether specific strategies would be helpful, especially, for example, expressions of affection. They may also need to be cautious about the imposition of any consequences, as at specific times in the meltdown cycle, this may exacerbate the situation.

When you have recovered from the meltdown, it is important that you understand the art of apology. You may be feeling better, but the neurotypicals can still feel upset, needing some time to implement their own methods of emotional recovery. Neurotypicals usually expect some type of apology or signs of remorse, and would be grateful for some way of restoring the relationship, such as your offering to help with household chores. Together you can then explore why the meltdown occurred and learn from the experience, and work out how to avoid future meltdowns in the same circumstances.

RECOMMENDED READING

Lipsky, D. (2011) *From Anxiety to Meltdown: How Individuals on the Autism Spectrum Deal with Anxiety, Experience Meltdowns, Manifest Tantrums, and How You Can Intervene Effectively.* London: Jessica Kingsley Publishers.

Artwork (See Plate 4)

Painting: Meltdown

Artist: Charlotte Poe

Artist's Commentary: There's too much bread in the bread aisle. Too much choice. Who needs that many variations of bread? The lights are too bright, too yellow. The under floor heating makes my legs feel strange and too warm. The freezers hum a constant undertone that buzzes like a wasp near your ear. There are too many things to catalogue, too many words, too many numbers. My legs want to buckle and I can't breathe. I want to throw up. I grip the trolley because it's the only thing keeping me upright. I wonder how other people manage to shop so calmly, when all around is this pressing in of noise and stimuli.

Painting: Meltdown

Artist: Michael Tolleson

Artist's Commentary: It was important to make the color sickening. I wanted the color to reflect the anxiety in the gut that comes from meltdowns due to too much…too much input, too much verbal, too many things to focus on, too many "anything." The person in this painting can do nothing but fold up due to this feeling that they cannot fight or do anything about. The moon hangs heavy over a slimy melting city. Nothing is attractive or right.

CHAPTER 5

Overcoming Depression

Stress Ranking: 5

Ranking of issue by stress caused

87%

Percent of respondents living with issue

76%

People with Asperger's/HFA may have issues with depression. Some examples of feelings of depression include: feeling hopeless, feeling sad all the time, feeling crabby towards others, wanting to be alone and away from people for extended periods, feeling like a failure with no future, and feeling like you don't want to live anymore. Do you have concerns about depression?

Garry Burge

As a teenager I experienced depression but didn't really know how to deal with it. I found that growing orchids helped me to retreat into a world where I could avoid the pain of being bullied and rejected. I had many orchids, and by the time I was 19, I had a considerable collection. I still grow orchids today and growing them has helped me cope through difficult times. Anxiety can be difficult to deal with and often a person needs to look for the warning signs. It can be a negative spiral and when it confronts you, you need to take action.

I got counselling when I was studying at the University of New England in Armidale, Australia. I found it impossible to make friends and to be understood by other students around me. I looked like them, yet could not make friends or fit in. Dr. Tony Attwood diagnosed me in 1978, which was the time I also decided to seek counselling. One of the counselling strategies that was recommended was cognitive behavior therapy. This is specifically designed to overcome negative thought processes with more positive and constructive thought processes.

When trying to deal with my depression, I found the biggest problem was attempting to make out that I was neurotypical. In doing this, I found that I was not able to be myself and, more importantly, I was exposed to expectations that were just not possible to reach. After being diagnosed with Asperger's syndrome, I came to the conclusion that in order to understand it better, I needed to accept my diagnosis. I also believed that now I knew I had Asperger's syndrome, disclosure was important so that I could help others to understand it. When dealing with depression, I remember Dr. Tony Attwood informing me of cognitive behaviour therapy which I tried to implement to control negative thought processes. These days I have come to terms with having Asperger's syndrome. I am more confident about disclosing my diagnosis, and do not feel as though I am a second rate neurotypical, as Dr. Tony Attwood puts it. I find that my advocacy work; such as writing blogs, and getting Aspie Support off the ground, has enabled me and other adults on the Autism Spectrum to accept each other more, and feel less isolated and abandoned. The advice I give younger adults and children is to recognize that being Aspie is not necessarily the problem; the problem is that non-autistic people do not understand that there are benefits of being Aspie. These include a mindset for detail, and a unique way of existing as a person. My thinking is individual to me and I shouldn't have to change it in order to be like others. I believe that for an Aspie, individual thinking is part of having the condition and it is how I exist.

It is also important to understand that when a negative spiral does develop, a person needs to know how to quickly find and implement a strategy from their emotional tool kit to handle it. I have found exercise beneficial in lifting and changing mood. Gyms often focus on physical appearance, but if you want a programme to help you feel less depressed, explain to an instructor that you have Asperger's syndrome and want to overcome anxiety. You will probably find that a cardiovascular programme will assist in lifting your depression. Another important point is that you should try not to develop a set of false expectations that may be impossible for you to reach. There will be expectations of you in the neurotypical world, but as an Aspie, it is better to just know what is best for you and to work within your own confines.

Bob Castleman

Depression is the fraternal twin of anxiety. They play together in the mind, harvesting mental energy, stealing it from things we want to do and think. My own experience with depression has given me an interesting "theory" about it. I suppose neurologists and psychologists will find this wholly unscientific, but it is a useful framework for understanding how depression works in me, and how I believe it works for others on the Autism Spectrum.

It reduces to simple cause and effect. Everyone wants to affect and successfully interact with his or her environment. Whether short term (satisfying hunger by eating) or long term (meeting a career goal), each of us wants to have our thoughts and intentions align with what is happening around us and, further, have those thoughts and intentions manipulate our environment according to our expectations. We spend our entire lives building a cognitive map of our world, adding and subtracting things that become our reality. When this cognitive map aligns well with the external world, we have a clear sense of cause and effect. If I do "A" then "B" will happen with a high probability. An accurate cognitive map allows successful interaction and manipulation of our environment. To the extent that this cognitive map is erroneous, our ability to successfully negotiate life is degraded. The less successfully we negotiate life, the more frustrated we become. Frustration leads to anxiety, which leads to degradation of cognition, which leads to more frustration, and so on. Depression creeps into the picture when this cycle becomes pervasive and exhausting. We run out of the mental energy to adjust our cognitive map and simply stop fighting. The deeper the depression, the more completely we stop.

How does this work for someone with autism? By definition, autism is a neurologically based difference in perception and processing. These differences lead to often profound and disabling variants in socialization, communication and cognition. If you live in a world where 90 percent of the people communicate 80 percent of their thoughts through body language and you cannot perceive body language, how can you begin to build an effective cognitive map that accurately represents cause and effect? If your core cognition is pattern based and not verbal, even if you can talk, your cognitive map is built on a truly foreign "language." Your sense of cause and effect is radically different than 90 percent of the world. You cannot easily learn to affect the world around you because the world truly thinks differently. You become frustrated, angry and anxious. You have shut downs, meltdowns, outbursts, and exhibit "random" behaviors. Then you run out of mental energy, tired of fighting with reality, and fall into depression.

The answer? Very simply—know thyself.

I was diagnosed late in life. I learned of autism at about 50 years of age and was formally diagnosed at 52. Simply knowing about this neurologically based difference has been astonishingly transformative. Years of frustration and baffling failure suddenly made sense. The feeling that I was always three steps off the beat was because I actually *was* three steps off the beat. But this isn't because I can't dance. It's because I couldn't even hear the music. But since my diagnosis, I know that there is a social language out there, one that I cannot speak well, but that is pervasive and influences everything around me. Just knowing that this other language exists gives me powerful tools to modify my own cognitive map and enable successful interactions with my environment. The more I learn about autism, the more familiar I become with the differences in the way I think and perceive. The more I learn about how the vast majority of the world thinks, perceives, and behaves, the better I get at understanding cause and effect. The better I understand cause and effect, the better I get at interacting with this crazy world. The better my interactions with this world, the lower my frustration and anxiety. Less frustration and anxiety equals less depression.

Truly, knowledge is power.

Debbie Denenburg

I am not ashamed to say that I spent many years of my life in a suicidal depression. I knew intimately the heartache of having unmet needs. I obsessed over not whether I would kill myself, but how. It was very clear that no one was interested in helping me figure out why I was in such a desperate state of mind. I had to learn how to deal with it on my own. This is the conclusion I came to.

If you are depressed, it is *not* your fault.

Depression is starvation of the soul. The soul is a living being and therefore it has requirements that must be met in order to feel healthy. Each of us is the only person on the planet who knows what our individual soul is lacking. This may include connection to other people. Therefore, relationships are soul nourishment. So is learning. Our souls crave knowledge because it satisfies curiosity.

Some souls need excitement and adventure. Those things allow us to feel life itself. It is up to each of us alone to identify the specific needs of our own souls. When we have accomplished that, then we can focus on fulfilling them. Those specific needs have to be a top priority in our lives. Asking for help in forming relationships, learning about new subjects, and feeling the life that comes from having adventures is the right thing to do. Feeding your soul is the starvation of depression.

Qazi Fazli Azeem

"What goes up must come down."

This quote is attributed to Sir Isaac Newton, who questioned why the apple fell on his head when he was sitting underneath an apple tree, and went on to discover the mathematical proof for gravity. Much has been said about Isaac Newton being on the spectrum, based on his behavior and abilities. I can say here that what goes down must go up. Those on the spectrum are driven strongly by specific interests, to the exclusion of other activities and people. This hyper-focussed behaviour may result in neurotypicals being distanced from us, not all of them understand our passion in things that make us happy. The lack of peer support and an absence of others who share our unique interests can result in being sad. Some of us may not desire the full attention of others, but, occasionally, being alone and having no one to share your interests with can result in sustained sadness (i.e. depression), which requires the help of doctors.

When we are focused and are really concentrating on the task at hand, we lose sleep and are awake for days. This causes a biological reaction in our brains and bodies, and depression will occur, particularly with those who do creative work, such as design or writing. Depression is inevitable, since life is not perfect, and our role in society has to be earned after years of service, struggle or contributions. In my case, I did not have any friends (outside my family) for most of my younger years, but this did not stop me from sharing my artistic ability (miniature clay modeling) with strangers and people that I met. This allowed me to avoid interacting with them, and concentrate on creating something that I could give to people or show them, which they would then take away, leaving me to my reading and comic books. I did this for nearly 15 years, moving on to other forms of art and design, so that people would interact with me in the context of what I created.

The reason why I mention this relationship of interaction based on practical purpose is that depression sets in faster once you don't have a routine. It is important to keep busy and create things, preferably artifacts and objects that can be admired by others, sold at galleries and fairs and shops (to fund the purchase of the raw materials), and if possible, to teach these skills to children and others after you master them.

The desire to help others and teach them my way of doing things became the singular purpose of my life a decade ago, as I became a part-time and then a full-time educator. Interacting with students has been the most rewarding experience of my life. Most of them are still in contact with me through email.

This social network I created through my experiences as a design educator does not allow me to think about my own weaknesses. This is how I overcame my inclination towards depression, by sharing what I knew, inspiring others to do the same, and using my abilities for good as opposed to thinking about what I could not do well. I am a role model to my students. My actions, achievements and goals continue to inspire my students as I share my achievements on social media. This desire to spread positivity through example allowed me to look beyond what I could not do and to overcome and remove depression.

Richard Maguire

Getting out into life, feeling good and succeeding are hard for us. Our development is delayed, we don't make enough contacts with people, our education is often a disaster, our family relationships are often strained, we have been defined by a series of things we failed at and did not achieve, and we have debilitating levels of anxiety all the time.

I was there at 21, old enough to move out from home study and do a job. But even though I was old enough, I was not developed enough. The whole lot came crashing down. I compared myself to my chronological peers and I felt awful. I got depressed and the only reason I am here now is because I got the dose wrong. Today, I am very pleased my suicide attempts failed. Where there is life there is hope. I clung to that back then, and I celebrate that truth now.

I was very depressed throughout the early decades of my life. I could see no hope for the future. I have found that this is a common experience for autistic people, and in my mentoring work I have found common themes and cures for this. Please read on, and I hope this helps:

- We are autistic, not faulty. We are different people with our own places in the world, and we complement the majority of non-autistic people. It is important that we feel good about this and that we find our places in the world. Our places are usually niches in human life. It can be fun and interesting finding out where we fit, and fun being there.

- Our development takes longer than non-autistic people, and this is fine. We need more time to bloom and get settled into our niches. Take heart and disregard what is thought of as normal development and timescales. Enjoy the extra development time—you deserve it. We are different; so be different—it's okay. Use time and your autistic passions and interests to find your place in life. Don't push it or worry, it will happen.

- Our education often happens best later than most people's. I got my degree when I was 44, and in my life that was the right time. Don't feel bad because school is or was hard. There is a lot of life to be lived, and you can find your own level and qualifications.

- Depression begins and ends. It is a part of life, not the whole of life. Most people will be depressed at some time in their lives. Depression is a creative state of mind. See how many creative people contend with depression in their life and art, and see what they create. You can too.

- Depression can and will end. The solution is within you. Depression can help you find the solution by teaching you to be persistent, strong and resourceful in life. You will be tested and refined beyond what most people experience. You can learn how to be strong and face life knowing that you have been tested to your limits and not broken. In fact, you will have survived and that is a very strong place to be in life.

I have helped lots of people through this process; where there is life there is hope; people prove that every day.

Depression helps you find out who your friends really are. And that is good. Share life with these people, grow and be strengthened, and depression will become less of a problem. You can even be happy and strong after all that. Lots of people make it; I know many of them.

Temple Grandin

Some people need to take antidepressants. A low dose of an antidepressant stopped my constant anxiety and panic attacks. I have a complete description in my book *Thinking in Pictures*.

You need to get out and do things. Mother never let me stay in my room all day. Go out and do some volunteer work. Good volunteer jobs are:

- working at farmer's markets
- delivering meals to seniors
- visiting people in nursing homes
- tutoring students
- walking dogs at an animal shelter
- working on repairs of a house in a low income areas.

Getting active helps to overcome depression. Another thing that helps is exercise.

REFERENCE

Grandin, T. (2006) *Thinking in Pictures: And Other Reports from My Life with Autism*. London: Bloomsbury Publishing.

Ruth Elaine Joyner Hane

Our viewpoint, how we think and feel, is determined by the messages we send ourselves after *an event happens*. This is our mindset. A positive attitude is important in overcoming depression.

Many on the Autism Spectrum struggle with depression, dejection and despair, while happiness and joy elude us. During high school, my business teacher asked me to stay after class. "I'm noticing that your response to other students is one of irritation and impatience." I was amazed that he would believe that. Since I did not recognize that this was the unintentional impression I was giving, Mr. Outwin promised to quietly say, when he noticed, "Your attitude is showing." Over the course of my senior year in business class, I began to see that on the days when I felt sad and dejected, my attitude was one of impatience. My teacher helped me reframe my attitude and change my mindset.

When something happens, such as not having homework done, our inner voice blames and shames us for failing. Melancholy creeps in and sadness and gloom persist, while gratitude and happiness are inaccessible. If our mindset is sadness, our life seems dark. Sometimes depression gains a foothold lasting for months or even years.

Feeling hopeless can trigger despair. My mother called to tell me, "The doctor found an aggressive cancer. I have a few months to live, and I don't want chemotherapy." It was the end of the winter term, and I had a major design project due the next morning. I pressed myself to concentrate on drawing lines and water coloring the perspective drawings. With each pencil line, I pondered life without a mother. I slept badly that night, as the wind pelted icy rain against my bedroom window.

In the morning, the elm branches glistened from the ice storm. As I turned left into the University of Minnesota, St Paul campus, my car slid sideways, the back end bumping over the curb. Fortunately, no damage was done to my car or anyone else, but the slide-out caused me to be angry and late for class. When the professor asked me to present my project for the usual class critique, a waterfall of suppressed feelings surfaced. The next week, I made an appointment to see a student counselor.

If my life feels lackluster, I ask myself, "How are you doing with depression?"

If I am not doing well, I can transform my negative attitude with a positive message of self-worth, affirmation, and gratitude. I change the naysayer voice that told me that icy morning: "Now look at what you've done! You deserve to crash your car! You're stupid and worthless! Why are you bothering to go to college when your husband and children don't support your dream of a degree? Everything is hopeless."

Reframing a situation is beneficial for me. Through counseling and group support, I learned to disclose my vulnerabilities and shame in a safe environment. I realized that by being loving and kind and changing my negative self-talk to positive affirmations, I could be patient and understanding of others and myself.

Transform your mood by spending quality time with supportive family and friends. *Predict a positive outcome* for yourself by posting affirmations on sticky notes where you will see them often.

"You are loveable, you are strong, and you are worthwhile."

In addition to counseling, there are many resources for treating depression, sadness and despair. Sometimes medication is prescribed for a lasting neurochemical imbalance in the brain. Maintaining a healthy lifestyle with good nutrition and exercise is important, and calming anxiety through meditation, yoga and other chi balancing endeavors is beneficial.

Mitch Christian

Depression really first hit me as puberty developed, although I was probably a little depressed when I was younger in a more mild way. By the second or third year of grade school it was pretty apparent that I wanted to spend less time with my peers and more time by myself at home or at school. My teachers eventually let me stay inside during recess, since I wasn't really involved in the activities of the other kids anyway. Adolescence just made things worse when socializing became a way to identify self, and being popular was equated with self-worth. I did some occasional hanging out with one classmate at a time over those years, but never really felt comfortable at anything like a group get-together. Mostly I would get lost at home in books, music, television, or doing art.

At college, I was nearly completely lost being away from home for the first time, and began to eat compulsively, such that I was obese by the time I was ready to graduate. I had switched my major from astronomy to art, and the resulting lack of a strict schedule was probably a mistake for me. During my final year, I began having random crying spells that didn't seem connected to anything going on in my life, but were accompanied by a persistent feeling of loneliness and sadness. Once I graduated, I moved back home and spent a year trying to get a job but with no success. This was most likely a low point for me. Finally I went back to school and got a degree in computer programming, and after earning my degree, I was hired and began working full time.

The stresses of an office workplace were considerable, but the routine of regular hours and a structured environment gave me a framework to build a plan for losing weight. Over time, I weaned myself away from unhealthy habits and began to slowly lose pounds, building up a little confidence at the same time. Eventually, I started an exercise routine that accelerated the weight loss and helped me maintain it for the long run. Unfortunately, by this time I had developed Type 1 diabetes. And due to my increasing exhaustion at work, I started drinking excessive amounts of coffee. That, and the diabetes, put me into a mental state where my moods would swing from manic energy and a more aggressive personality at work, to nearly complete lethargy once I got home. I lost interest in making art or even reading anything besides magazines. This went on for a number of years until, after several attempts, I was able to break out of those habits and create a lifestyle that suited my needs more closely.

Now I stay well regulated with a stable calendar of activities that I maintain pretty closely throughout the year, including all of my favorite interests in moderation, along with periodic chores that help me appreciate and look forward to the fun times. A simple organic diet and a consistent exercise schedule are very important factors for me in that equation. Over the last few years, I've become more involved in online social media sites, especially those where I can find others on the spectrum. In understanding others like me, I gain a deeper understanding of myself. Seeing that many people have been through similar experiences to varying degrees creates a sense of belonging that can be comforting when life is not going so well.

Dr. Tony Attwood's Advice on Overcoming Depression

There are many reasons why a typical person can feel depressed, but why are people who have an ASD more vulnerable to feeling sad and depressed? There are several reasons, including intense feelings of social isolation and loneliness, low self-esteem, often due to being rejected by peers, and the internalizing of peer criticisms and torments. Other reasons include the mental and emotional exhaustion from socializing, not being able to tolerate intense sensory sensitivity and excessive change, and a cognitive style that focuses on what could go wrong, which leads to a pessimistic outlook on life. Another potential cause of feeling depressed is the perception of a diagnosis of an ASD, such as Asperger's syndrome, as a disability, and a self-perception of being irreparably defective and socially stupid.

The characteristics of ASD can also prolong the duration and increase the intensity of depression. People who have an ASD have considerable difficulty conceptualizing and disclosing in conversation with others their inner feelings, preferring to retreat into silent solitude and to resolve the feelings of depression by subjective thought, or by using their special interest as a thought blocker for depressive thoughts. Neurotypicals are better at articulating and disclosing feelings. They know that another person can provide a more objective opinion and validation of emotions and cheer them up by reassurance and words and gestures of affection or compassion. Another person can provide distraction by initiating enjoyable social experiences, or using humour. People who have an ASD, on the other hand, can have considerable difficulty resonating with, or being infused by, the happiness of others, and may not perceive social experiences as an antidote to feelings of depression. Indeed, social interactions may reinforce the reasons to feel depressed.

Everyone feels sad sometimes, but a clinical depression is a deep sadness that can be difficult to break out of. One in five neurotypical people suffer a clinical depression at some point in their lives, so you are not alone in feeling sad and experiencing a clinical depression at some stage in your life. The good news is that we have a range of strategies to reduce the depth and duration of a depression. Effective clinical treatments exist in the form of cognitive behaviour therapy conducted by a clinical psychologist, and a range of antidepressant medications that can be prescribed by a doctor.

Strategies to Feel Happy Again

IDENTIFY PERSONAL STRENGTHS, QUALITIES AND ABILITIES

Chapter 2, on self-esteem, included an activity to identify personal qualities, particularly in the areas of abilities and personality. Low self-esteem is a major cause of feeling depressed and this activity can be used as an antidote to these negative feelings, providing clear, visible evidence of personal strengths.

CHANGING THE PERCEPTION OF ASPERGER'S SYNDROME

Those who have an ASD are not defective but different, and indeed, ASD can be associated with great achievers. There are famous people in science, the arts and information technology who have had the characteristics of ASD in their profile of abilities. They include heroes such as Albert Einstein, Alan Turing, Mozart, Andy Warhol, Bill Gates and Steve Jobs.

It is important to recognize that ASD may have given you specific talents. People who have an ASD can be very loyal and dependable friends; are interested in meaningful conversations rather than "small talk"; have a determination to seek the truth; demonstrate an advanced use of visual reasoning and problem solving; show great attention to detail; have exceptional long-term memory for facts and information; show great determination; and have a unique perspective for problem solving. They may also be able to sing in perfect pitch, draw with photographic realism, or write wonderful, imaginative fiction.

Congratulations, you have Asperger's syndrome! This has given you specific abilities: please use them wisely and appreciate those abilities, and they will be appreciated by others—and then others will appreciate you.

A Happiness Repair Tool Box

The many strategies and techniques that may be employed to help ward off or overcome depression can be thought of as tools in your emotional repair tool box. The authors of this, and many other chapters in this book, have confirmed the value of techniques such as physical exercise, self-belief, good sleep and nutrition, relaxation and meditation, and sharing your feelings with someone you trust, as effective emotion repair tools. They know what they are talking about and have empathy for your situation.

Some of the additional tools that have great value in overcoming depression are:

- *Having a caring role*, such as being a volunteer for those who need help, or caring for animals and pets: Being needed and appreciated is a powerful antidote to feeling lonely and depressed and can be a major reason why thoughts of suicide remain just thoughts.

- *Exploring aspects of spiritual, personal or religious beliefs*: Spiritual support can alleviate depression and encourage a feeling of optimism and happiness.

- *Engage in positive, happy activities*: Feeling depressed deprives you of energy, pleasure and initiative, so you may have to be brave and summon the energy to restart old hobbies, activities and interests, or discover new sources of pleasure and happiness.

- *Creativity*: The depth of emotion experienced when depressed can be expressed and alleviated in drawing, writing poetry or music, and creating lyrics to songs. If you cannot find the words to precisely express your despair, ask someone to listen to a song or section of music that you have chosen that expresses your feelings more eloquently than you can do in a conversation. Another option is to go to Google Images, type in the word "sad," and select and print images that you can then share with others to communicate your feelings of depression. A picture is worth a thousand words.

- *Cognitive behavioural therapy (CBT) strategies*: Clinical psychologists have devised strategies within CBT programmes for depression, to change pessimistic and distorted thinking. These can include challenging the belief that the derogatory comments of those who have teased you are accurate descriptions of your personality and abilities. The CBT strategies can also include examining the actual evidence for certain beliefs that cause feelings of depression, putting specific events into perspective, and exploring ways of changing your self-perception and your perception of past, current and future events.

Employment

From my extensive clinical experience, I have come to recognize that a good and satisfying job is a far better antidote to depression than even CBT or medication. Enjoyable and productive employment provides structure for the day, a sense of self-worth and an income to purchase sources of enjoyment. Part of a programme to combat depression can be to seek support in finding, maintaining and enjoying successful employment. There is more information on this in Chapter 12.

Strategies that are Not Recommended

Finally, there are some strategies to cope with feeling depressed that are clearly not recommended, such as using legal substances such as alcohol and prescription medication, or illegal drugs such as marijuana, opiates or amphetamines, to induce a sense of emotional isolation or detachment—a safe, emotion-free "bubble"—that helps numb the pain. It is important to note that long-term use of alcohol and recreational drugs such as marijuana actually increases the risk of experiencing and maintaining a deep clinical depression. You may need to seek help if you use such strategies and have difficulty reducing or eliminating self-medication for depression through illegal drugs and the misuse of alcohol or prescription medication.

RECOMMENDED READING

Attwood, T. and Garnett, M. (2014) *Exploring Depression CBT Program with Young People with ASDs Manual.* London: Jessica Kingsley Publishers. (to be confirmed)

Dubin, N. (2014) *The Autism Spectrum and Depression.* London: Jessica Kingsley Publishers.

Artwork (See Plate 5)

Painting: My Blue Face

Artist: Debbie Denenburg

Artist's Commentary: Depression is starvation of the soul. This blue face represents what a starved soul looks like. A voice that has not been heard. Feelings that have not been validated. A life that has not been approved. This face lives in a world where it has surrendered to the conclusion that it does not belong there. Nothing can be done to change that. It is starved for acceptance. The real shame is that this soul has so much to offer. If only it weren't invisible.

Painting: No Escape

Artist: Michael Tolleson

Artist's Commentary: The feeling of depression cripples and reduces this person to sitting on the ground and covering her face to shield herself from the waves of despair. There is no escape as the weight of this feeling leaves her hopeless. When in this situation, there is no future or hope, only the desire to physically fold up, away from everything.

CHAPTER 6

Living with Sensory Issues

Stress Ranking: 6

Ranking of issue by stress caused

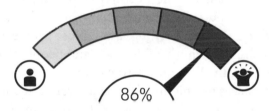

86%

Percent of respondents living with issue

83%

Many people with Asperger's/HFA have sensory issues. Some examples of this are: being affected by sounds, lights, smells, touches and tastes. Do you have sensory issues?

Lisa Morgan

In dealing with sensory issues I have learned to know myself well enough to avoid areas that are difficult. Also, to take care of myself if I have been exposed to an environment that has been hostile to my senses.

I have accepted that I must live a bit differently than others. For example, I never go to amusement parks, fairs or festivals on busy days. I might go on a wet, rainy day rather than a beautiful day when it will be very crowded. I will go very early to the most popular exhibits or make the decision to not see them at all. I will not go to a popular local amusement park unless it's right at opening time on Sunday morning, when most people are at their places of worship. When it's about noon and people start coming to enjoy the park, I will be on my way home.

There are places like nightclubs that are very difficult sensory-wise. I tried to go to nightclubs when I was younger, and tried to enjoy them, but it was always a disaster. I couldn't hear any of the conversations going on, the noise was painful, people were crowding me in, and I felt completely overwhelmed. I have learned to enjoy a quiet place where there might be music playing in the background, with just a couple of people, so I can participate in the conversation and not be overwhelmed.

If I must take the subway, I bring noise-reducing headphones, listen to my favorite music, or wear earplugs. I will also stay close to the doors where there are fewer people. If I must ride a bus, I try to stay close to the front.

At work, I have learned to be open and honest with my sensory issues. My colleagues understand my sensitivity to noise and smells. They also appreciate my ability to hear and smell things they can't. Several times in my life I have smelled hot wires or smoke when no one else has, and have been able to stop a possibly dangerous situation.

I do not make my sensory sensitivities a huge issue where I demand the environment to be completely adapted to suit me. I do the best I can to be comfortable in the environment I'm in and will quietly ask whoever is in charge to make some changes if necessary.

I have learned to make taking care of myself a priority if I have been exposed to a hostile environment. I might get into my most comfortable clothes, in my favorite place, and do something I love to do. It might be listen to music, read a book, watch a movie, do a puzzle, whatever makes me happy and relaxed. I might enjoy a favorite food, or go for a walk, take a bath, or a myriad of relaxing activities.

I have stopped making excuses, feeling inferior, or being sad that I don't enjoy what the majority of people look forward to. Accepting who you are, what you enjoy, and what makes you overwhelmed is something we all must do to live peacefully with ourselves.

James Buzon

I guess I've always had sensory issues, but it took a while for me to realize how much I was affected by sensory overload. I mostly noticed that all of a sudden I would feel tired. I didn't know what was making me tired until I spoke with fellow Aspies. It all sounded a bit odd to me at first; how could things like sound or light or even textures exhaust one's energy levels?

I started looking at the circumstances that preceded the times that I felt drained. Sure enough, the situations were loud, brightly lit and full of activity. My mind couldn't parse the various sources of input. It was like putting everything in the room inside a giant dryer, and turning it on. I was inside the tumult. At such a time, I'd react strongly, and either run away or feel like curling up into a ball.

While I was attempting to understand my sensory issues, I found some evaluations from when I was very young. I discovered a statistic measuring central auditory processing and was curious. It turned out that my processing speed in regards to sound was below the tenth percentile, or below 90 percent of my peer group.

I always wondered why sometimes my understanding of others was impaired, and why their voices sometimes didn't make sense. Now I had my answer.

I haven't been properly diagnosed as having Central Auditory Processing Disorder, but my experiences coincided with the symptoms. I have a suspicion that my difficulty with processing sounds (specifically voices) is connected with the difficulty I have separating other sensory input. Just knowing that my experiences aren't unique seems to help me when I feel the need to escape.

Additionally, I've found that if I block out some input to one sense, it generally helps me tolerate a stressful situation. Colored sunglasses help block out harsh white light from indoor lighting; I have both yellow and rose lenses. This helps when I'm feeling stressed out between college classes and I can't escape from noisy environments. I started buying large aviator shades with mirror tints on a whim, and found they really help block everything out. I feel like I've gotten some sort of respite from the chaos. In the future, it may pay to look into expensive colored glasses, but for now a 10- to 20-dollar pair of sunglasses works just fine.

To a lesser extent, good headphones and music help me retreat into a less stressful world. Music at least has structure, more so than human speech. The sounds of conversations running over each other and fighting for their places can be torture when every other sense is likewise overstimulated. If I can manage it, I have my favorite music available on an MP3 player (or laptop if I'm sitting still). It helps even more if the headphones have a good lower register. The bass combats the sometimes tinny sound of human speech.

If all else fails, a dark or dimly lit room is a last resort. In fact, I've fitted every light in my room with a low wattage bulb (60 watts the highest) and invested in colored lights. Depending upon my mood, I can choose a slightly reddish hue supplied by string lights, a yellowish glow from a 25-watt "stained glass" bulb, or just have one low wattage incandescent bulb from a lamp burning. I also made sure my own private space has textures that I've chosen myself. I tend to prefer plush and flannel textures. When combined with subdued lighting, I have a perfect Aspie getaway. I find I've been able to hold my frustration in check when I know I have a comfortable setting waiting for me at the end of the day.

Richard Maguire

This is advice from both living with sensory issues and having worked with other autistic people.

- Sensory issues will not go away, we have them for life.

- It is better to deal with them than retreat into a limited life dictated by sensory issues.

- Sensory first aid; this phrase comes from a mother who helps her son pack a sensory first aid kit for when he is out and about. I carry earplugs or a music player to use in the event of loud noises. I carry a calming stim object: personally, I carry a camera for this purpose—you may want something else. Carry scents that calm you. Wear clothes that are sensory-friendly. Carry dark or colored glasses if they help. The list could go on.

- Ask people close to you—family, friends and good colleagues—to be more understanding. If you can deal with sensory issues, you are far better at everything else. Help these people be calm and not comment about sensory issues. This can help other people feel better about your sensory needs.

- There will always be some people who do not understand your sensory needs. People in the above category help just by understanding and being empathic.

- Each day is different and sensory needs can vary. This is life: do not worry about it. Take each day as it comes and do what is needed.

- Feel good about eating a limited range of foods. You need to, and that is fine: you are not hurting anyone by doing this. Learn to be kindly assertive when people question what you eat; this will help them get the idea and not bother you.

- It's okay to wear clothes that are comfortable. Ask a good friend to advise on fashion and looks with clothes you can wear, so you can look and feel good.

- Have a sensory profile done on you. The information helps.

- Read Olga Bogdashina's *Sensory Perceptual Issues in Autism and Asperger Syndrome*. This is a very good book and will explain lots. Ask family and friends to read it. If they won't, you will have lots of things to say and explain after reading this book yourself.

- Give yourself permission to be who you are, with your sensory issues. This can help you feel a lot better. Other people can be helped to feel better about your sensory issues if you do.

- Do not be a sensory issues bore. No one will like that, and they may be less likely to be accommodating of your sensory issues if they are bored and fed up of hearing about them.

- Get enough sleep. This will help you feel better, stronger and less bothered about sensory issues.

- Some events and places can just be too much. Give yourself permission to limit the time you spend in them, or avoid them altogether.

- Take a rest from sensory irritants if they cannot be avoided. Recharge your coping abilities.

- Use home as a sensory-safe comfort base. From there, you can then enter into an unpredictable sensory world. One rule is: do not hide from this unpredictable world. Learn to cope with it through sensory first aid, getting respite, dressing comfortably and having understanding people on your side.

- Remember, you are not going mad and you are not inferior. You are autistic, and you will have a very different sensory profile. This comes with being autistic.

- Be happy, that helps lots. Smile and laugh as often as you can. I go to YouTube for laughs every day—it's good medicine.

RECOMMENDED READING

Bogdashina, O. (2003) *Sensory Perceptual Issues in Autism and Asperger Syndrome.* London: Jessica Kingsley Publishers.

Anita Lesko

Life with Asperger's is like living with Dolby Surround sound, wearing 3-D glasses like those used in movie theaters, and having your sense of smell and touch jacked up to the max. Simple things like going to the grocery store or a restaurant are anxiety-provoking events that only we can understand. These issues affect every aspect of our lives, right down to our choices of clothing. Trying to explain this to a neurotypical is actually pretty entertaining—to watch that look of absolute disbelief come over their face, the furrowed brows, the squinting eyes and the head slightly tilted to the side. It makes me feel truly special that I have all these "extras"!

First I shall discuss clothing. Most Aspies have their uniform, as I call it. We tend to wear black or some dark color. Prior to discovering I had Asperger's, I always assumed that I was drawn to wearing black because it makes you look slimmer. No, it's an Aspie thing. We all select an outfit, then have 20 sets of it. I nearly fell off my chair laughing at a cartoon I recently saw of Steve Jobs standing in front of his closet, scratching his chin saying, "Gee, I have a keynote tonight... I wonder what I should wear?" as he peers in at 20 black turtlenecks and 20 pairs of blue jeans on hangers! Whatever we're wearing, you can bet it's soft and comfy. We don't do fashion. We do soft.

Auditory, visual and olfactory issues are more difficult to control, and often the workplace has one or more areas you need to deal with. If your work environment affects your ability to concentrate or function, you need to talk with your supervisor to let them know this, and work together to correct the situation. You must become your own advocate. Identify what bothers you, think about how it could be made better, then talk to your boss to let them know what the distractions are and what can be done to minimize it or alleviate the stimuli.

As an anesthetist, I am exposed to two forms of stimuli: extremely loud music of the one particular genre that I *absolutely cannot handle* (i.e. anything heavy metal or angry, with those electric guitars). The other is any kind of case that smells. There are a number of types of cases that fit this bill. Years ago I'd be assigned to rooms that either had the loud music playing, or the case smelled. Since my diagnosis, I request to not be on those cases.

You must also learn to advocate for yourself in public places, such as restaurants and grocery stores, that are playing blasting music. I go talk to the general manager, explain that I have Asperger's and kindly request that the volume is turned down just while I dine or shop. Just be sure to ask in a very pleasant fashion. I've never had anyone turn down my request.

If bright lights are an issue in your workplace, wear tinted glasses or even sunglasses if need be. Always be sure to have a pair of sunglasses in your vehicle to wear while driving, and use your visor to its fullest advantage. I can't tolerate the strobe light effect that occurs while driving when the sun is shining through the trees. I'll get my visor and swing it to that side and adjust it to maximize sun blocking.

My main point is simply that you need to be an advocate for yourself. Don't be afraid to take charge of your life.

Paul Isaacs

For me, sensory issues I live with are very complex, but nevertheless, through understanding them, I have been helped with my self-esteem and confidence.

- *Face blindness:* I have problems with recognizing and processing faces. This has been an issue for me for a long time because the face is far too complicated to process and understand. At times I have problems recognizing my own face.

- *Object blindness:* This is being visually "mono-tracked." I can only process my surroundings one piece at time, much like a floating jigsaw puzzle. This is also is the same with people; I focus on one area and "lose" another part of them.

- *Meaning blindness:* I have problems with understanding objects and the meaning behind them. I live in a world which is full of patterns, shapes and colors, but with no meaning. When I was a child, I would lick, sniff, tap, rub, mouth and touch objects, trying to get the "meaning" of what I was feeling.

- *Comprehension blindness:* I have problems with understanding what text means. Filling out forms and reading letters can be confusing for me. I may be able to pick out the letters and words, but not the meaning. This causes confusion and annoyance.

SOLUTION: IRLEN LENSES

In the summer of 2012 I was diagnosed with Scotopic Sensitivity Syndrome. This confirmed the diagnosis of the sensory issues I described above, and also gave me an understanding of how they affect my perception of the world. Irlen lenses have "pieced my world back together" by helping me with facial recognition, body language, identifying objects, even comprehending letters. They have also reduced my headaches, lethargy and anxiety. They have truly improved my life and my sensory system. They are enabling me to do so much more with my life.

Dr. Know

My approach to sensory issues is to avoid them and protect myself from them.

LIGHT

- Get sunglasses and use them—possibly more than one pair, and if you use regular glasses, consider getting prescription sunglasses. Using hats or hoods can restrict the amount of light that goes into your eyes as well. If you are indoors and the amount of light is bothering you, don't be ashamed to use these protections and don't worry too much about what others think.

- If possible, try changing, dimming, obstructing or turning off sources of light, or instead move them or yourself to reduce your exposure. In the workplace, discuss these possibilities with Human Resources or your boss, as appropriate.

- Avoid activities or places where the lights bother you (e.g. headlights while driving after dark, when you probably should not use sunglasses).

SOUND

- Get earplugs; I like silicone but there is a variety on offer. Or get noise-blocking headphones, either in-ear or those that cover the ear. Use them, and don't worry too much about what others think.

- Covering your ears with your hands helps for sudden loud noises, such as sirens.

- Avoid going to places where the loud sound bothers you (e.g. concerts, discos).

PRESSURE CHANGES (AS IN AIRPLANES, WATER IN EARS)

- In some circumstances, earplugs can help as well, but be sure that it is safe for you to wear them.

GASES AND PARTICULATES (SUCH AS POLLEN)

- There is not much to do other than trying to avoid the sources, holding your breath or mouth breathing while you try to distance yourself. Unlike sunglasses or earplugs, a gas mask is not something I would generally advise wearing, though you can try nasal screens for blocking larger particulates like pollen (if you cycle, a cycling mask can block some pollution).

- If you are cooking at home, don't suffer from acid in your eyes (onions)—try swimming goggles (silly looking, but it works). Food smells can usually be avoided with some ease and if odors on your hands bother you, you can rinse them through water together with some stainless steel (a knife blade should work, but be careful not to cut yourself; otherwise get a "stainless steel soap").

- If smoke particularly bothers you, avoid cars and places where smoking is allowed.

- To avoid perfumes or body odor you need to keep some distance from other people, which may entail not using certain types of public transportation. If your concern is perfume, I believe in some workplaces you can bring your issue to the attention of Human Resources, or your boss, as appropriate.

FLAVORS AND TEXTURES

- If you are not an independent adult, communicate your issues clearly and reasonably and get them to be taken seriously. Otherwise, it is best to not put in your mouth something you don't want in contact with your tongue.

- Try to avoid getting stuck in situations where you get surprised by food you don't like when there are no other options (ask in advance, and also keep some food with you so as not to go hungry).

- If you have frequent issues with flavors or textures, you may need to prepare your own food to avoid the problematic ingredients.

- Finally, try new things only in controlled environments.

TOUCH AND FEEL

- Use fabrics and clothes that you like, avoid those you don't like.

- Protect yourself with gloves, and so on, to handle textures or sensations you don't like; this may include using socks with sandals.

Lars Perner

Historically, sensory vulnerabilities have not been part of the DSM (Diagnostic and Statistical Manual of Mental Disorders). Since the DSM characterized the Autism Spectrum primarily in terms of social functioning, many of us were not aware that our feeling of sensory overwhelm had anything to do with the condition. Sometimes, we may not have been aware that ordinary people experienced things differently. Interestingly, those of us on the spectrum may be either highly sensitive or very insensitive to a particular stimulus. A friend of mine, for example, would amuse others by sucking on car battery terminals, completely oblivious to the sparks flying, while being reduced to panic when exposed to the bright lights of retail stores.

In the general population, most people have what has been identified as an optimal stimulation level. Even for ordinary people, sounds that are too loud become too much. On the other hand, without sufficient stimulation, most people find their experience boring. Sometimes, those of us on the spectrum may actively seek out strong stimuli. I, for example, love hot, spicy food. On the other hand, I am a rather picky eater and find the tastes of many foods that a lot of people seem to enjoy rather unpleasant. The point is that those of us on the spectrum may reach and exceed the desired level of stimulation much more quickly—and sometimes more slowly—than most people.

Since sensory vulnerabilities differ between individuals and may not be obvious to others, it is important to identify those stimuli that one finds particularly troublesome. Some can be relatively obvious—loud sounds, bright lights and strong smells— but in some cases, it is not just a matter of the magnitude of the stimulus. Certain sounds can be much more bothersome than others, irrespective of their actual volume. It should be noted that people on the spectrum might experience stimuli that the general population can't consciously detect. If a child complains about a humming sound from a refrigerator several rooms away—something we might think that no one could detect—the experience may be very real and painful. Things that are obviously not painful to most people—such as having one's hair cut—can be severely so for some of us.

Sensory overwhelm can be particularly stressful if it comes as a surprise. If it is anticipated, at least we can mentally prepare. Since sensory overwhelm can greatly interfere with thinking and planning, finding the most effective coping strategy "in the heat of the moment" can be problematic.

In my experience, sensory overwhelm is significantly magnified when I am tired. Things that I might have been able to handle when better rested become unbearable when I am worn out. This is a vicious cycle, since sensory overwhelm contributes to growing exhaustion and fatigue.

On a very practical note, I was taught that networking is essential. Therefore, I would always dutifully attend cocktail parties and receptions at conferences. The problem here was not actually social. People at conferences, for the most part, were there to pursue the same interests as me. The problem, instead, is that it is very difficult for me to separate the voice of the person who is standing right next to me talking from the blur of all the background voices in the room. Finally, I gave myself permission to skip the receptions and a get a good night's sleep. I would then talk with people individually during breaks, building connections much more effectively.

Mitch Christian

Noises are a major irritant to me. Any sort of rattling, clanking or jingling noise can be annoying, and sudden sharp sounds can make me jump. Loud volumes of noise can be physically painful, depending on the pitch and duration of the sound. The high-pitched, sudden beeps of alarm clocks, microwave ovens and elevator bells are on my list of least favorite things. If I control the source of the noise and know what to expect, the problems are often reduced, so, for instance, I can play music quite loudly or enjoy a loud movie if I choose which song or film I'm exposed to.

Certain kinds of light, such as glare and reflections, can bother me, and pulsing or strobe lights can be nearly intolerable. Just the intensity of a light source might be enough to make me cringe. Sometimes just simple acts such as squinting, shielding my eyes or turning away is enough to reduce the problem to a manageable level. Wearing shades in bright sunlight helps a lot, or just placing the edge of my hand against my forehead can block enough of the light to reduce the stress. Non-glare computer screens are a big plus for working in an office.

Touch sensitivities run the gamut from the need to wear only all-cotton clothes, to light brushes on my skin that I recoil from. Massages are pleasant, though, and I think it's the deep pressure that helps relax me. I've never been fond of handshakes, but I've grown to accept them as part of the expected social demands. In situations where I encounter these problems I try to direct my attention away from their source to something else around me. So, for instance, if one part of my body is in contact with an unpleasant texture I try to concentrate on another part of my body that isn't being irritated. Or just mentally focusing on a different object to the one that is touching me can help, so in the case of a handshake I might think about the person's face or clothes instead of their hand.

When I was growing up, I couldn't stand slimy foods like tomatoes or the gristle on meat, which would cause me to have a gag reflex. Gradually, my tastes expanded with time and I've been able to try a wider diet over the years. I still avoid spicy food and oysters, though. In my late twenties, I began noticing issues with certain foods that would give me digestion problems, and had to start eliminating some of them from my diet. Pork was a big one, and I haven't had a hot dog for many years. Still, I try to eat a variety of food that is as unprocessed at possible so it doesn't contain added ingredients. I like to try new foods once in a while, too, and I've found that starting with small portions can be a good way to get used to a new taste.

I have a strong aversion to certain odors, such as chemical smells, and I usually hold my breath in the grocery store aisles that carry cleaning products or gardening supplies. Some perfumes are just as bad, and I avoid cigarette smoke and hairspray with a passion. Luckily, there are a lot of unscented products available these days like soap, lotions, detergents, fabric softeners, and so on. Sometimes, pleasant odors such as vanilla or cinnamon from a scented candle can help mask an unpleasant one; air filters also work.

Dr. Stephen M. Shore

Been there: After sitting at our table and ordering our meals, I begin to realize that the restaurant we chose is too noisy or there's a bright light over my head. I tell my friend we have to leave—now! Bad-a-boom!

Done that: Another meal ruined. Both I and the other person are bewildered by the sudden departure. The waiter is also left wondering what happened. And all that comes from the experience is anxiety from the incident and a sense of dread about returning to that restaurant.

Try this:

- *Build a strong foundation of self-awareness:* The above is an example of an undiagnosed sensory issue. All that I knew at this point was extreme anxiety and a need to leave the situation, without understanding why. Realizing that I have sensitivities to lighting and noise makes it easier for me to modify my environment as needed.

- *Conduct a sensory scan of the environment:* Sitting under recessed lighting fixtures for me is like looking into a spotlight for most other people, and knowing that I am hypersensitive to light noise makes me realize that the first thing I need to do upon entering a restaurant or other location is to take stock of the lighting and noise levels. Should the lighting and noise levels constitute what I consider a sensory overload violation, I will look for a quiet place in the restaurant and make sure I am not seated under a recessed lighting fixture. Finding myself in a location that fails these two criteria results in my choosing another place to eat.

- *Develop and implement an advocacy plan:* If I am in the restaurant I will ask for a quieter location. Should my table become noisy at a later point, perhaps due to a large party sitting down nearby, I will ask the waiter or waitress for a quieter place to eat. Similarly, with recessed lighting, I may ask the person I am seated with if they would mind switching chairs with me because there is a recessed lighting fixture above my head.

Dr. Tony Attwood's Advice on Living with Sensory Issues

At last, the DSM-5, a clinician's textbook that defines Autism Spectrum Disorders, has included "hyper- or hypo-reactivity to sensory input" as a diagnostic criterion for ASD (American Psychiatric Association 2013). Thus, sensory sensitivity will be evaluated during a diagnostic assessment, recognized by clinicians and academics as one of the defining characteristics of ASD. This will subsequently lead to the development of conceptual models of sensory sensitivity and effective treatment.

To date, we do not really know why sensory issues occur in association with ASD. However, we do know that this characteristic tends to be a life-long issue. The good news is that adults with an ASD have greater opportunities to create and maintain a lifestyle that minimizes experiences of sensory sensitivity, and greater maturity enables the person to temporarily endure the experiences, rather than have an irresistible need to escape from them.

It seems that all the sensory systems can be affected in ASD, and often the person has various levels of sensitivity in not one, but several sensory systems. The most common is auditory sensitivity, with tactile, visual, olfactory and taste sensitivity often co-occurring. There can also be sensitivity and a disturbance of proprioception (a sense of the position of the body using information from internal signals) and vestibular systems (sense of balance and orientation). It is not simply hypersensitivity; there can be hypo-sensitivity, especially a lack of perception of, or reaction to, some sensory experiences such as pain and temperature. There can also be temporary fluctuations in sensory perception, such that the same experience is perceived as less or more intense from day to day or hour to hour; fragmented sensory perception (focusing on parts and detail rather than wholes); and sensory agnosia (difficulty interpreting from which sensory system a sensory experience comes). There can also be a desire to experience more intense sensations that might be unpleasant to neurotypicals, such as the taste and feeling of exceptionally spicy or "hot" food. The reactions to such sensory experiences may be perceived as eccentric by neurotypicals, but are a recognized characteristic of the sensory profile associated with ASD.

ASD is also associated with synaesthesia, or cross-sensory perception, such as seeing images in association with specific sounds, and prosopagnosia (face blindness, that is, a difficulty recognizing people's faces). There can also be an association with Scotopic Sensitivity or Irlen Syndrome, a visual perceptual dysfunction that affects reading abilities by distorting print and the visual perception of the environment. Thus, sensory experiences can be extremely intense, confusing and frightening for those who have an ASD.

Strategies to Cope with Sensory Issues

The Aspie mentors have provided several personal strategies for coping with sensory issues in this chapter and you may find that you benefit from having an assessment of your sensory profile by an occupational therapist or psychologist, which could provide valuable information on which of your sensory systems are affected. You may also find it helpful to read literature (see the end of this chapter for suggestions) on the sensory sensitivity associated with ASD.

Occupational therapists have designed assessment instruments for the sensory sensitivities associated with ASD, and often use sensory integration therapy for both sensory sensitivity and difficulties with sensory processing. Irlen lenses, developed by Helen Irlen, can also reduce visual distortion.

AVOIDING OR TOLERATING AVERSIVE SENSORY EXPERIENCES

As an adult, there can be greater opportunities than as a child or adolescent to create a lifestyle that minimizes the risk of encountering specific unpleasant sensory experiences. You will need to explain to others why you are perhaps choosing to engage in such eccentric avoidant behaviour, but there will be greater understanding and support when the neurotypicals around you know why you are avoiding certain situations. Most neurotypicals will not have experienced personally the intensity, pain and distress that you experience because of your sensitivity, but may have greater understanding and sympathy if you make reference to the sound of fingernails scraping down a blackboard—many people hate this. Almost all neurotypicals find some sensory experiences mildly unpleasant; try asking them which sensory experiences they find difficult to tolerate, and then explain how for someone with an ASD, there are many more sensory experiences that are perceived as unpleasant, and to a much greater degree, than there are for neurotypicals. The problem in ASD is that the distress or pain is so much more intense, and is often in response to common daily experiences. This should elicit more compassion than the somewhat heartless comment, "Just try to ignore it."

The good news is that with maturity there can be greater ability to temporarily endure the sensory experience, using cognitive strategies such as reassuring self-talk ("I will be out of here in ten minutes," or "I must be brave and try to keep going"), which can inhibit the impulse to escape. Mature adults with an ASD may also have the assertiveness to ask for changes in environmental experiences, for example, requesting that the volume of music in a store or restaurant be turned down, or to be seated in a secluded area of the café.

REDUCING THE INTENSITY OF THE EXPERIENCE

Sometimes the intensity can actually be reduced. For example, in the case of auditory sensitivity, you might choose to wear industrial noise-reducing headphones or earplugs, or listen to music using earphones. This strategy can camouflage the external auditory sensory experience in community settings, such as supermarkets or shopping malls.

Tactile and visual sensitivity can be reduced in some cases by choosing clothing carefully. The problem can be the uncomfortable feeling of the fabric on skin, and the scratchiness of labels and seams; but you may also find bright patterns and colours visually overstimulating. People who have an ASD may prefer to choose subdued colours, and often wear clothes that are all black; this also solves the problem of the colour coordination of clothing. However, a problem for women with an ASD is the expectation by neurotypical women that one should be fashion conscious, which often involves wearing uncomfortable and impractical clothing that may be brightly coloured or highly patterned. It may be more important that you feel comfortable rather than fashionable.

ALTERNATIVE SENSORY EXPERIENCES

It may be worth considering having with you a portable "repair kit" of alternative sensory experiences that neutralize specific sensory sensitivity. For example, have a scent that you perceive as very pleasant in a spray bottle, and when you experience olfactory sensations such as someone's body odour when using public transport, spray a tissue with your chosen scent and inhale it as an antidote to the obnoxious olfactory experience. The sensory repair kit could also include a good book or a small computer game console that could act as a temporary distraction, mesmerizing enough to block out specific sensory experiences.

A common characteristic of sensory sensitivity for those who have an ASD is an aversion to fluorescent lights, which may appear to flicker, and downlights in ceilings that provide too intense a level of artificial light. An alternative is to ensure greater access to natural, but not too bright, light, or to wear a baseball cap or visor indoors to stop the effect of downlights on visual perception.

Strategies that Do Not Seem to Work

Neurotypicals may assume that if you have repeated exposure to an unpleasant experience, you will gradually habituate to it and it will be perceived as less intense. They may also believe that if this does not work, you should just try to ignore it. Neither strategy works in reducing sensory sensitivity; it is an interesting characteristic of ASD that repeated experience of an aversive experience (desensitization) does not lead to habituation, and if an experience is particularly unpleasant, it is almost impossible to ignore. You need compassion and cooperation to help you either avoid or tolerate sensory experiences.

REFERENCE

American Psychiatric Association (APA) (2013) *Diagnostic and Statistical Manual of Mental Disorders, 5th Edition.* Washington, DC: American Psychiatric Association.

RECOMMENDED READING

Bogdashina, O. (2003) *Sensory Perceptual Issues in Autism and Asperger Syndrome: Different Sensory Experiences—Different Perceptual Worlds.* London: Jessica Kingsley Publishers.

Bogdashina, O. (2010) *Autism and the Edges of the Known World: Sensitivities, Language and Constructed Reality.* London: Jessica Kingsley Publishers.

Artwork (See Plate 6)

Painting: The Fire Within

Artist: Michael Tolleson

Artist's Commentary: I live with sensory issues daily. Warm clammy hands on me might as well be sandpaper, as well as the typical clothing label discomfort issues so many of us experience. This painting has to do with sensory issues with water. For me, it is a daily experience I brace myself for. Simply put: water hurts. This painting shows the cool, refreshing stream of water becoming flames as it hits. He stoically braces himself and receives the cool stream knowing how painful it will feel when it hits his body. There are no other choices or escape from this daily routine. For someone not on the spectrum, sensory issues are something that cannot be imagined or truly understood.

Painting: Living with Sensory Issues

Artist: Jennifer Healy

Artist's Commentary: In this image, the snake adds a sense of dread and anxiety. This is exactly what having sensory problems can be like. Sensory overload often results in shutting down after no release from the flight or fight mode. But, even though it's sometimes a hurdle, life around us can still be a beautiful thing. That's why I chose the inviting color scheme and the nature elements. Sensory issues are difficult but there is always hope.

CHAPTER 7

Making and Keeping Friends

Stress Ranking: 7

Ranking of issue by stress caused

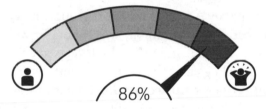

86%

Percent of respondents living with issue

82%

Many people with Asperger's/HFA have difficulty making and keeping friends. Some examples of this are: "I don't know how to start a conversation," "I don't know how to be a friend," "I don't understand what to do when my friend doesn't call or write me." Do you have difficulty making friends?

Anita Lesko

Making friends is one of the most complex issues facing everyone with Asperger's. We've all been there and done that! We all know the feeling of thinking we've made a friend. You trusted them enough to confide in them and believe in them, only to have that belief shattered. It's a sickening feeling. You feel lost and wonder why you fell for it again. Being very naïve can play into this problem; it certainly has for me.

After starting my Asperger's support group, I met an Aspie my own age. We had lots in common, and I thought we'd be friends forever. For the first time in my life, I felt relaxed enough to share my innermost feelings and thoughts—something I'd never done before, because I never trusted anyone enough to do so. For the next year and a half, this went on, only I didn't recognize one small issue that I should have. On our very first lunch get-together, this person, a female, had announced to me she was gay. That did not bother me—I am very open-minded and accept everyone. What I didn't recognize was that this person was thinking of me in a romantic way. There were signs along the way I didn't see. Or perhaps I simply chose not to see them.

Then one day it all came crashing down. I was *extremely* busy one week and had forgotten to respond to her text message. During that time I did send out a reminder to my support group for our next meeting. This friend, who also received that group email, became angry. She texted me that I seemed to have time to email all those people but not her. She then sent me an email of all the things I did that annoyed her. It was pretty ugly. It was then I realized it was the sort of thing an angry female does when her boyfriend cheats on her. I discussed it with a number of people for second opinions. They all said the same thing—that I was correct in my analysis. I took that whole thing badly, because I thought I had developed a strong friendship for a lifetime. I was too naïve to recognize what the other individual was hoping for—a relationship that I would never be interested in. I felt lost for a *long* time.

However, I never give up. Over the past two years since my discovery of Asperger's, I've been meeting more and more people on the spectrum. I've also been meeting endless neurotypical (NT) people who choose to work with people on the spectrum. These are all the people I wish to surround myself with. I finally came to the realization that a friendship with an NT who has no prior exposure to Aspies will probably never work out. Maybe one day those folks will come to accept us. Until then, I'll focus on Aspies and NTs who work with us by choice.

My best advice to Aspies is to get involved with helping other Aspies. This will put you in situations of meeting other Aspies and NTs who understand and accept us. This will provide you with people who are potential friends. It is a win-win situation. You will be helping other Aspies, and you will be helping yourself. It will provide a sense of belonging and acceptance.

Don't let one bad incident keep you from having the courage to try again. I didn't let that unfortunate situation sour me on finding friends. I look upon it as a learning experience. Not the end of the world.

Lisa Morgan

While growing up, I had only one friend at a time, sometimes none. I couldn't handle more than one, and didn't handle just one very well either. One by one, friend after friend, they would leave me in a terrible, hurtful way. Once, my friend wrote terrible things about me all over a nearby building in chalk so everyone could see. Another time, in front of a lot of other kids, this "friend" teased me again. And once I had a friend who would have nothing to do with me anymore because I didn't answer a letter she wrote me in college that I never received. She would not listen to the fact that I never saw it. She just had nothing to do with me anymore. I never saw any of these "breakups" coming.

What I have learned over the years is that it's not just all me. In fact, most of the time the difficulty had more to do with my friend than with me. I am a loyal friend. I don't know the word quit when it comes to friendships, so I would forgive my friends and allow myself to be in an emotionally abusive friendship.

What I have also learned is that there are safe people, and people who are not safe. By "safe" I mean being able to sustain a healthy relationship built on mutual trust, respect, boundaries and caring. Unsafe people have qualities such as being inconsiderate, selfish, cruel, controlling and immature. Although this sort of person can be an acquaintance, and can be part of your circle of friends, they would still be considered unsafe as far as being included in your inner circle of trust goes.

Learning to recognize safe and unsafe people can be difficult. I watch people constantly, and if I see someone who, over time, does not gossip, is caring, can be trusted, and is respectful, that is a good candidate for a safe person. Although no one is perfect, this person should consistently show these positive qualities. I try to get to know this person better, and see if we have common interests to share. Eventually, this person may become one of my "safe" people I can trust to be a close friend.

I'm not always correct, and if I find out one of my safe people is not safe, I will slowly stop spending time together until we drift apart. There is the possibility of confrontation to share your concerns, but it can go either way. Confrontations can either be a tool to strengthen a friendship, or reveal what you may already be suspecting, that your friend is unsafe.

Always remember, you are worthy of being in a relationship with a safe, reliable, caring person. Although they are sometimes hard to find, don't give up; they are out there and are worth looking for. It is worth putting the time into building a friendship based on mutual respect, caring, trust, and common interests.

Jennifer Cook O'Toole

Have you ever watched people in the grocery store trying to pick out the perfect melon? Some people shake them. Others sniff them. A few knock on them. They may be "in the market," so to speak. But I'm pretty sure that most of those shoppers haven't a clue as to how to actually find what they want.

The same can be said of Aspies and friends. We know we want friends; often, though, we don't really know how to choose good ones. In fact, you may not even realize that you should—or that you can—*choose* whom you befriend. When you are lonely, feel rejected or afraid, the want of companionship can feel bottomless. It's easy to compromise who we are and accept far less kindness than we deserve just to have someone by our side. I know. I've been there. I've accepted bruises and excused them. I've been the popular one, too, standing in the center of the crowd, yet feeling utterly alone.

There are so very many things I have learned about friendship that I want to tell you—about levels of intimacy and trust and listening more than you speak. There is far too much to say, and it's all far too important to gloss over. So, let's cover one moment thoroughly—the one moment common to every relationship, romantic or platonic, when we actively choose who and what we will allow into our lives. Stop with me here, and realize this: *you do have a choice.* And you deserve to make a good one.

"The minute you settle for less than you deserve," it's been said, "you get even less than you settled for." That's true in all things, be it fruit or friends. You have to "shop" for the right relationships, too. You need the right people by your side and at your back…not necessarily the obvious people.

Here's what I mean. In any crowd, class or club, there are naturally "attractive" people. Whether because of looks, confidence or power, they draw others in. These "obviously attractive" folks—who may be wonderful people—already have busy social lives. They don't need to make the effort to begin yet another friendship.

Don't spend your energy on obvious. Approach people who have room for and need of an extra someone in their lives. That's who will most value your company and probably work hardest to deserve your friendship, too.

So really, just be the kind of friend you'd want to have. Be yourself. Be real. Ask questions. Listen to the answers. Ask more questions. Don't just *think* compliments, give them. Take turns. Smile. Notice kindnesses, and say thank you. Relationships are about balance and reciprocity in communication, in invitations, in expense (of time and money). They are about being kind more than about being right, and about glad humility—not thinking less of yourself, but thinking of yourself less.

When you want something (or someone) new, you have to try something new. My husband, a police officer, had a panic attack before he asked me for our first date; he left the office where I worked, sat in his car—sweating and sick—giving himself a pep talk before he could walk back inside to find me. He was more terrified of approaching me than an armed robber. But in hindsight, he's awfully glad he risked it. So am I.

How do you make a friend? In the end, it's really very simple. You decide to take a chance. You say, "Hi." You may be ignored. You may fall in love. There's no way to tell. In fact, only one thing is certain. Every friendship, every love, every adventure and reunion began with a risk and a single simple word. Everything wonderful begins with, "Hello."

Qazi Fazli Azeem

I know the times you must have wondered if you are the only one out there who is interested in unique subjects that most people don't talk about. Turn your weakness into strength. Write about your interests. Make a drawing, an illustration, an animated video or a computer presentation. Share it online; show it to people in your class, at your university, on the internet. You will find others interested in the things that you like. Master your favorite subject—make your hobby into a career.

Can you work with computers? Start teaching others. Can you make art? Practice and get better and start displaying and selling it. Conversations can be easier if they are about your work and your interests. Do you like talking about your interest? Start teaching it to people. Have you got a lot of experiences that you can share with others? Write a paper, an article or a book about them, and share it with people around you and online. The internet is full of special interest groups, for people who get together to talk about Lego, cooking, computer games, books, comics, and every topic that could be your interest. You need something to talk to people about. If you don't know what to talk about, how about visiting the opening show at a museum or an art gallery? Observe people and listen to them, see how they start conversations, sustain them, and then end by exchanging business cards.

You don't have to look directly into someone's eyes all the time when talking to them; you can point at something, like a painting, and talk about that. Or look at their eyebrows or hair. I don't look at people's eyes longer than a few seconds when talking to them. Eye contact is really important though, I can't emphasize it enough. You really need to pretend to look towards people's eyes, particularly if you are meeting them the first time. This can be done by looking at their eyebrows or brow or nose, rather than directly at their eyes. I increased my tolerance of eye gazing by looking at my own eyes in the bathroom mirror for hours, for many months. The hardest thing to do after talking to someone about a topic that you both are interested in is to maintain conversation for long enough that you could find ways to collaborate later, or exchange business cards with them.

You have to learn to listen to the other person talk, no matter how much you want to say about your own feelings, or your favorite subject. Sometimes I consider listening to others as the most important part of conversation; let them do all the work by talking, and learn from their issues and obstacles. Give them advice if you can, or just hear them talk. I learnt more about teaching not by teaching others, but by hearing them talk about what they wanted to learn and what they wanted to do with the skills that they wanted to learn from me.

Making friends is about sharing public activities, such as going to the movies, having dinner, visiting a museum or a public lecture. Sometimes talking is not important. What's more important is being there for the other person, sharing the same experience in the same physical space, whether it is a private or public space.

I don't have friends my age. Most people who understand what I talk about are more than ten years older than I am. I met them through sharing, teaching and presenting my work at different forums.

Share your interests online with the world: there are many websites which allow you to meet others who want to share and talk about the same things as you. Reach out to the world, and if you don't know how or have not learnt about this, ask for help from others.

Richard Maguire

The first piece of advice I have is: don't try too hard to make friends. Friendships happen in life when we are not looking for them. A friend is someone we connect with in a special way. Friendships happen, they are not forced. If we try too hard to make friends, people will become uneasy and stay away. People will want to be a friend because of who you are, not the image you try to project. Learning and developing good social skills helps lots. We need to communicate with people so we can meet and make friends.

Being autistic, we will struggle to make friends in the sort of social situations in which other people find friends. We like to share interests; I have seen friendships made and develop in clubs for people who share interests. Sharing an interest helps us get round a lot of the social things that can be hard for us. For example, I am a keen cyclist and I have made friends in bicycle clubs. We can ride together, make conversation about cycling to get started, and find we get on well. We are also likely to share similar values and lifestyle. This all helps with friendships.

If you are young and at school or college, you can use interests and seek out the "alternative" people. We don't usually make friends with people in the popular crowds—our social skills are not up to it. I used to be around the cycle sheds at break times and made friends with the alternative set, and I found interesting friends. That is what my son does, as well. However, as we grow up something interesting happens. Unknown to us, some of the popular students liked us, and with adult maturity and the passing of time, we meet them and make friendships with them. They will often say that they did not know how to get on with us when we were younger, and they liked our integrity and independence. They say we were able to be ourselves, while they needed to conform; they valued our example, they thought we were freer than them. We take more knocks and surprisingly learn to be more mature and accept people for who they are—this is wonderful for making friends.

Anxiety can cause us to come across as aggressive and put people off. It's a strange thing, but other people can interpret anxiety as aggression. It helps if we physically loosen up with people and show fewer signs of anxiety; we can meet and find friends that way. Ask someone you know well to help you with how you come across to other people. They do not know what is going on inside us, so have to rely on reading our behaviour and body language to work us out. It helps more than I can say to learn how to come across as relaxed and open to other people. They are nervous too, and love to be with people that help them feel good. They too need friends.

Learn to smile. Smiles are not just a facial expression. They come from inside, and are an expression of our souls and state of mind. A forced smile is worse than no smile. I practise smiling from inside. My technique is to think of happy things, and to watch YouTube videos that make me laugh. I listen to music that produces lovely emotions inside me. I connect with all this and practise holding these emotions and states of mind so I can smile a warm smile from inside. That helps with friendships more than anything else I know.

Debbie Denenburg

I never had a best friend until I was 45 years old. She was 86. Kind of an odd pairing, yes, but it worked for us. I did not know at the time that I had Asperger's. All I knew was that other people had friends and I didn't. I could see clearly how easy it was for everyone else to naturally attract friends. It *looked* so easy. I wondered what I was missing. Until one day…I met Sophie. I had just moved into a house and this little elderly lady and her husband, who were our new neighbors, saw my husband and me outside one day. They introduced themselves. Sophie began talking. She was so unbelievably open and honest. Sol, her husband of 63 years, rolled his eyes at some of the things she said. It was really funny. I loved this woman immediately! As time passed, we all got to know each other well. Very often, when the four of us went out someplace, Sophie would hold my hand because she was afraid of falling. She confided in me all the time because I was the first person she ever felt safe talking to about personal subjects. Things like feelings and aging and how she was rarely able to make close friends. She shared her obsession with books with me. My husband and I remained very close with Sophie and Sol until their deaths.

After they were gone, I was getting heavily into my research of Asperger's. That's when I realized that Sophie was most likely an Aspie. That's why we connected. After her funeral, people kept coming up to me and saying how special I was to her. Even her own children had never seen her bond with anyone like this before. For the first time in my life, I knew what it meant to be a friend.

Since that time, I have found a new best friend named Audra. We met in a women's group online. We connected because Audra felt like she was always being criticized for being honest. I happen to love honesty. I let her know that I wanted her to be her true self with me. I didn't care about things like being politically correct. I wanted to know *her*. Well, she is an Aspie. We began talking more often. Then one day I got extremely ill. I had to go to hospital. Things weren't looking good for months. All during that time, Audra kept posting things to my Facebook page, always letting me know that she was there. She was my cheerleader rooting me on to get healthy. She even sent me a bouquet of flowers. She was exactly what I needed and I didn't even know it until I had it. This woman who lived 2500 miles away from me became my soul sister. Then one day, she wanted to meet me in person. She made arrangements to visit me. She faced her worst fears and booked her first flight. She stayed at my house for ten beautiful, crazy days. We are as close as ever.

My suggestion for making friends is basic. The hardest part is where to find friends. For Aspies, this usually means pursuing our personal interests and meeting like-minded people in the process. Next, it is crucial to take the time to communicate. Even if it's just email, communication is the glue that bonds human connections. Let the relationship grow at its own pace. Coax it along by asking questions. Get to know the other person's opinions on things you are interested in. Make a sincere effort to take an interest in the things they deem important. Always have respect, even when you have opposing views. Just because you don't agree doesn't mean that you can't be friends. Remember that we are all here for a limited time and ask yourself, "Is this someone I want to share my limited time with?" Your answer will tell you if they are a potential friend.

Henny Kupferstein

I love Facebook. It matches exactly what my needs are. I get to put out little blurbs so that people can take my "pulse" and check if I'm alive. This way, they don't have to call me and annoy me with mindless chitchat. I also get to keep in touch with people that I ordinarily wouldn't, without having to play the "calling to check up on you" game, where I am the loser due to my own anxiety. This prevents many uncomfortable interactions that I used to avoid. I now have a tool to bypass that.

Through Facebook, I have become adept at appropriate social interaction, but only by making enormous mistakes without intending to. I had to unfriend people that were constantly misunderstanding me. I now have many friends of the "hybrid breed" who are *this* close to the Autism Spectrum. They are the coolest people, because they comfortably straddle both worlds with grace.

Online communication perfectly supports turn-taking. I changed my face-to-face understanding of turn-taking by practicing online, and adjusting appropriately. From the internet, I learned that in order for you to comment on a topic, you must actually read and process the whole thing. If not, you run the risk of commenting on a part that caught your eye, and you will immediately expose your stupidity if you did not carry through reading until the punch line.

I also learned that people have different styles of getting to their point. Some make their statement right from the start, and then spend the rest of their turn supporting that thesis. Others begin with a small fact, and then spend their turn explaining why it is relevant, interesting, and connecting to the following small facts. Then there are those (me) who engage in the shock-and-awe style, where I drop a dramatic bomb, so that I fully engage the listener until I am done explaining. Many find it delightful and captivatingly clever, while others find it arrogant and rude, and take offense.

On the internet, I am never plagued with the panic of interrupting without meaning to. That greatly benefits me, as I am without stress and the "conversation" flows beautifully. Because I am a content-orientated listener, I don't need the gestures and body language to tell me how a person is feeling. Emoticons serve a very clear purpose, and are concrete indicators for me to reciprocate appropriately. I do get in trouble with violating ethical and social mores because of my twisted humor. I am particularly fond of puns, and I often turn words around to mess with people. My Aspie friends engage in such banter all the time, and we snicker and get great entertainment from that. But others who do not grasp the weight of the puns accuse me of being inappropriate and offensive. As the joke goes, I work well with others, as long as they leave me the hell alone.

Technology enables information to travel at lightning speed. This means that while I never knew what my relatives were doing over the course of a whole year, I now know what they are having for lunch, thanks to Facebook. So too, my first experience with cell phones was a woman back in 1998, crossing the street, oblivious to the honking around her, shouting into the phone, "put it on three fifty!" She was obviously rushing home, and delegating dinner tasks to her kids. I was humiliated. For her, for me, for all of society. I value a conversation. I treasure interpersonal connections that are pleasurable. To use a phone that was very costly back then, more than a dollar a minute, to yap about oven settings, just made me worry that the world as we know it was about to fall apart. Sure enough, people now use their gadgets to order pizza, swipe it as a credit card, and break up with boyfriends.

The directness and instantaneity of online communications sweetens the messages so that hits home. Therefore, I can easily accept it even if I do not agree with it. In contrast, unscripted and unplanned in-person conversations are highly cryptic to me, and counterproductive. My belief is, "Hey, whatever works." But I'm not alone in this. A group of individuals were monitored for change in depressive symptoms during and after internet interventions. The success rates were so enormously high that the study proved that "both cognitive behavior therapy and psychoeducation delivered via the internet are effective in reducing symptoms of depression" (Christensen *et al.* 2004). So bring on the grumpy cats.

REFERENCE

Christensen, H., Griffiths, K. and Jorm, A. (2004) "Delivering interventions for depression by using the internet: randomized controlled trial." *British Medical Journal 328*: 265.

James Buzon

Making friends is difficult, especially for us Aspies. Sometimes we come across as too intense. Other times, we're too shy. The middle ground can be hard to find. And we wonder…is it us or the other person?

It's a little of both. Some people, no matter how hard you try, will be difficult to connect with. Sometimes we tend to take it personally, because we're unsure of how to read social signals. It makes it difficult when you really like and admire someone, but that person doesn't quite see you as the good friend you'd like to be.

When I feel safe around a group of people, I tend to be more focused on making friends. People fascinate me, and I want to be around them. This seems to make NTs a bit unsettled, as it comes across as intense, and slightly intimidating. In the past, I would hover or continually try to show that I was a good person. That seemed to make potential friends nervous, and make it harder to form friendships. To top it all off, the words "creepy" or "weird" would start to be directed towards me: I'd close right up and become very shy. Shyness makes it equally hard to make and maintain friendships.

Most of the time, my impulsiveness was working against my efforts. Whenever I felt a bit of interest from anyone, I jumped at the possibility of a new friend. I never thought it was anything I was doing wrong; it all seemed mysterious and somewhat unfair when things did not work out. Why did everything seem so difficult?

I started to notice something peculiar amid my efforts. When I wasn't trying so hard, people seemed to come to me. It all seemed even more mysterious than what was happening to me when I really tried. I really began to recognize this pattern when I went back to school for another degree. The less I was obsessed with making meaningful connections, the more friends I seemed to be attracting. I kept myself available and open to conversations, of course, but didn't attempt to steer interactions in one direction or another. I think it allowed others to become more comfortable with who I was and let them discover my personality. It sometimes reminds me of approaching a timid cat for the first time; the more you let the cat discover you on its own, the more likely it is that it will allow you to approach in future interactions.

It's difficult for us on the spectrum to be patient with friendships. We can visualize the end result, and it makes us all the more eager to actively pursue interpersonal bonds. However, I think when we find the strength to be patient and allow others to come to us, we form tighter bonds with those who choose us as friends.

Dr. Tony Attwood's Advice on Making and Keeping Friends

Neurotypicals seem to find, make and keep friends easily, so they often have great difficulty understanding why this is so elusive for someone with an ASD. If a person with an ASD does not have any friends, the naïve response of an ignorant neurotypical can be, "Well, you should just try harder." Unfortunately, it is not that simple.

A number of important skills are necessary for an adolescent or young adult to make friends. These include the ability to read and interpret body language and understand social conventions and boundaries; the art of conversation and self-disclosure; and the ability to gauge the correct balance in terms of intensity of engagement in the friendship. None of these abilities are intuitive or easy for a person with an ASD. In addition, he or she may be particularly vulnerable to friendship "predators," who may abuse a genuine desire to be a friend, and find the ending of a friendship, with the resultant sense of grief, especially difficult to cope with. However, these are all skills that can be learned, though this takes time and considerable intellectual analysis and effort, which can be exhausting.

During the adolescent and young adult years, there can be an intense feeling of loneliness, which is especially agonizing when surrounded by so many peers and potential friends at high school, college or university. Each person with an ASD has a very unusual profile of abilities, interests and personality. If one were to use the metaphor of a person being a piece of a jigsaw puzzle, it is as though neurotypicals have shapes or profiles that fit together easily. Those with an ASD, however, may have to meet many more people before they find others who are like-minded, who match and connect, or that special person who fits perfectly—in other words, an Aspie friend. However, as there are several billion people on this planet, somewhere there is sure to be someone who matches or complements you and would be the friend you seek and need. Please be patient—but do ensure you are meeting new people.

There can be difficulties for those with an ASD at every stage of friendship. The first stage is to find a potential friend by participating in social events, and not marooning yourself in your bedroom, feeling lonely. This takes considerable courage and a careful choice of where to go to meet people. At school or college, you might choose to join groups that share a common interest, such as a choir, voluntary service organization or computer games club. It is best to avoid situations that involve loud music due to both sensory sensitivity and the difficulty of hearing someone's speech and being able to engage in a conversation. It is also wise to avoid situations where the excessive consumption of alcohol is expected, as intoxication by alcohol temporarily "dissolves the frontal lobes," the part of the brain associated with intelligence. You need that intelligence to process social information while making a friend.

When an acquaintance has the potential to be a friend, a very important social skill is to know the degree of intensity and frequency of interactions required to encourage rather than stifle the friendship. Those who have an ASD tend to be at the extremes of friendship intensity, either extremely shy, withdrawn and appearing to lack interest or commitment to the friendship, or too intense, intrusive and dominating, where the description "wearing his or her welcome out" would be apt. The skill is in knowing the right intensity level for the person and the situation. It is valuable to ask the friend if you are appearing to be very shy and seem not to be committed to the friendship, or too intense and overpowering. You will need that information as a response to a direct question rather than relying on your interpretation of subtle verbal cues and body language. Those with an ASD can find groups of people too complex and overwhelming, and may prefer one-to-one interactions, bearing in mind that "two are company, three a crowd."

There can also be issues of how frequently to meet and engage in text messages or correspondence, the disclosure of inner thoughts and feelings, and the development of loyalty and trust. A part of friendship is repairing a friend's emotions, cheering that person when he or she is sad, reassuring when anxious and calming them down when angry. Several chapters in this book have included advice on how to repair your emotions and that advice can also be used in making and maintaining friendships.

There will be times when either friend may feel neglected and it is important, as in any relationship, to have open and honest conversations and communication, as well as regularly reviewing the friendship. Those who have an ASD can be extremely loyal and trustworthy friends, eager to share practical and helpful information. However, friendships sometimes have a "use by date," and the ending of the friendship may not be accepted by both parties at the same time. Those with an ASD may have had several transitory friendships and be unsure why the previous friendships ended, and thus feel betrayed. The ending of the friendship reinforces and seems to justify a feeling of low self-worth. It is important to recognize that it is rare to have a lifelong friendship. Mutual circumstances and interests change over time and it is important to enjoy the friendship while it lasts, and to know that there will be new friendships.

Artwork (See Plate 7)

Painting: Just a Marble in a Box

Artist: Marilyn Cosho

Artist's Commentary: This collage is about a round person who likes being alone in a square box where everything is calm and familiar.

Painting: The Gathering

Artist: Michael Tolleson

Artist's Commentary: Making and maintaining friendships is difficult for many of us on the spectrum. The scene in this painting is about "gathering." The townsfolk are on their way to a social gathering while the woman gathers her twigs. So often with autism, we busy ourselves with our obsessions and ignore the need for bonds with people. Here in this painting, there is little concern with bonding with others in this small town.

CHAPTER 8

Living with Personal Management Issues

Stress Ranking: 8

Ranking of issue by stress caused

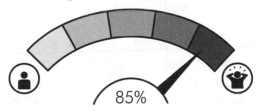

85%

Percent of respondents living with issue

72%

Many people with Asperger's/HFA have difficulty being organized without becoming overwhelmed. Some examples of personal management issues include: being able to make decisions on "what is *most* important," being on time, completing projects when they're due, managing your clothing, and personal hygiene. Do you have difficulty with personal management issues?

Mary Robison

I can be an organizational disaster, but I have learned a few things that work for me.

Every morning, if I am going to school, I take a shower. Every other day I wash my hair, as my scalp gets too dry if I wash it daily. I use conditioner. After I shower, I dry off, apply lotion (in the winter) and deodorant, then dress. If I'm not going to school, I may only shower every other day; I have very dry skin, so if I haven't been too active, it's all right. When in doubt, I shower. Underwear and socks must be changed daily. Pants can go two or three days, but shirts no more than two; look and sniff before putting them on. If there are any stains or smell, get clean clothes. For shoes, it is best to have at least two pairs and swap them, wearing different pairs on alternate days. I do my laundry at least once each week, washing sheets and towels, too, all with soap and disinfectant.

In the summer, I tend to wear black pants, a tank top and a matching (solid color) polo shirt. The tank top underneath keeps the shirt cleaner. In the winter, I usually wear black pants, tank top, a long-sleeved shirt and a wool jacket. If it is cold, I also wear a sweater, a black fleece vest, or both. I have several wool jackets: gray, black, purple and red. I try to wear only a single color (in addition to black/grey/white), as I have trouble matching things. Almost everything I purchase is solid-colored. I prefer to wear bright colors such as red, blue or purple. When I am teaching, I tend to buy solid-colored silk shirts that are machine washable; they look professional but aren't too difficult to maintain. I like to have at least three weeks' supply of underwear, bras, tank tops and socks. I stock up, because it can be difficult to find intimate apparel that doesn't irritate my skin.

I only wear pants with at least two pockets. In my left pocket, I keep my Swiss army knife and my keys (when I am out of the house). In my right pocket, I keep my inhaler and my cell phone. If the pockets are small, I keep my keys and inhaler in the front pocket of my purse.

My purse has a back pocket, where I keep my little notebooks with important information. The center area is where most things are kept; my wallet is attached to a cord, in turn attached to the strap so I can always locate it quickly, and so it cannot fall out and get lost. My makeup is in its own zipper pouch, and I have another zipper pouch with my credit card case, my change purse, any loose coupons, tax-deductible receipts, a small loose-leaf notebook and a pen. My checkbook has another pen and stamps in its pocket. My computer glasses in a case, a camera and its battery charger round out the center area. I go through my purse every few weeks to get rid of loose debris.

I have a hook in my kitchen to hang my keys as soon as I walk in the door. I usually hang up my purse, also, so I know where it is. Before I go to bed, I take my various medications and plug in my phone to charge. I keep my vitamins and medications in a large decorative pot on my table. At night, I empty my pockets and stack everything—my Swiss army knife, any notes and my inhaler—with my phone on top of my closed laptop. I have a computer bag, separate bags for each class, and a bag with generic teaching supplies (whiteboard markers and erasers, ruler, pencil case, laser pointer, thumb drive and notebook). That way, in the morning, I can load up my pockets, grab only the bags that I need, my keys and purse from their hooks, and be ready to go.

I use lists all of the time to make sure that I complete my tasks. I have little notebooks that are earmarked for specific things. One is only for my electronics projects. One notebook includes my shopping list. The list is divided by store, but I also keep a list on my cell phone. When I go shopping, I check both lists. I write notes to remind me of things that I need to do. I keep these notes either on my cellphone or on bits of paper in my cell-phone pocket. I check all pieces of paper before I go to bed and again before I leave the house. In this way, I don't forget to do things.

I have a calendar on my cell phone and a paper one on the wall in my kitchen. I write important dates on both. My school has a computer calendar application. I check all my calendars daily and set the alarm function on my cell phone for appointments.

The key to daily organization is habit. I try to always do things the same way. If I don't hang up my keys, I'll never be able to find them. Occasionally, I fail to hang them up and must spend hours searching for them, which can be overwhelming. I'm not naturally organized so I must really work at it. This is what works for me. You must find a scheme that works for you.

Anita Lesko

Many Aspies live extremely busy lives. I'm no exception. Long before my diagnosis, I realized I needed a very structured system to manage my life, and very early on I mapped out a system that I hope helps you too.

I have a clipboard that I use to make a list of everything I need to do for the coming month. I break this down by weeks, and then by days. Each task/goal is written down, along with any specifics for each one. I use a yellow marker to highlight the critical items.

This list is reviewed each day, often multiple times per day to check off each task as it is accomplished. Some flexibility has to be maintained, as occasionally something comes up that throws everything off. When that happens I can look back over my list and rearrange things to fit in what I couldn't do because of the emergency. I can maintain a feeling of control with this method, and it keeps me focused.

I also have a big calendar onto which I write appointments and any special dates. I am always sure to write down all appointments on this calendar or else I'd forget them. I keep both the calendar and clipboard on my desk. When not at my desk, if I think of things I need to do I write them on my iPhone notepad for later reference.

Sleep is a *very* important issue to discuss. There's no getting around it—all the latest research shows that everyone needs seven to eight hours of sleep each night, including REM sleep. The Dr. Oz Show is a great place to get plenty of information on this and many other topics. Visit www.doctoroz.com and search sleep. As a person with Asperger's, I know being well rested is a key factor in being able to maintain maximum performance.

Be sure to create a peaceful sleeping environment. I always need to have "white noise" when I sleep, which I get from a small fan on my dresser. I also *highly* recommend something with lavender fragrance in the room. I make handcrafted soaps and I get lavender oil from Provence, France, for the soap, as well as lavender buds. I get small soft sacks and fill them with the lavender buds and place one on my pillow, being sure to give it a gentle squeeze every few days to continue releasing the fragrance. I use a reed-diffuser to put the lavender oil in to fill the entire room with this beautiful, soothing fragrance. This fills my heart with joy and makes me feel overwhelmingly relaxed, ready to sleep.

Another key factor is food. I eat extremely healthily, mainly red quinoa, fresh vegetables that I grill, wild rice, tuna, chicken, fruit, nuts and very little red meat. I drink plenty of spring water too. I avoid fast food, as it makes me feel very lethargic, which equals decreased productivity.

Meditation is extremely important. Nothing fancy—just being alone in a quiet, peaceful environment allows you to tune out everything and concentrate on nothing. I use a Himalayan salt rock lamp that emits a mesmerizing peach-colored warm glow when lit.

Exercise is another important aspect of my life. Taking care of four horses and ten acres generates plenty of exercise, but I regularly walk 30 minutes each day after the farm work. No thinking is allowed. I just enjoy the outdoors and fresh air and recharge my batteries.

Bob Castleman

Rather than dive into all the various aspect of personal management, I am going to stick with something of critical importance to any person with autism who has or wants a career. To be successful in any career you need to be able to set goals and, further, be able to make and execute plans that enable the achievement of these goals. This is practically a cliché, being part of nearly every self-help book and career-planning guide ever written. But goals are not all equal. The type of goal that drives a career must be connected to something passionately felt. This passion pushes the goal deep into your thinking, informing and affecting your actions. Such a goal infuses perception, shuts out distraction, and allows a ruthless editing of the flood of information we endure in a technological culture.

It is tempting to think that someone with autism would be good at setting such goals. One of the curious things about autism is the ability to maintain intense, singular focus on a very narrow range of interests. This can become pathological when the focus is so complete that meals are skipped, bills are not paid, personal hygiene falls to the wayside, relationships are ignored, and all the other distractions of daily life are pushed aside. This is passion without direction. It is a state of mind that has no goal and no purpose other than to be in that state. It is a unity of mind that is impossible to describe, but one that all autistics recognize. We like being in this state of mind. We actively seek it, arranging our lives so that we can slip into our reveries as much as possible.

Such an intense focus left unchecked destroys careers. Even if such a passion is a talent or ability in high demand, without the capacity to integrate this passion into the ebb and flow of a work environment, it is nothing more than a wildfire that scorches everything it touches.

The difficulty with autism in the workplace is not passion or commitment. The difficulty is that goals are primarily a social construct. Many of the milestones that measure progress towards a goal are things like college degrees, awards, promotions, recognition from peers, and financial benefit. The singular focus of an autistic passion does not allow these considerations to even become part of the process. It's not that these things recede into the background and become minor elements in a bigger picture, but rather that they don't exist at all within that cognitive space. When operating fully within this space, there is nothing but the interest itself.

Worse, creating and executing plans to achieve a goal is almost entirely a social exercise. You need to network with people. You need to be able to understand the intentions and needs of others so that you can build cooperative relationships. But, by definition, autism includes clinically significant deficits in socialization. The very thing that enables career advancement is also the one thing that escapes those of us on the spectrum.

The only answer I have found to this paradox is that I must sacrifice a piece of that favorite mental space. I must cut a chunk out of my cognition and devote it to understanding a world that speaks a language utterly foreign to me. And even this is a partial solution, because the processing of the social world still *cannot* enter that place in me where I am most at ease. It never integrates, but only exists as a compartmentalized area of consciousness that I must acknowledge and accept. I cannot unify social thinking with the part of me that feels most free and natural.

Fortunately, this is not as hopeless as it may sound. The truth is that while sacrificing a small part of that cognitive space where I prefer to live and giving it over to dealing with the social universe, a curious side effect appears that allows me to navigate this heavily social world more successfully. The more successfully I navigate the world, the more I am able to enjoy my "zone" because I am not nearly as anxious and distressed about daily life. So although I must give up a piece of myself to have any chance at a career, it is a sacrifice I am willing to make.

Debbie Denenburg

I don't have a particular incident of my own to place here. This is the way I do things. I am compulsively organized because it alleviates stress.

Begin your personal management with these letters: OTAAT—MIF. This stands for "One Thing At A Time—Most Important First.

All good management is the result of a system. Every system is made of smaller parts that are put together. A good manager knows how to manage each small part of the system—one thing at a time—starting with the most important one. Your life is a system. If a part of your life is stopping the rest of it from functioning properly, then that is the most important part. Put that part *first*. An example would be if you were sick. You need to attend to your illness and get it under control. If you don't, then you are risking making everything worse. Your system is not being managed correctly. It is only when that part has been managed that you can move on to something else.

Another component of good management is knowing that everything has a place. All important papers should be kept in files. These files need to be divided into categories. These may be bills or records of any kind, such as medical or school. Each file folder should be arranged by date. The oldest date is in front. That way every time you get a new paper, you simply put it at the back of its file and everything stays in date order. This method can prevent meltdowns when you have to find a particular document.

Last, but just as important, is having a big calendar that you can write on. Write down all of your appointments and other events. Put times and names and addresses so your information will be there all in one spot. Then you can avoid the frustration of searching when you need that information.

Dr. Know

- *Keep track of time:* A simple countdown stopwatch can be a great help; for example, it can remind you to get back to work after a short break of some minutes. You will find this mode available in many wristwatches. If you need help not to lose track of time, or need a reminder about important dates, try setting an alarm. There is also good software available for computers or mobile phones that can be set to remind you automatically.

- *Organize your time:* All other things being equal, if you start earlier, you will finish earlier. Plan ahead, and allocate a reasonable amount of time for unforeseen events. Help yourself to prioritize and schedule your tasks by having a large calendar where you can see the various deadlines simultaneously across multiple weeks or even months; this can be on paper or using software. You can create intermediate milestones and set your own deadlines for them.

- *Deadlines:* There is a difference between what is urgent and what is important. Be aware that it is often easy to let urgent things take your time even though they are not important at all. Avoid this tendency when your time is too limited.

- *Leave home on time:* If you don't want to be late when leaving home, have a backpack or some other container ready with everything you need, so that you can just pick this up and know you have all your requirements.

- *Clothes:* It may help to have several identical copies of the same items. You don't need to go to extremes, but, paraphrasing fictional character Seth Brundle, it may save you the mental energy of deciding what to wear each day. Allegedly, Albert Einstein did this to some extent, having several versions of his formal suit for ceremonies, and in more recent times, Steve Jobs often appeared with his trademark uniform of jeans and black turtleneck, and Mark Zuckerberg confirmed in an interview that he had about 20 duplicates of the same gray t-shirt.

- *Individual hygiene:* If you have trouble with this (e.g. don't like to wash because of sensory issues or because you have other things you would rather do with your time) I suggest asking a dermatologist what the minimum frequency of showering for health reasons is (dermatologists will probably tell you it is actually better for your skin to not take a shower every day). Then just get your bathing done like any other unpleasant chore you have to do. For example, set a fixed schedule and keep to it—think of days when you exercise, and so on, and match the dates to minimize your body odor.

Lars Perner

One could reasonably say that I am highly organized or that I am highly disorganized. This all depends on how you look at it. Executive function problems mean that, unless I put in planning and safeguards in advance, I will end up quite disorganized. This, on the other hand, has caused me to develop explicit compensatory strategies, resulting in systems of organization of which many people would be rather envious.

To make sure that I bring the right things to class, I have a cart into which I put materials as I get them ready. This means that I do not have to remember and find things I need as I am about to head off to class. I find that I am not very good at maintaining file folders. If I have to rely on actual paper, I prefer binders that are more robust. Generally, when I get an important document such as a W-2 tax earnings statement, I immediately scan it so that it is on my hard drive. It is a lot easier to find my scanned file than to find the actual document.

To make sure that I remember my appointments and important dates, I use the Outlook calendar. It reminds me of events such as birthdays and meetings. This calendar includes even my regular classes so that I will get a reminder 15 minutes in advance of the need to leave for class. To be sure that I bring important things with me to work in the morning, I will often put a reminder on a Post-It® note on my door to remind myself.

To make sure that I remember to cover what I need to in class, I make a list of topics, including a list of any audiovisual material that I need to show.

Rather than collecting assignments on paper, I mostly ask students to turn them in online. I can then copy the text of a student paper into an email and type in comments there. That way, the paper goes directly to the student without having to be handed back. If the student comes in to talk about the paper, I can easily access the outgoing email. There are some paper documents that students have to turn in. Therefore, I bring plastic zippable folders to class and put everything I receive into these. The documents can then be sorted later, but I ensure that everything gets back to my office and is placed in the stack of documents to be processed.

Learning faces can be very difficult for me. To track student participation in class, I assign each student a "participation ID number." I print out a sign with the number in large letters and the student's name below that in smaller, but still rather large, letters. I ask students to "flash" their ID sign each time they participate. That way, I can take down participation on a pre-printed sheet with student names and numbers. The nice thing is that each time I take down a "participation incident," the student's name is refreshed.

When traveling, I need to carry a number of documents. I have a passport pouch that I keep around my neck when I travel internationally. When I first book them I save e-tickets, airport shuttle bookings and hotel reservations as PDF files into a directory for the specific travel event, and then print them all out before the trip. I carry these in a plastic folder so that they can be easily found on the trip. I can then add receipts as I receive them so that I have them for reimbursement or tax purposes as needed.

Ruth Elaine Joyner Hane

Organization in some areas seems logical and effortless; in others, a challenge. Since I have strong management skills, I have worked as secretary, business owner, and a store buyer. My kitchen is well ordered, with a place for each dish, pan and utensil, and my closet is arranged by color and season. However, tossing, donating and repurposing saved things that have an emotional attachment is difficult. Personal management challenges may be in some, but not all, areas of our lives. If chaos is a problem, the first step is to make a practical plan.

Personal management includes, but is not limited to: time, home and work environments, legal records, finances, recreation/hobbies and transportation. A lack of organizational skills can result in a messy lifestyle, and even become a full-blown addiction, resulting in hoarding and saving every item, without a storage plan or an assessment of need. Having no rules for order may seem appealing, especially to some teenagers, but lost items, rotting food and missed appointments are the consequence.

Frequently, those with autism find that judging time is difficult, since time management depends upon a notion of how long things take for you and for others to accomplish. Each task can vary depending upon your attitude and energy level. When our executive function is not effectively connected to past experience, personal management is challenging.

At the Edinburgh activity gym, I overheard a parent give a five-minute time boundary to a child, who nodded briefly, as he raced past. "Five more minutes and then we need to get our shoes and go home." Ten minutes passed. The next time I saw the child, his parent was distressed. "I said five minutes, not ten!" The child had appeared to agree with the five-minute rule, and seemed dumbfounded that climbing the tunnel and chutes tower had taken longer.

Some people have ADD and ADHD (attention deficit disorder, and attention deficit hyperactivity disorder) in addition to autism. With attention distractions, developing a system for order is elusive, with daily habits for placing keys in a designated catch box, hanging a jacket in a closet and dropping mail in a central container impossible to acquire. If we are to make organization a lifestyle, then a more rigorous plan needs to be made, including a system for rewards that influence the pleasure center of our brains. We are motivated as human being by pleasure more than by pain. If you have piles of clutter, with narrow paths, there is a major personal management problem.

There are many sources for learning and implementing good personal management skills. Checking on the internet, I see several sites for creating order out of chaos. One site suggests making an appointment *with yourself* to schedule a block of time, with no distractions, to do a task. Then, give yourself a reward. Tackle one small area at a time. For example, a messy drawer can be sorted, with the unused or useless items tossed and the remaining things placed in small boxes, or bins with dividers. Then you can find what you need.

Richard Maguire

Personal management is something I struggle with, as do many autistic people I know. People often ask me if I need a system for helping with my chaotic personal management. Trouble is, a system on top of what I have to do already just overloads me even more; I have to manage the system as well. I have mastered the art of minimizing everything that needs organization. I say I can do the task plus one thing related to it, never two or more. I have worked on planning my life with video scripts in my head. I cannot lose my head, it goes where I go and it contains all my life, thoughts and plans. I live my life out in conjunction with my videos in my head. I plan in videos, 3D photo realistic. I think in videos. I can stim in videos, really vibrant psychedelic stuff. I recall the 1960s and psychedelic art: it formed a deep impression on me and I learned to think in these colours and forms. I use them to plan and hang thoughts and tasks on. Find out how you think so you can use it to plan and give shape to your life.

I do not use any external device other than a blue diary where I put my bookings and events so I have a linear time line of places to be and things to do. A diary, that's all. The diary goes everywhere with me, it's my brain—without it I would behave like a lost ant.

It is common in autism to have organizational difficulties. People I know and have worked with have ways of coping. We tend to be either very organized and make precise frameworks to live our lives in, or we are disorganized and scatterbrained. I am the latter; my office at home is a complete random pile of stuff with a desk in it. But I like it that way. I just cannot organize, so I don't. That makes things simpler—I am happy with that. The diary is the only organizational thing I have, the only organizational thing I *can* have. It is task plus one thing.

When I speak in public, people are amazed that I seem so natural and do not use notes. In fact, I cannot use notes: their preparation, position and use overloads me; that would be task plus three things—so, no notes. But I do have those videos with sound in my head, which I play and act out in real life when I am speaking or performing any task. People just don't see them or the thousands of hours every year I put into making new videos and refining existing ones. I do my entire personal organization this way.

I have pre-made scripts. I was lucky my mother was a domestic science teacher and I learned all household tasks, including cooking. I could not organize these things myself, so I do them in a pre-learned pattern. This is something I'm good at. I cannot manage money in any exact way. I only have a sense of what I earn and where it goes, so I have an accountant who does what I cannot do.

I would advise working on ways of organizing yourself that you know work, and using them. Don't try to use too many systems, you can get lost in them. Use your passionate interests to hook things onto. Then rote learn the rest, and set up patterns in your life you will go back to again and again, so you can pick up on the things you need to remember. You can also ask family for help in planning. They may prefer doing this rather than helping you pick through your organizational mess. I know mine prefer it that way.

Dr. Tony Attwood's Advice on Living with Personal Management Issues

The term "personal management" includes many daily living skills, from personal hygiene to completing assignments on time. Psychologists use the term "executive functioning" to describe personal management abilities such as planning and organizing, the perception of time, working memory, prioritizing and flexible thinking. Unfortunately, a characteristic of ASD is to have difficulties in all these areas. Other specific characteristics that affect those who have an ASD are a vulnerability to being easily distracted by internal imagination when bored, problems working out how long it will take to complete a project, and difficulty remembering spoken instructions. Those with an ASD are not unique in having such problems, and children and adults with an attention deficit disorder (ADD) are similarly affected. Fortunately, we have some effective strategies that were first developed for those who have ADD, which can also be of great benefit for those who have an ASD.

Personal Hygiene

As a child, personal hygiene is the responsibility of parents, but as an adolescent and adult, it is the responsibility of the individual. The responsibilities include regularly washing all of your body, including cleaning teeth and hair, ensuring there is no pungent body odour, and checking that clothes are clean and appropriate for the situation. These activities may appear to be boring and time consuming, but are essential for health and are also very important in friendships and at work. One of the most effective ways of losing a friendship or failing a job interview is a lack of basic personal hygiene. For more information on personal hygiene, I recommend a book on puberty written by my wife Sarah, entitled *Making Sense of Sex: A Forthright Guide to Puberty, Sex and Relationships for People with Asperger's Syndrome*, published by Jessica Kingsley Publishers. The book covers many aspects of puberty from personal hygiene to sexuality (see Chapter 9).

Planning and Organizing

When it comes to planning and organizing, those with an ASD seem to be at the extremes of this particular executive functioning ability. They can be either disorganized and chaotic with regard to planning, organizing and especially prioritizing, or almost obsessively organized, with excessive neatness and an inflexible plan and expectations. Both groups have difficulty changing a decision when presented with new information and being flexible in considering another way to achieve a particular goal.

When planning an activity such as a project or even the schedule of activities for the day, it is important to carefully consider the range of options and the potential outcomes for each option, and the essential priorities, and to be prepared to make changes when necessary. This requires careful thought and flexibility in thinking.

A strategy that may help is to write or type the range of options and create a flow diagram to clearly see the options and potential outcomes. Drawing and creating a diagram can be much quicker and more effective than mentally thinking about and having to remember what to do.

If a decision is needed and there is considerable uncertainty or ambiguity as to which decision to make, I recommend the "On Balance" activity of imagining, drawing or using an old-fashioned pair of scales and placing coins on each side of the scales, with one side being one option and the other side being the alternative option. A greater "weight" of a particular aspect of each option is represented by more coins and eventually, on balance, one option tips the balance and is the wiser decision.

It will also help to have the schedule for the day in visual form, with time allocated for each activity. Software automatic reminders can be used to prompt when to end a particular activity. There will also need to be a list of material or resources needed for each activity, and a checklist to indicate what has been achieved and what is needed for the next priority.

The Perception of Time

The perception of time can vary according to how much the activity is enjoyed. Time engaged in a special interest seems to go so quickly and reminders to switch to another activity are at first disbelieved, as there must surely be more time remaining for this enjoyable activity. Again, modern technology can help, with the alarm clock function on cell or mobile phones being employed.

A difficulty for those with an ASD is accurately estimating how long it will take to complete an activity or assignment, often erring on the side of underestimating the amount of time required. It may help to seek the advice of a relative, colleague or friend on the time that needs to be allocated to a particular activity, and to work back from the due date or time to ensure that you have planned sufficient time to complete the activity.

Working Memory

Working memory is the temporary mental store for recent information. Those with an ASD can have an excellent long-term memory for facts and information, but a relatively limited capacity for remembering what has been said recently (auditory working memory) and quickly forget a thought; hence the need to interrupt others before the thought is lost. Thus, complex or lengthy spoken instructions are quickly forgotten. It will help reduce the effect of this characteristic if you use the voice recording facility of a cell or mobile phone to accurately record what was said, or at the time of listening to the instruction or information, mentally visualize or imagine the scene where the information will be needed. A "mental video recording" of what to do or what needs to be remembered may be easier to recall than spoken instructions.

If there are problems remembering a specific spoken instruction, it will help recall to return to where the instruction was originally given, as contextual cues may facilitate recall. If there is a tendency to forget where something has been placed, one strategy is to make a momentary mental photograph of where the item has been placed at the time it is placed there to facilitate recall of where it is.

Other Strategies for Personal Management Issues

Since psychologists use the term "executive function," you may need an "executive secretary." This is someone, perhaps a parent, who can provide guidance in executive abilities and daily living skills. However, this should only be temporary support, as eventually there will be a need for you to be completely independent.

A personal management skill which can be elusive for those with an ASD is flexibility in thinking, and being prepared to change your strategy or decisions with new information. It is wise to change strategies sometimes and also to be able to admit to others if you are confused about what to do, or if you have made a mistake and need to seek their help.

It is also important to recognize your attention capacity or attention span for a particular activity, and to take regular breaks to ensure that your concentration is maintained. There is also a range of medication available for those who have attention difficulties such as ADD. It may be worthwhile seeing if medication can improve your attention and executive function.

Having difficulties with personal management skills can be a significant cause of stress and disappointment in your abilities, especially when you know you have the intellectual capacity to complete the activity to a high standard. It is important that you and others know that these difficulties are not due to laziness or a sign of a character fault, but genuine difficulties that are a part of having an ASD.

RECOMMENDED READING

Attwood, S. (2008) *Making Sense of Sex: A Forthright Guide to Puberty, Sex and Relationships for People with Asperger's Syndrome.* London: Jessica Kingsley Publishers.

Artwork (See Plate 8)

Painting: Strings Attached

Artist: Marilyn Cosho

Artist's Commentary: Making a living is difficult when a person has lots of strings attached. The thread symbolizes getting tangled up in details and worry.

CHAPTER 9

Understanding and Succeeding with Intimacy, Dating, Sex and Marriage

Stress Ranking: 9

Ranking of issue by stress caused

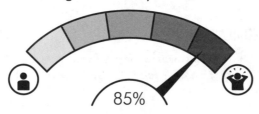

85%

Percent of respondents living with issue

77%

Many people with Asperger's/HFA have difficulty understanding all the complexities of intimacy, dating, sex and marriage. Some examples of intimacy, dating, sex and marriage issues include: being uncertain about what is expected or what is appropriate (i.e. in a social and/or sexual situation), not knowing your response to sensory issues involved with intimacy, and not knowing or even identifying a partner's needs. Do you have difficulty with intimacy, sex, and marriage issues?

Jennifer Cook O'Toole

As my husband, John, recounted a minor disagreement we'd had, I listened closely. Every so often during the story, I interjected to make a few "corrections." The intent wasn't to be rude…only to "fix" some of the "facts" he recalled. As I saw it, those mistaken facts were causing him unnecessary hurt. And, if a simple fact check could spare wounded feelings, everyone would be happier. Right? Nope. Turns out, that was one "fact" I definitely had wrong.

You see, I know there's no such thing as a "wrong" feeling. But, I have always reasoned, there are wrong facts that can cause unnecessary feelings. I wouldn't want my best friend to experience frustration or heartache for any reason…especially if a "better" understanding of the facts could prevent any discord from the start.

And right there would be the part where yours truly messes up. Without realizing it, in my quest for perfect accuracy and all the comfort it would bring, I was actually being quite condescending, a bit cowardly, and apparently irritating, to boot. Yikes.

The truth is that misunderstandings are *really* uncomfortable for me. You know how TV sitcoms often rely on "comic confusion" as the basis for the plot? Even as a child, I didn't like them. Instead of laughing along with the audience, I'd cringe along with the characters, changing the channel or leaving the room to escape.

Feelings aren't about facts. They are about perceptions. That much I know. But I had yet to learn that caring about someone means you respect him enough to bear his discomforts without protest or correction. His feelings—which will *always* be different from yours—are the reality to which you must respond.

Yes, I was trying to prevent John from avoidable hurt. But in digging deeper, I realize there was more to it. "Fact checking" serves me, too, just as changing the channel had before. In hyper-focusing on particulars, I, too, dodge discomfort. By parsing facts instead of accepting feelings, I avoided sharing his hurt. I discounted his experience. You might even say that I changed the channel.

Avoiding, deflecting, distracting. It's all very human. When John messes up or feels that he's let me down, he often gets irritable. He turns his frustration outward, where it can't harm him. Some folks blame others, pout or even hide. Whichever method we use, what we're really doing is hoping to escape the fallout of our less-than-best selves. The irony is, though, that by running away, we create more hurt than we avoid. If we want teammates who will share our journeys and trials, who will "cringe along" with us, then we can't change the channel on them. We have to stay tuned in.

If "the truth" can only be one person's version or experience, and if you argue your perception as fact until the other side gives in or gives up, has truth prevailed? Nope. "Your" truth won via endurance, not kindness or justice. Hurt feelings won't respond to your facts. And you can't grow without considering different perspectives. When one person's "truth" overpowers another's, everyone loses.

All right then, is there one "truth" that will apply to everyone? Yes. And here it is: How you *respond* to a mistake is far more important than having made one. Or two. Or many. Or even whether you agree you've made a mistake at all.

Forget the excuses. Nix the blame. No whining. No correcting facts. No arguing away others' feelings. No pity-party or grouchy, sassy attitude. Accept the consequences. Accept your responsibilities. Respond to others' feelings…not to your perception of the facts. Clean up any mess you've made. Stick around. Don't change the channel. Show you are eager for another chance. Then, when you are given that chance…make good. And do better.

Lisa Morgan

Relationships are all about communication and compromise. In communicating, honesty is crucial. In order to compromise, one has to be able to understand the other person's needs and desires. Relationships also have to be held together with trust. When one person becomes the most important person in his or her own mind for any reason, the relationship is in trouble.

The ability to compromise is important. In a relationship, there are many times when both people share common interests, beliefs, likes and dislikes; however, there are times when each person needs to be flexible and support their partner even when it's not their favorite activity, restaurant or hobby.

It's been many years since I've dated, but my previous experience is that most young people aren't looking for a long-term relationship. There can be a lot of empty talk from one person to the other just to get what they want or need. It can be difficult to discern truth from fiction. Again, honesty and clear communication about expectations and long-term plans is very important.

Listen carefully for consistency in your date's words. Watch them interact with other people to see if they are basically the same person in public as in private. If you feel uncomfortable, there is a reason, and don't let your date talk you out of it. If your date wants to go faster than you in the physical aspect, be clear and stand your ground. Communicate very clearly. If that's a showstopper for them, then go out and celebrate that you have saved yourself from a person who didn't have your best interests at heart.

Over time, find out as much as you can about your date and watch them interact with as many different people and in as many different situations as possible. Watch for inconsistencies, as well as consistencies in their actions, words and beliefs as they interact with you and with others.

Listen to the people in your life who love and care for you. They won't tell you the person you're dating is wrong for you just because they are bored and have nothing better to do. They will have valid reasons, and it's a wise decision to at least listen to them and give their reasons serious consideration.

Spend time investing in a relationship that is important to you. Try to find out what is important to your partner, whether it's spending time together, writing love notes, giving gifts, or nice spoken words of encouragement. Once you have figured out how to show your partner you care, spend time creatively showing them.

Also, if one partner needs time alone, respect that and don't take it personally.

After 26 years of marriage, I have discovered that all these scenarios and more fall under the two very important skills: communication and compromise.

Debbie Denenburg

Like so many school girls, when I was growing up, I was boy crazy. I thought that getting a cute boyfriend was the ultimate life experience. I thought that if I had one, I would finally be accepted as a valid person. Well, life doesn't work that way. I didn't get any boyfriends. Part of that was because I couldn't tell "signals." I didn't understand flirting, so I didn't know when someone was interested in me. If I was interested in a boy, I had no clue of how to pursue him. It was all a big mystery. Eventually I figured out a little bit of it, but it felt fake.

As I got older, I was completely unprepared for any kind of relationship. I had no regular friends and I surely didn't know anything at all about having a romantic relationship. I just knew that I wanted someone of my very own who would love me unconditionally. I felt that I was capable of providing that to them also. I fell in love quickly and deeply, sometimes being utterly obsessed. Well, that just ruined any chance of success. Trying to "own" a person doesn't work. As a result, I ended up having a long series of painful attempts at love.

I finally figured things out when I was in my late thirties. I have been married for many years now.

If you are seeking a relationship or trying to improve on a current one, here is what I suggest you try. Honesty. First be honest about yourself. Ask yourself these questions. Are you heterosexual, homosexual, bisexual, none of these? Do you want a permanent relationship with marriage and family? Or maybe kids are not for you. If they're not, *don't* have them. You're not doing anyone any good if you do. Some people are perfectly content childless or having just pets. Whatever it is you want for your life, that is the right thing. If someone you are interested in wants something different, then they are not the right person for you. A bit of solid advice would be to stay away from anyone who tries to make you do something that you have no interest in. That's a path to failure. Next, trust your gut. It doesn't lie. If something doesn't feel right, then it isn't. Finally, be willing to cooperate in order to make the relationship work. Be respectful of each other's individual traits and supportive of each other's desires. There are always going to be situations where things don't fit nicely, so you have to figure out what steps to agree on that would provide the best results for both of you.

Ruth Elaine Joyner Hane

Media, not parenting, is defining our culture's values in intimacy, dating, sex and marriage. The persuasive social media is replacing parenting, with emerging adults and children inspired by seductive messages sent through music, video games, virtual connections, sex-texting and online eroticism. Tweeting, with its limited character requirement, is fostering crude and disrespectable interchange. Lethargy abounds, without the incentive to learn *how* to have a successful friendship, one that could lead to dating and a long-term relationship.

Surfing the internet is more interesting than following intergenerational values and using old-fashioned communication like a traditional date. Making a movie date or social plans is an exception for young adults on the spectrum of autism, who prefer the stimulating video games and virtual reality. Cyber romances instead of actual, face-to-face relationships proliferate, exposing vulnerable adults to disappointments, and even danger. Posting online, individuals with autism are increasingly without safeguards, and there are few real opportunities to meet others.

My husband and I met in a social group, Singles Altogether. We were raised with old-fashioned values, where a mother was the nurturer and a father provided financial support. Although our parents felt that we rejected their values, our choices remained rooted in a mid-century norm, with a nuclear family. Since both of us were divorced, we chose to live together for six months before we married. We wanted to learn how to live amicably, while doing a home remodeling project to build bedroom space for our kids. Working long hours together contributed to better communication. We learned how to tolerate our differences, and foster our skills and talents. We resolved our different processing styles, and planned our future, "fight by fight." Through respectful disagreements, we realized that we have similar values and integrity.

Today, cohabitation is the norm for couples, who often live together for months and even years before marrying or making a commitment; often this is considered to be the "next step" toward marriage. A step process is conducive to building a strong relationship.

Although my husband and I have attempted to resolve our blended family differences, two of our four children are "taking space" from us for an unstipulated time. I believe that with hours in front of a computer screen or TV, skills for solving disparities, setting boundaries and making amends are not practiced.

Increasingly, generations of families are torn apart and grandparents banished from further contact. The next generation, our grandchildren, are affected with the missed connection and left with issues of abandonment. Children are being raised by *social media*, not parents. Unfriending is the accepted model for broken relationships; lovers, friends and family are disposed of with the click of a button. What possibility is there for learning authentic intimacy?

I began a social group, the Aspie Get Together, after meeting young adults at the Autism Society's state conferences. The emerging adults told me that they felt lost and lonely staying at home without employment, after aging out of the education system. The Aspie get-together is governed by its members with rules and guidelines they created. With a forum for communication, and guidance by a facilitator, people on the spectrum meet and learn natural social skills. Several couples have begun dating after meeting in the group. Parents engage with their children by offering peripheral support and by providing car pools.

A social group is a return to community engagement, with gatherings focused on celebrations, hobbies and interests, athletic endeavors and volunteering. With face-to-face relationships in a safe environment, skills for dating are learned, one by one.

Jeanette Purkis

When I was a teenager, I never quite knew what was involved in intimate relationships. I had read some novels and stories that discussed relationships, but I didn't quite know how it worked in real life. I quite liked the idea of having a boyfriend, but the whole concept of sex seemed very invasive and scary. I wondered if I could go out with somebody who didn't want to have sex, but I thought that there was probably nobody on earth who would want that.

When I was about 16, I had my first sexual encounter with a man who was much older than me. This experience was very unpleasant and left me wondering if maybe I should be a lesbian. So I spent the next few years looking for a girlfriend. I didn't have much luck in finding a partner from either sex at first, but when I was 20, I started going out with a young woman who was still in high school. I didn't know how to act around my new girlfriend. I had no idea what was expected of me and the relationship was soon over.

I didn't quite look or act like what people might think of as the "average" lesbian, so over the next ten years or so I had no end of trouble finding female partners. I was also in a very negative place emotionally and in terms of my living arrangements, so the kinds of people who were attracted to me were no good for me at all. One partner ended up stealing all my possessions and moving to Queensland!

My low self-esteem and desperation to be in a relationship meant that I had a succession of difficult and negative relationships. I didn't have anything in common with my partners and I didn't know how to "do" the relationship thing. I would either feel intimidated by my partner or I would feel superior. When I was intimidated, they would walk all over me emotionally and treat me badly. When I felt superior to a partner, I would judge them mercilessly and find their every action annoying. Relationships require give and take. If you're the person doing all the giving, or all the taking, the relationship will simply not work.

Now I have a much clearer picture of what I want in life in terms of intimate relationships. I have discovered that I'm probably asexual rather than lesbian or anything else. I do not have much interest in sex and sexuality. I've also discovered that I am quite capable of living a single life and that's okay. The only thing I miss about having a partner is the companionship. However, I have largely overcome that by having a cat that is just as pleased to see me when I come home from work as a partner would be.

TIPS FOR ASPIES

- Most Aspies in successful relationships seem to be either going out with someone who is very similar to them, such as another Aspie, or who is very different.

- Having no relationship at all is far better than having a damaging or exploitative relationship.

- A lot of Aspies are asexual or uninterested in sex. This is perfectly okay.

- Aspies are just as capable of having a loving relationship as the rest of the world.

- Aspies can make amazing partners and parents. For that matter, so can neurotypicals!

Anita Lesko

I haven't been on a date for over 15 years now. I realize that is eye popping to most reading this! To be perfectly honest, I do not feel like I have been missing anything. I have a very demanding schedule that I have crafted to work well. There are not many people I personally know who could maintain all I do. I am very content with my life. I feel fulfilled by all I am doing to help others on the spectrum. Years ago things were different.

Back in the day, I had my share of romances. I was engaged twice, to men not quite mainstream. One was a highly strung neurosurgeon on an ego trip. The other came from royalty and taught me the Viennese Waltz. There were several others, each a story in itself.

Back in my early twenties and through my thirties, I had a drop-dead body, as it's called. Aside from my university studies, I had plenty of time for working out. I was built like Barbara Eden on *I Dream of Jeannie*. At that time, however, I *really* had limited facial expressions. Nevertheless, my raging hormones overrode that, and the men found me. I was *extremely* sensual and savored every second of my passionate encounters. I never had any problems with sensory issues, such as touch, when it came to romance. One big issue was for both of us to be freshly showered prior to commencing activities. That in itself could be accomplished together!

I have learned many things since that time in my life. I was in love with the two men I was engaged to. But I was in love with them for the wrong reasons. I can see that now, as hindsight is always 20/20. Had I married either one of them, it would not have lasted, partly because of them, but also because of my Asperger ways. The Austrian guy had many friends and galas to regularly attend. It literally wore me out. I desperately needed down time after each one. I simply couldn't handle being around hundreds of people for hours at a time. I loved the music and Viennese Waltz, but it was massive sensory overload. That was a constant point of contention.

In these past years, I have evolved to the point of not having any interest in finding a man. Frankly, I don't see where I could squeeze one into my schedule. Trust is another big factor that plays into my thoughts on relationships. In this day and age, I would find it extremely difficult to trust anyone. All I have to do is look on the TV or listen to co-workers to hear of infidelity. Aside from the emotional matters of the heart, there are way too many sexually transmitted diseases to get. People these days treat sex very casually, like it's just a sport. The romantic era is gone forever.

With all that said, if I did meet someone who struck my fancy, a romance would have to blossom from a friendship first.

As for dating, I have no clue about all the rules of the dating game—and "game" it is. I find it both exhausting and entertaining to listen to neurotypicals (NTs) and their rules for dating. Either I like somebody or I don't. All the games people play are beyond me. I also realize I'd need to meet a guy on the spectrum for it to work. I'd make time for a good man if I found one.

In the meantime, I've got plenty to do!

Dr. Know

I consider mutual friendship to be possibly the best foundation for relationships, though this does depend on the individual personalities. Much of my advice here reflects this opinion and is therefore consistent with what I suggest for friendships.

I believe in being true to oneself, and this really applies to lasting relationships. Know what you want. There is some pressure from society to be in a relationship, but it is fine not to be in one or not to want one.

I have not really looked for relationships, and I suggest not actively looking for a relationship, particularly if that requires you to do things you don't want, for example, going to bars or clubs where you may feel uncomfortable. Instead, do things you like and meet people that way—this may still require you to go outside your comfort zone, but at least it is for something you enjoy. You may also make friends, and gain experience and personal growth. If you do meet someone who you think is a good match, then at the very least you share one interest. If you don't meet someone who is a good match, you won't resent your time as wasted, since finding a match wasn't your goal in the first place.

If you do know someone that seems like a good match, I suggest getting to know each other better. This may be tricky and can lead to a lot of anxiety, but there are ways to deal with this. First, it is important to present yourself truthfully, though you can highlight your qualities. Communicating in writing can be very helpful—and may indeed be how you met.

Rather than going out alone with the person, you can try spending time with a group of mutual friends first, as this may greatly reduce the pressure. If you become more certain that the person is a good match, you can then propose sharing some time without the group. If your feelings are not reciprocated, you may still be a good match in the sense that you can be good friends, but only if both of you are comfortable with that.

If you are in a relationship, consider the difference between "needing" and "wanting" to be with someone. If you don't need each other but choose to stay together it should be because you really like each other. Conversely, you need air to breathe, whether you like it or not. I consider that relationships based on "need" are, or can too easily become, unhealthy. It is best to retain some independence, not because you are paranoid that your partner might decide to leave you—incidentally, I recommend against such thoughts—but because accidents can unfortunately happen. It is better to be happy about what you have already enjoyed, rather than worried about the relationship ending. If it does end, it need not spoil the past. It is healthy to be sad, but avoid being bitter—you may even get to continue being friends.

As for improving your relationship, there is some literature; I greatly recommend the book by Ashley Stanford, *Asperger Syndrome and Long-Term Relationships*. Communicate with each other while taking special care to ensure that the communication is being correctly understood. It may be helpful to do this in writing, even if you are in the same room.

It is important that both of you recognize that nobody is perfect. Identify particular difficulties that each of you has, noting the respective individual behaviors and traits, regardless of whether those traits are autistic or not. Recognize your own weaknesses and acknowledge your responsibility without excuses. Strive to improve yourself, with the primary motivation of being a better person for its own sake. All being well, your partner will be motivated to do the same without pressure from you, as it must be a personal decision.

RECOMMENDED READING

Stanford, A. (2002) *Asperger Syndrome and Long-Term Relationships*. London: Jessica Kingsley Publishers.

Richard Maguire

Okay, I want to run away from this subject right now. The trouble is that advice in these areas needs to be finely nuanced and contextual, something hard to communicate on the written page. We autistic people find this subject matter difficult. We can get into trouble by not grasping the complexity and contextual nature of knowledge and skills. Many of us get into trouble, sometimes with the law, because we have taken advice, followed it and not contextualized it or understood when it is to be followed and when it is not to be acted upon. Too often, I meet people who have been advised that a strategy helps them find love. They carry the strategy out, then get into trouble because they do it in the wrong context and/or with someone who is not interested in them and is upset by their attention. This can lead to hurt and pain all round, and a retreat into isolation. For that reason I will not give specific advice.

I mentor many lonely adults who want to be in love, marry and have sex, who live scared of these things yet in great need of them. This needs a lot of careful unpicking, learning and confidence. It is a big and complex part of my work. I believe that the help from someone who can be completely trusted and who knows this territory very well is essential: someone who has good professional indemnity insurance if they are being paid. Detail, detail and more detail are needed so the person can get some sort of grip on the complexities of these subjects, their feelings, sexuality, relationships, intimacy, dating and marriage. Just try to break these things down into autistic bites of information—your head will hurt.

First, I would advise addressing friendships and being able to negotiate those before getting into the more complex and sexual aspects of relationships. I can recommend *Friendships: The Aspie Way* by Wendy Lawson. This book is very Aspie friendly and explains just what we need to know in ways we can understand. Please start here with friendships: they are foundational to all the rest of this subject and will be very useful in relationships and marriage. Intimacy and sex in a long-term relationship will need a basis of friendship and good, free and honest communication.

I stumbled and fumbled my way into intimacy and sex in a most gawky and horrid manner. Oh, I wish I had had someone to guide and advise me through all that. I am married: 21 years at the time of writing, and being this fortunate was more through luck than judgement. I met a lovely empathic lady through a shared interest, our Christian faith. I recall seeing her playing her flute at an evening service. I remember going to the pub afterwards with members of the congregation, getting steamed on beer, sitting next to her and making conversation with her and plucking up the courage to ask her out. I think that worked because we were both similar people with similar histories and lots in common.

Staying married has not been easy. We have needed to learn to grow and develop our relationship over the years. Please remember to do this and avoid the autistic practice of not changing through time by not picking up the cues and adapting to them. If that happens, then the whole relationship comes apart because nothing changed or grew.

As for intimacy and sex, a whole book would not do this justice. A good friend or parents who are open about these subjects would be good places to start. But please, get the friendships right before taking on these things.

RECOMMENDED READING

Lawson, W. (2006) *Friendships: The Aspie Way*. London: Jessica Kingsley Publishers.

Dr. Tony Attwood's Advice on Understanding and Succeeding with Intimacy, Dating, Sex and Marriage

Perhaps the greatest challenge for someone with an ASD is to experience an intimate and lasting relationship. So many abilities are needed to succeed at the dating and relationship game, from recognizing the signs of mutual attraction, to the communication and experience of emotional, conversational and physical intimacy. Typical teenagers and young adults gradually progress along the continuum of intimacy, from looking intently at each other and holding hands to sex. During adolescence, they will probably have several partners with whom to share the journey along the continuum, each learning the dance of romance, love and intimacy and how to maintain a relationship. There will also be friends who will share their personal experiences and provide guidance, encouragement and support.

Those with an ASD usually have their first mutually enjoyable romantic experiences many years after their peers. They tend to be late developers in terms of romantic and sexual experiences. Their sources of information on sexuality may not be peers or personal experiences, but more likely the media, literature and possibly pornography. There can also be confusion regarding social and sexual conventions and boundaries in a relationship, reading the body language of attraction and rejection, as well as confidence and knowledge of being attractive. Despite all these difficulties, there can still be a yearning for a successful sexual and long-term relationship.

Pornography as a Source of Information

People who have an ASD tend to be socially isolated and detached from peers who can provide each other with information on sexuality and intimacy. There is still, however, a craving for information, and if this is not provided by peers and personal experience to a satisfactory level, an alternative source of information on sexuality can be pornography. Unfortunately, this may become problematic should the information obtained this way be used as a guide or documentary on dating, sexuality and physique. It is very important to understand that pornography is fiction, designed for adults, to provide sexual stimulation. It does not represent real relationships or situations, or even real bodies, as the images are often digitally manipulated and enhanced. Seeing should not be believing.

People who have an ASD tend to have a well-developed imagination and have previously escaped into imagination when socially isolated or bored. Pornography can provide the imagery for sexuality in the safe sanctuary of home. There is no risk of ridicule or rejection, and a sensory response can be enjoyed in solitude by someone who is comparatively deprived of pleasurable romantic and sensuous experiences. This is both positive and harmless. However, there is a very real risk in pornography, because it provides such pleasure, becoming a new special interest. One of the characteristics of a special interest is the collecting and cataloguing of a wide range of examples of the interest. In the case of pornography, the person with an ASD may want to "complete the collection," and in so doing, view illegal pornography, unaware of the social and legal boundaries and consequences. It is very important that people with an ASD are aware of these boundaries and do not cross them, as the consequences are strict and severe.

The Stages of a Relationship

Those with an ASD tend to have a very poor body image and cannot believe that their personality and abilities could ever be attractive to someone. Perhaps, then, the starting point is exploring the concept of attractiveness. Typical adolescents have experienced flirting, which provides useful information on what someone would find appealing about them. The art of flirting requires the ability to read and know how to respond to some of the most subtle and fleeting body language. This ability is often quite mysterious for the person with an ASD, and actually quite difficult to teach. However, guidance is needed on being attractive, knowing when someone finds you attractive, and what your attractive qualities are.

For those with an ASD, some of the most attractive qualities are being kind and compassionate, interesting intellectually, and honest and trustworthy. These qualities in men tend to become more appreciated by women as they become more mature— possibly more maternal. I often advise adolescent and young adult males with an ASD to try to be patient, as girls are more likely to notice and value who you are from their mid-twenties onward.

One of the challenges for someone with an ASD is the tendency to misinterpret another's intentions. For the person with an ASD, who may frequently experience rejection and ridicule as an adolescent, a simple act of kindness or compassion can be misinterpreted as meaning more than was originally intended. The experience of compassion, interest or kindness can be so rare and so enjoyable that the person with an ASD would like to have the same experience again. They may think that perhaps the act could have been an indication of more feeling than just compassion.

It can also be difficult for the person with an ASD to recognize that the person to whom they are attracted because of such acts of compassion may also be someone who tends to be physically demonstrative in expressing appreciation, which is expressed frequently to many people. This affectionate response may be misinterpreted as personal and exclusive, without the realization that it is simply an indication of the person's personality or culture. Ultimately, this can lead to accusations of stalking, due to the original signals being misunderstood, and the new signals of discomfort not being read accurately.

The next stage in the dating game after the recognition of mutual attraction is to decide where to meet and what to do together. The wise advice is to let the relationship progress slowly. This is important for both men and women with an ASD. For the men, it is important not to be perceived as only interested in a physical relationship, and women with an ASD need to be sure the partner has honourable intentions. It is also wise advice for girls with Asperger's syndrome to be careful not to use their sexuality as a way of being popular. This only makes them more vulnerable to predators, and unpopular with the very people whose support and advice they most need. Both men and women with an ASD tend to focus on what someone says or promises rather than his or her personality and previous history in relationships. For this reason it may be valuable to have friends or family members who are more skilled in the area of character judgements provide advice about the integrity of the potential partner, and on how far they can be trusted.

When choosing a venue for a date, it is wise to go somewhere that is not isolated and has people nearby, and to avoid situations that involve the consumption of alcohol unless you are very sure of the integrity of the person. The first dates can be with a group of friends, and should provide opportunities for both of you to enjoy shared social experiences that are enhanced by having a partner.

The inevitable question will then arise of when during the relationship there should be more intimate touch and intimate experiences, as well as where and how to sensuously touch each other. It is important to seek agreement and consent for any sensuous or intimate actions and especially to be able to accept a rejection of the request. This does not automatically mean the end of the relationship, but it does mean you need to be patient and discuss what each of you expects in the relationship, and perhaps find a compromise.

The quality of the relationship will be improved by the exchange of compliments. Unfortunately, people with an ASD may not intuitively know when, how and on what ability or quality to give a compliment. Neurotypicals have many friends who can give advice on what to do or say and how to respond to a compliment, which may not be the situation for people with an ASD. However, a parent or family member may be able to provide some advice on the art of giving and receiving compliments.

There will be times during a relationship when there will be breakdowns in communication and misinterpretation of intentions. The measure of a good relationship is that these challenges are approached and resolved in a positive way. There will be a need for compromise, constructive conflict resolution and apologies. These skills can be difficult for a person with an ASD, but certainly not impossible to learn and implement.

There is also the issue of the frequency, intensity and quality of affection exchanged in the relationship. People with an ASD often need guidance in the expression of affection, with neurotypical partners complaining that they experience too few acts of affection, or too many, and at inappropriate times. The couple may need to talk to each other regarding the level and types of affection in gestures, words and actions. With regard to physical intimacy, those with an ASD can have issues in terms of sensory sensitivity, especially tactile sensitivity. It is important that the non-ASD partner recognizes these aspects of ASD, and that a mutually enjoyable compromise is achieved.

It is also important to know the signs of a mutually healthy relationship so that you can recognize signs of abuse, or that an ending of the relationship is imminent. For adolescents, it is a point worth remembering that the romantic relationships of teenagers, neurotypical or ASD, tend to be brief and there will be a grieving process when the relationship is over. There are strategies to help you move on emotionally and to be prepared for another relationship in the future that may well last longer, and may be more enjoyable.

Sexual Identity

From my clinical experience there seems to be a greater percentage of people with an ASD who are asexual, that is, not interested in an intimate relationship with anyone, male or female. This can be due to several factors, including being vulnerable to teasing during adolescence about any romantic attachments, difficulty identifying dishonourable intentions, lack of certainty and feelings of being overwhelmed by the complexity of the romantic codes of conduct, and a preference for autonomy, with companionship achieved through pets. It can seem safer to be celibate, and achieve life fulfilment by measures other than a relationship. We now have literature to help with the dating game such as *The Guide to Dating for Teenagers with Asperger Syndrome* by Jeannie Uhlenkamp, and Jessica Kingsley Publishers have published over 15 guide books on relationships where one of the partners has the characteristics of an ASD. Psychologists and teachers will be interested in *Asperger's Syndrome and Sexuality* written by Isabelle Hénault, also published by JKP.

A person with an ASD can achieve a successful and intimate lifelong relationship. If you are seeking such a relationship, please be patient, be available to meet people, and be assured that there are strategies to help in areas such as expressing affection and experiencing intimacy. It is important to recognize that ASD can affect relationships in many positive ways, too, such as your natural tendency to be honest, trustworthy and loyal.

RECOMMENDED READING

Hénault, I. (2005) *Asperger's Syndrome and Sexuality: From Adolescence through Adulthood.* London: Jessica Kingsley Publishers.

Uhlenkamp, J. (2009) *The Guide to Dating for Teenagers with Asperger Syndrome.* Shawnee Mission, KS: Autism Asperger Publishing Co.

Artwork (See Plate 8)

Painting: With a Heart That Beats for No One

Artist: Michael Tolleson

Artist's Commentary: The person in this painting wanders the streets alone with their heart beating red hot and clearly visible. We all want at some point in our life to be loved and to be needed. A relationship with one of us on the spectrum can be a roller coaster for anyone brave enough to try to understand us. This person is alone because they are unable to be seen and recognized for who and what they are. The city and sky are alive around them, but they are undefined and not understood. The world lies just on the other side of the street, a short journey to the world they long for. But the street turns into a rushing canal that is a barrier from a life they so desire. Ultimately, they have a heart that beats for no one.

Overcoming Anxiety

Anxieties
Charlotte Poe

Paralyzed by the Fear
Michael Tolleson

Plate 1

Overcoming Poor Self-Esteem

Mirror Image 2
Kimberly Gerry Tucker

Wrong Planet
Michael Tolleson

Plate 2

Accepting and Working with Change

The Visitation
Stephanie Tihanyi

Plate 3

Living with Meltdowns

Meltdown
Charlotte Poe

Meltdown
Michael Tolleson

Plate 4

Overcoming Depression

My Blue Face
Debbie Denenburg

No Escape
Michael Tolleson

Plate 5

Living with Sensory Issues

The Fire Within
Michael Tolleson

Living with Sensory Issues
Jennifer Healy

Plate 6

Making and Keeping Friends

Just a Marble in a Box
Marilyn Cosho

The Gathering
Michael Tolleson

Plate 7

Living with Personal Management Issues

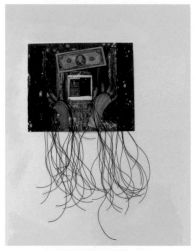

Strings Attached
Marilyn Cosho

Understanding and Succeeding with Intimacy, Dating, Sex and Marriage

With a Heart That Beats for No One
Michael Tolleson

Plate 8

Understanding and Expressing Emotions

Something About Us
Victoria I. van Rooij

Flowers for One
Michael Tolleson

Plate 9

Faking It

Faking It
Lea Morschel

No Strings Attached
Nekea (Kea) Blagoev

In a World of Billions
Michael Tolleson

Plate 10

Getting and Keeping a Job

The Interview
Marilyn Cosho

The Thirst
Michael Tolleson

Plate 11

Disclosing a Diagnosis

Freedom
Nekea (Kea) Blagoev

Don't Kill the Messenger
Michael Tolleson

Plate 12

Bullying

Brain in a Box
Marilyn Cosho

Red Badge of Cowardice
Michael Tolleson

Plate 13

Choosing a Career

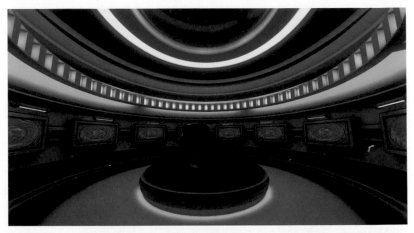

Quiet Room
Derran Rootring

Fork in the Road
Michael Tolleson

Plate 14

Improving Empathetic Attunement

Trying to Read Between the Lines
Marilyn Cosho

Plate 15

Should I Be Tested For Asperger's/HFA?

Coming Out
Marilyn Cosho

The Exam
Michael Tolleson

Plate 16

CHAPTER 10

Understanding and Expressing Emotions

Stress Ranking: 10

Ranking of issue by stress caused

85%

Percent of respondents living with issue

80%

Many people with Asperger's/HFA have difficulty understanding and expressing emotions. Some examples include: not being able to feel sad or excited for another person, not knowing how to identify what you are really feeling, and not knowing how to control your own anger. Do you have difficulty understanding and expressing your emotions?

Dr. Know

You can improve your understanding and expression of emotions with some dedicated effort, perhaps in a way similar to learning a foreign language.

Some individuals are more eloquent than others and I recommend relying on your own strengths. If you have trouble talking, try non-verbal expressions—writing is an obvious choice; if you are artistic, create some art. It is often believed that actions are worth more than words. So do not feel disadvantaged. You can express your positive emotions with gifts or by doing nice things, like cooking for someone or helping them. Despite, or in addition to, the previous examples, it can be important to use words. Personally, I think that if you like someone, "I like you" is a great, simple approach that has little risk of being misinterpreted. Words also have their place to express negative emotions. I favor very direct approaches. Just say (or write) "I'm anxious/afraid/angry," and explain why, or add other details, if needed.

I think understanding your own emotions should typically be easier than understanding the emotions of others—so perhaps start with your own and do your best to generalize from there.

This may leave some significant gaps in understanding, and I still have trouble understanding some emotions, such as jealousy. Ask directly for clarification whenever possible. It is better if you have people you trust enough to know what they tell you is genuine, even if it doesn't make too much sense to you; and let them know when you don't understand and what is confusing you.

Qazi Fazli Azeem

There are two ways that we regulate and check for emotions: by sensing the intonations, volume and pitch of voice used in conversation, and by making eye contact to read facial expressions. Those on the spectrum who have difficulty maintaining eye contact will need to rely on understanding the meaning and hidden social cues in words, idioms and the tone and pitch of voice. This is particularly hard and requires training, and my personal mastery in this process came through watching hundreds of hours of comedy TV sitcoms, mainstream comedy shows about people having humorous conversations about random and seemingly boring things.

There is hidden knowledge in such an auditory experience, as the same humor and terms of engagement can be used in real social settings to create, hold and sustain conversations. I memorized most of that dialogue and used different forms of it to connect with people, quickly shifting the conversation to the subject of my interest.

The other way is using eye contact to visually read emotion. This is something I am not good at, but I have gradually tried to increase the duration of my eye contact, since, when meeting people the first time, it shows that you are serious and confident. Avoiding eye contact is common for so many of us. It makes me uncomfortable, too. I have read about neurological reasons for it, one possibility being an enlarged amygdala, which triggers a fight or flight response to prolonged eye contact.

One way that I tried to minimize this communication problem was to look at my own eyes in the bathroom mirror for hours, over many months and years. Another way to prolong eye contact is not to look directly at the eyes of a person, but to look at their eyebrows or brow or ears or nose, focusing very hard and not looking directly into the eyes.

The second real component to being "emotionally present" is to *really listen* to what other people have to say, even faking interest sometimes. I tend to take my teaching skills and apply them to conversations with people. I encourage and advise people when they show me what they have been doing and working with, and I advise them or give my opinion about their topic and subject of conversation, if I have something relevant to share or teach them. My teaching experiences enabled me to keep a frame of reference; they helped me create a database of memory where I can simulate what to say and when to say it, when to listen, and when to interrupt and give advice.

The last part took the longest, since I used to interrupt conversations too early, and didn't know when to end conversations. I have seen that I have grown the most when I have tried to understand others' points of view, and more specifically, how they use and work with emotions. I had to fake my interest sometimes, and keep myself from yawning when listening to boring conversation in social settings, but this paid off in the long run, since people started trusting me and actually listening to my own eccentric ideas.

When we show interest in other people and hear what they have to say to us, they do the same for us, and also help us achieve our plans and goals. I learned this over a very long period of time. I am not perfect at this process, but I am learning and getting better at it.

If you want meaningful relationships with other humans, you will have to learn to listen and care for others.

Debbie Denenburg

Delayed processing. That is the first thing that comes to mind when emotions are involved. I cannot show emotions and intellect together at any given moment. I never could and I doubt I ever will. My feelings and facial expressions have always been misinterpreted. For example, there was one time when I was with several co-workers. We had gone out to lunch on a workday. Suddenly, one of the women started having some kind of physical attack, like asthma. Everyone else was panicking. I did not. My experience has taught me to not panic but to assess the situation and get the appropriate help. After our colleague was taken to the hospital and the rest of us got back to the office, I was accused of being uncaring. They said I looked scared. I wasn't. I was the complete opposite. I was in total control and remained calm in a charged situation. The last thing a panicked person needs is to have everyone else around them panicking.

I just don't care anymore what other people think they know about me. The people who truly take the time to know me understand that this is how I am. They know that I always care. I am not callous. I remain calm because going into a panic does no good. There have been times when this trait saved my life. I am, in fact, very emotional. But because mentally I am built differently than the general population, my feelings are seen as wrong or invalid. They are not.

This subject is very sensitive for Aspies for just this reason. I am not an expert on how to handle it and I am always interested in knowing how other Aspies deal with it. My suggestion for showing that we have emotions is to calmly explain to others that not all people exhibit emotions the same way. That doesn't mean that the feelings are not there. They are. We happen to have different "timing." Where others may show emotions in a specific way in a situation, we are often on a time delay. We may have a tendency to cope with facts first, so that when the emotions take over—and they will—we are not overwhelmed with emotional/ intellectual overload. Our minds don't work in two dimensions at once. This is one of the core differences between Aspies and neurotypicals (NTs). We store our emotions. Then later, when they have accumulated to an intolerable level, we have meltdowns.

Henny Kupferstein

The internet has helped me tremendously. It has now become acceptable to exchange written words as part of full-time communication, rather than face to face. Because I can get quite wordy, people tire easily in my conversations, but they tend to love my vivid, graphic writing. I use words to describe pictures of my feelings as I see them in my head. People often laugh at the vivid descriptions, but they like to hear my visuals. Although I don't use the expected "feely" words, I describe the scene of the emotion, and they can derive their own thoughts about which word best fits that scene. "After I finished that meeting, I felt like I was seeing splatter red spots." If they say, "Oh, you mean furious," I nod my head submissively. Sure, furious. Yeah. Whatever. Even if it doesn't exactly feel like furious to you, let it go. Accept that they have a word for it, and you have a picture for it, and be grateful that worlds met briefly for a moment.

When I am proud of myself and am very delighted, I see glittering purple stars in a midnight black sky. When I'm working too hard at school on homework, I see myself lugging two gigantic pails of water up a hill, and I'm sweating. What mental health professionals label as "racing thoughts," I describe as a car that has flipped upside down in a pothole, with its wheels still spinning.

I learned that criticism should be carefully crafted. In music, it is quite a challenge when someone expects you to give feedback on his or her work. First off, you may not know what the person is capable of musically if you only see them in this one light. As a result, you cannot even talk about what they are good at, as you must stick to the program. Additionally, what if you are reacting to a personal preference? From the comments I got for my music, I valued most the ones that included "I" statements: "I like the cadence on the B section; it really captured the dynamics of the composer," rather than "You shifted from the B to A section in the cadence flawlessly." Even though it seems like a compliment, it also gives us material for our brains to go haywire—because now we begin judging ourselves internally based on the new clues we were given. So cut it out. Leave the person out of it. And stick to what *you* liked, as a person. And that's how people can learn. We learn by the effect we have on others, not by what we see in the mirror. So don't be shy, just say it.

Suppose you are working with a tutor on an essay for class. The tutor reads through it and marks the paper with a bunch of corrections. You know you need the help, but when confronted with it, your self-esteem plummets. Auditory learners might find it helpful to read their homework out loud, so they can hear how it sounds. Many people struggle to piece their words together on paper. Hearing it as they read it gives a whole new dimension to the sentence structure. I suggest you learn what triggers you emotionally, and seek an alternative that works for you without that trigger.

Mitch Christian

Over the years, I've gradually become better at expressing an understanding of the emotional states of people that I'm talking to. Typically, I try to nod my head or make affirmative sounds at appropriate times in order to show that I empathize with them. The skill of mimicry comes into play here, as well. Picking up on the body language and vocal inflections of the other person gets me in tune with them. It's helpful to think in terms of rhythmic patterns in the give and take of a conversation, kind of like the flow of music. I might not actually feel anything until later when I think over the conversation, though. I've also learned that it's better to stay on topic, and to try not to interject my own interests unless it fits into the overall theme of the discussion.

The emotional expression that some people display can be uncomfortable for me to watch or be around. It seems exaggerated, and I keep asking myself why they need to be so overly demonstrative. Their gushing is disturbing, partly because it feels like the release of something personal that would embarrass me to show in public. I'd rather keep those things to myself, but I try to react appropriately in order to get along with them. I don't try to imitate their drama, but try to show sympathy for their feelings, and I try to understand that it's natural for them to be that way.

Knowing what my own emotions are has often seemed like a problem, and it may be partly due to my emotional state remaining at a low level most of the time, as long as I'm not in an environment that causes me to become anxious or excited for some reason. That seems natural to me. I think that it's often the expectation of others and myself that bring about the idea that I should be aware of this or that emotion going on inside myself at any given moment, even though my mind is actually absorbed in more interesting topics. Expecting to always find an identifiable emotion can lead to the false conclusion that I'm missing something that I should have, when in fact I'm fine the way I am. So, I've learned to not try to express emotions the way others do, but to accept the way *I* express them.

Occasionally, I might burst out in what seems like an overreaction to something funny or annoying, and it might appear that I'm either deliriously amused or that I'm dangerously angry. To me, it's just appreciating a good joke or humorous situation, or a temporary release of built-up frustration that comes out through my whole body instead of just a facial expression, like most people. I feel engulfed by laughter or exasperation, but the behavior usually passes pretty quickly, even though the state of mind can linger within me for quite a while. I've learned to play down those situations by sensing when I'm becoming overstimulated before it reaches a peak level, and by letting it out ahead of time in small doses, instead of one big one.

Ruth Elaine Joyner Hane

Actually, being able to understand another person's feelings and demonstrate appropriate emotional support is directly related to our ability for reading faces and understanding body language. Emotional availability is generated in a safe, loving environment. If a child does not have a safe environment, one that builds trust and love, intimacy with others is thwarted. Emotional availability is compromised when trust is broken.

Sitting at a window table at the Lotus, a Vietnamese restaurant, while sharing vegetarian spring rolls, a good friend tearfully ended our close friendship. "I just can't be your friend anymore. It's as if you have a glass wall that I can't penetrate. Whenever we get close, you distance from me."

I did not understand Mary Lou's feelings. We were best friends, like sisters. I had helped her prepare the nursery for their first child. Although I could not assist at her delivery as she wished, I cheerfully babysat for their first date after her son's birth, and continued to give childcare for five years.

Two weeks before our lunch meeting, Mary Lou and her husband were preparing a will, and asked to name me as their son's godmother and to raise him if anything unforeseen happened. I thought about their request and believed it a tribute to our relationship. Sorrowfully, I could not make a commitment. By declining, I may have hurt their feelings. I could not give a valid reason.

It was not until my next therapy session that I began to understand. The psychologist asked, "Can you remember another time when you wanted to trust, but couldn't?" "Yes, I wanted to trust my father." He was patriarchal, believing he was entitled to do whatever he pleased, as the head of our household. His emotions were unpredictable, charming one moment, angry the next. My father's "at home" behaviors contradicted his position as a deacon in the church. I learned that often a perpetrator's own shame is projected onto the victim, through demeaning words and actions.

My father considered me to be obstinate, incorrigible and evil, needing the heavy hand of discipline, including twice weekly spankings, leaving welts on my legs. I often hid from him, in an obscure cubby space above my closet, so small that only my shoebox of treasures and I could fit. I was afraid of my father and his strong emotions and uncontrollable rage. Sometimes his mood would lift if I hid long enough. I determined *never* to be like him.

Mary Lou's trust and love was genuine, unassuming and honest. I felt uncomfortable with so much emotion. She was raised in a culture where physical touch accentuated a conversation and affirmed a friendship. I am uneasy with proximity, and sudden touch is disconcerting. Playful, loving sentiments are overwhelming. Neurotypical people experience an endorphin rush of pleasure from socializing. For me, I believe that in the presence of strong emotions, too many excitatory chemicals are released, causing me to feel overwhelmed, not pleasurably enthusiastic.

Many people with autism retreat into seclusion rather than try to learn how to read and understand facial expressions and body language. I suggest starting at the very beginning. Infants observe from an early age the body movements and, a few months later, facial expressions of their caregiver and others. With autism, this early mirroring is compromised.

Start by looking in the mirror at your own face. Practice making facial expressions, observing where in your body you are feeling the emotion connected to your expression. Watch others making expressions, and notice if you are looking at their face, or only a part of it. Eye exercises many help.

Steve Selpal

Stop worrying. All Aspies are different when it comes to sensing emotions in other people or experiencing appropriate emotions in response to others. There is a time and a place for dealing with emotions.

When you are at a job, it's easier. The workplace is the place to be unemotional. Stifle your feelings and never whine or complain, even if others (mostly NTs) entice you into expressing anger with bosses or gossiping about peer employees. The job is where you can act unperturbed and get into your work. You are probably paid by the hour and it's the work that counts.

At home or in a social setting, you can practice at learning how others feel by listening. Stop talking about yourself and *start listening*. By listening you can gauge how the other person is feeling. The only way to gain a friend or even a sexual relationship is to listen to what the other person is saying. If he or she is talking about a personal loss, realize this and take note. Don't change the subject and talk about your interests. It's not about you. It's about the other person.

Friends want to share a joke or talk about something funny that happened to them. You have to stifle your thoughts and open your mind to listen to what the other one is saying. That way you will learn about what is funny or if it's appropriate to laugh. It's always okay to laugh if others are laughing. That's true even if they are laughing at you. If you can laugh at yourself, it makes others relax more around you and that way you can make friends.

Know your surroundings. Don't laugh at a funeral. Be aware about what other people are doing. It really doesn't matter to other people what's going on inside your mind. Nobody can sense what's going on in your mind. Learn how to act by watching others. That way, you can see when they are sad. You may not feel sad yourself. Just be polite and be appropriate. Appropriate behavior is important. Acting silly or attempting to cheer people up when they are sad may not be appropriate behavior at a funeral. Eventually, you may understand grief and empathize with the grief felt by others.

Do you trust anyone? Does anyone trust you? Part of trust is emotional. If you forget to do something for your mother or for a roommate, they may act with disapproval or anger. Why? It's because you broke trust. You just put your relationship on probation. You have to build trust and take things seriously, even if you feel it's trivial or uninteresting. If it's your turn to take out the garbage, make sure you remember to do it. If you don't perform what is expected of you, then people can't trust you. Building trust is actually rewarding by avoiding bad feelings. Life is a give and take situation, and the key to gaining trust will build your relationships. There are always emotional attachments to trust. People can relax around people that they can trust.

You might feel exhausted after a day at a job or at school. That's common for Aspies, who need some alone time to recharge their batteries. Sometimes you have to wait for your alone time. Your alone time is important, but you can't always have it when you want it. When others need you, that means they want to trust you. Don't get angry. It's better to be polite and do what is expected of you.

Anita Lesko

Understanding emotions is extremely complex. Expressing them even more so. After 53 years, I can finally understand the whole gamut of emotions. There are many, and varying degrees of each. It has taken a lifetime to achieve this ability. To neurotypicals, it comes naturally. Not so to an Aspie. I've had to study people… observe their every move…put myself in their shoes…imagine how I would feel if I were them at that very moment. It is not a simple process, but one that can be accomplished if you want to.

Understanding emotions can only be done if you first stop obsessing over yourself. Aspies tend to get self-absorbed, focusing on their Asperger's. Get over it. That is my first word of wisdom I give fellow Aspies. Stop focusing on it. Put yourself out there with other people. Only by interacting with others can you begin to truly recognize and understand their emotions. This in turn will also help you understand your own.

Watching the news is an excellent means of studying facial expressions and the emotions that go with them. The Nightly News with Brian Williams and CNN's Anderson Cooper 360 are my favorites. Over time they all start becoming second nature. This is the easy part!

Expressing emotions is still one of my biggest downfalls. It is so unnatural and extremely uncomfortable. After learning of my Asperger's, my mom shared something from my childhood. She described how heartbreaking it was to her when I'd stiffen my arms out indicating I didn't want to be touched or hugged. Yet we are incredibly close. Females are often all "huggy-kissy" in groups such as cheerleaders. I cringe just looking at that—it's not my cup of tea.

I am better able to express my emotions in a one-on-one situation. If I'm talking to one person, I feel comfortable enough to let my guard down and share my inner self. I think I have become proficient at verbalizing my emotions. Not so with matching up my facial expressions! I could be feeling something quite profound inside, yet on the surface my face is saying something very different.

I have learned that a smile goes a very long way in expressing emotions. Studies have shown that smiling can improve your inner well-being. It also helps melt the ice when interacting with someone. You might not know what to say, but smiling is a universal language, and it makes you approachable. You are less likely to seem as though you're from another planet!

Being able to express your emotions in writing is a great attribute. However, nothing tops straightforward human interaction. This skill took many years for me to develop. I am still a work in progress. To me the biggest factor is trust. If I feel I can trust someone, it is much easier to express my emotions. Expressing your emotions can make you feel very vulnerable. You have to be willing to take the risk of divulging your inner self. In order to attempt to build a friendship you have to put yourself out there. Even if it didn't work out in the past, that doesn't mean it won't work now. Men's figure skating olympic gold medalist Scott Hamilton has a quote I love; he says, "It isn't about falling. It's about getting up." This holds true for being brave and expressing your emotions.

As with anything, practice makes perfect. Continue working on expressing your emotions. The more you do it, the easier it becomes. Don't worry about it to the point you become paralyzed with fear. Just let it happen—like an orgasm!

Dr. Tony Attwood's Advice on Understanding and Expressing Emotions

It seems that a constitutional component of ASD is a difficulty understanding the subtle emotions expressed by neurotypicals and a difficulty communicating and managing emotions at the level neurotypicals find acceptable. A person with an ASD will at times feel like an alien on a strange planet where members of the dominant species (neurotypicals) are constantly exchanging fleeting facial expressions, tone of voice and body postures to express an excessive range of emotions. For example, neurotypicals have several hundred facial expressions that they expect to be easily identified by members of their species. Neurotypicals also expect other people to express emotions at just the right intensity and to be able to resonate with the emotions of fellow neurotypicals. They assume that everyone can easily, effectively and efficiently repair others' emotions. But for those who have an ASD, the world of human emotions seems illogical, confusing, overwhelming and alien.

The difficulties experienced by those with an ASD include the inability to intuitively and instantaneously "read" the feelings of another person, and problems in accurately reading and interpreting internal feelings and communicating those feelings at the right intensity for the situation or the relationship. Neurotypicals have never really experienced these difficulties themselves, and thus can be very critical and dismissive of those who struggle to understand and express emotions.

However, understanding and expressing emotions are skills that can be acquired by those with an ASD, although they will need significant guidance and encouragement. In my opinion, children and adolescents who have an ASD need at least an hour a week, from pre-school to high school graduation, devoted to learning how to read emotions, from happy and sad for very young children, to jealousy and being in love for adolescents. The educational programme for those with an ASD should focus on reading and analyzing emotions both within themselves and others, and expressing emotions at the right level of intensity. They also need to learn how to manage and express specific emotions, such as anxiety, sadness, anger and affection, at a level which does not cause personal and interpersonal distress. In some ways, it is equivalent to having lessons in a foreign language and culture, but since it is the universal language of neurotypicals on planet Earth, it is necessary that those with an ASD become fluent in that language and familiar with the culture if they are to succeed with the dominant species of the planet.

Strategies to Understand and Express Emotions

The early signs of difficulty communicating emotions can be recognized in infancy, with the very young child tending to express extreme levels of distress and agitation that parents find difficult to repair with the usual strategies of affection and distraction. The next sign is the young child being bewildered by the myriad facial expressions made by adults. Information from facial expressions also has to be integrated and congruent with hand gestures, body posture and the prosody of speech. Without an intuitive understanding of these fleeting cues that communicate feelings, the ability to read emotions becomes an extremely complex, and at times overwhelming and elusive, cognitive rather than intuitive skill.

In the education of very young children who have an ASD, a useful metaphor can be employed, where the face is equivalent to traffic lights. The child is given guidance as to whether a particular facial expression, such as a smile, is a green light face, such that you can continue the conversation or activity, an amber light face, such as a frown, where you need to check the other person's feelings before you continue, or a red light face, such as an angry expression or tears, indicating that you need to stop. Other games might include matching facial expressions to body language and tone of voice, and identifying the appropriate emotional response and level of expression for a particular situation.

Psychologists use the term "affective education" to describe these activities, and many suppliers of educational resources include in their catalogue games and activities on recognizing and expressing emotions. There is one recommended resource specifically designed for those with an ASD, with an age range from child to mature adult—*Mind Reading: The Interactive Guide to Emotions*, which is an entertaining and informative interactive DVD available from Jessica Kingsley Publishers.

Sometimes, the greatest difficulty for someone with an ASD is recognizing and reading (and expressing) his or her own internal feelings rather than the feelings of other people. For help in the acquisition of this ability it would be wise to seek the guidance of a psychologist, who can use a range of strategies and resources. One of the components of psychotherapy for those with an ASD is the development of the ability for self-reflection and self-disclosure: that is, to precisely identify a current emotion and communicate the level of expression. If the vocabulary for words to describe the various levels of emotions needs to be developed, there are resources such as *The CAT-kit* for cognitive affective training developed by myself and colleagues from Denmark. *The CAT-kit* is available from Future Horizons: for more information see www.catkit-us.com. A clinical psychologist can use cognitive behaviour therapy and other psychological therapies to help manage and express emotions of clinical concern such as depression, anxiety and anger.

People with an ASD have the greatest difficulty communicating emotions using speech during a face-to-face conversation. There can be a greater eloquence and insight when typing rather than talking, for example, sending an email or typing an entry into a diary; or expressing feelings through music, such as identifying a song that expresses the feelings in a personal and accurate way; or writing a poem, or creating a drawing or work of art. Great works of art have been made by those who may have had the characteristics of ASD, and experienced particularly intense emotions, for example Michelangelo and Vincent van Gogh.

It is important that family members and friends are aware of the difficulty with the communication of emotions associated with ASD. They may be able to read the signals of increasing emotional intensity within the person with an ASD better than the person him- or herself, due to problems with self-reflection and monitoring internal emotional states. Parents, friends, and perhaps in later life, a neurotypical partner may have the ability to read the signals of increasing emotional intensity, and know the situations that can cause agitation. They can then provide guidance and encouragement in managing and expressing emotions at an appropriate level and will be able to soothe, reassure or console their partner with an ASD when he or she is emotionally distressed or agitated.

RECOMMENDED READING

Attwood, T., Callesen, K. and Moller Nielson, A. (2008) *The CAT-kit: Cognitive Affective Training: New Program for Improving Communication!* Arlington, TX: Future Horizons.

Baron-Cohen, S. (2007) *Mind Reading: The Interactive Guide to Emotions – Version 1.3* (DVD and CD). London: Jessica Kingsley Publishers.

Artwork (See Plate 9)

Painting: Something About Us

Artist: Victoria Ingemann van Rooij

Artist's Commentary: We are in a quiet and sleepy town late at night, where not much noise is heard—only the sounds of a few cars driving slowly over the rainy roads. We see two very different and unique creatures. The male wolf is giving a flower to the female robot, expressing his emotions for her, even though their differences are so great. The female robot is having a hard time looking him in the eyes and accepting the flower, even though she wants it. The wolf has covered his eyes to make things easier for the female robot. I chose to bind them together because even though they are different there's some sort of undefined magic between them.

Painting: Flowers for One

Artist: Michael Tolleson

Artist's Commentary: Trying to be understood emotionally is never easy. And given the single-minded hardheadedness that is part of my Asperger's traits, I feel it is even harder for someone on the spectrum to share their feelings with others. There is an old song that came to mind when I painted this. The lines are about lovely flowers displayed in a home. Although the singer supplied the flowers for themselves, it was still important they saw them in their home. My painting is about how we, with Asperger's, would rather supply our own emotional needs than depend on others. Many times in my many relationships, I have picked and supplied my own flowers.

CHAPTER 11

"Faking It"

Stress Ranking: 11

Ranking of issue by stress caused

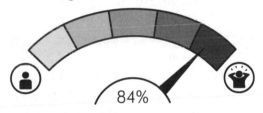

84%

Percent of respondents living with issue

78%

Some people with Asperger's/HFA feel that in order to survive in an "NT (neurotypical) world" they need to "fake it." An example of faking it would be to not let anyone see the "real you." When in social situations, you intentionally "wear a mask" and play a role that you've learned works better than being the real you. Most also find this practice exhausting and need time away from people to recuperate. Do you have concerns about "faking it"?

Bob Castleman

There is a paradox that autistic people deal with daily, with every interaction they have with the rest of the world. In our schools, children are taught: "be yourself." Self-help books speak about finding your inner warrior/goddess. We are to self-actualize, flow from our true selves, find our true path, and so on. Unless you are autistic.

If an autistic person is true to their nature, they will rock, flap, twitch, mumble, pace, wear the same color clothes every day, not look you in the eye, not want to talk about "Grandma's bunions," and so on. Yet we are taught from an early age, *don't do that*. We are taught from as early a point as possible to be social, make eye contact, don't rock, don't stare. We are taught through persistent, institutionalized mechanisms to be anything other than ourselves.

Worse, this is something that seems mostly directed at autism. Someone with cerebral palsy will get medication, physical therapy, and accommodations, but they will never be told, "Don't walk like that." But with autism, variants in gait, posture and hand movement are all considered movement *disorders* and must be trained away through 40 hours weekly of applied behavioral analysis. Except that my neurology *wants* to move. So for me not to have weird movement, I have to make myself not be me—a direct contradiction to what is inculcated by force of culture.

This goes deeper than just movement. Autistic flapping and rocking is the most visible aspect of our intrinsically atypical neurology. I am a very non-linear person. I don't think verbally nearly as fluently as I think in patterns. These patterns have no verbal referents. They are patterns, not words. To communicate with people, I have to translate these patterns into words. There is a processing delay that exhibits itself in the cadence of my speech. If I were in grade school today, I would be sent to speech therapy. But they would teach me how to speak properly, never addressing my need to translate my pattern thinking into words. Because I am really smart, I would actually learn to speak properly. *Success!* High fives all around! But I would be taught a set of behaviors that pulls me further away from my true self, never learning how to communicate the part of my consciousness that actually flows. To my speech therapist, I am "cured" and I can go on to a rich and expressive life. There is no awareness of the wall that such competent speech has erected around my true nature.

Let's be clear. Autism can be severely disabling. Movement and cognitive differences can be so profound that they interfere with basic self-care. I would never suggest that symptoms and behaviors that won't allow someone to thrive should be simply accepted as self-expression. But neither should such things be dismissed simply because they are not within the current basket of social parameters called "normal."

This is not just a simple issue about tolerance and accommodation. I've spent my entire life suppressing my natural self. It is exhausting to constantly self-monitor my behavior simply to ensure I do not appear weird in public. I have to actively regulate my interactions simply to prevent saying or doing things that intend no offense, but are perceived as such by many people. At work, I have to force my cognition to operate in the linear time, task switching, and multiple sensory input modalities that pervade the contemporary workday. My brain doesn't work that way. But I have to. It is terribly inefficient and draining. I have to force myself to not be me. I have to fake it.

One of the most important lessons I have learned since my diagnosis at age 52 is that I must have a space somewhere in my life where I don't have to fake it. I must have a place where I can just fall into myself and wander around in my own cognitive universe without worrying about how others will react. And I would advise all people on the spectrum to find such a place for themselves as well. The hard truth is that it will never be acceptable in many situations to simply be yourself. This is true for everyone, not just people with autism. But when your true self is so far outside the accepted norms, and you need constantly to monitor yourself and actively fake it, then you need a place to go and recuperate and recharge. Find such a space in your life and make it part of your routine.

Liane Holliday Willey

When I wrote *Pretending to be Normal*, it was the first time I realized there were others like me who had spent lifetimes crafting a variety of personalities to help them fake normalcy through situations they could not easily nor quickly figure out. These days, the word "normal" has been challenged enough to make most people realize the concept is very subjective, but this doesn't mean we with Asperger's syndrome don't often want to fit in better, even if it's only to secure employment or keep a friend. And to be honest, the harsh reality is that homeland security police, employers, and a still judgmental society keep their standards of acceptable behavior rather rigid. Normal may be subjective, but it isn't a castoff concept for most people.

To keep myself from doing things that may bring unwanted attention or may cause people to decide I'm not friend or employee worthy, I do tons of research before I take on new adventures, talk to people in my business or attend a social event. I study everything, from the business jargon, the clothing style I'm expected to wear for any event, to the menu a luncheon might have, to self-help columns on how to get through any number of personal or group situations. In effect, I study as if I'm about to take a test. Life for me is, after all, kind of like one big test after another. With my studying in place, I take my new knowledge, and practice in my own mind how I will act and dress, and what I will talk about when I get to wherever I'm going. I picture myself casually turning down a food I can't eat, or look online to find an example of the clothing style the event is likely to have so I can mimic this with my own clothes. I think of things to ask other people so the focus will be on them and not on me. I practice exit strategies such as saying, "I've had a lovely time, but I need to get home to let my dogs out of their kennel."

I find faking it is really about cracking the code, which can be a mental turn-on, much like a detective probably has when on a case. I see faking it as acting, and acting is just plain awesome, especially if we know our parts very well. Crack the codes, research the necessary information and practice your acting skills! Then go act the part and take pride in the fact you can use your smarts to get yourself through most things!

RECOMMENDED READING

Willey, L.H. (1999) *Pretending to be Normal: Living with Asperger's Syndrome*. London: Jessica Kingsley Publishers.

Jennifer Cook O'Toole

Somebody once said that what messes us up the most in life is the picture we have in our heads of how we are *supposed* to be. Oh sure, the world may claim to celebrate the original among us. "I don't care what you think about me," scoffed designer Coco Chanel, "I don't think about you at all." But truth be told, for most of us, life in the middle of the bell curve looks a lot easier.

"Normal" is, after all, the norm. It's unthreatening, expected and comfortable. The word itself comes from the Latin name for a carpenter's square. So, if you'd like to fit neatly into a tidy, safe corner, "normal" is the way to go.

However, "normal" has also been done. Many times. And it isn't very interesting.

Why? Real life isn't a neat right angle, and you're not normal. Neither am I, thank goodness. Don't get me wrong: I understand the longing to blend effortlessly. But how many of us would truly—*truly*—be content to be anonymous and unremarkable? Most everyone we admire for anything *isn't* normal. Genius isn't normal. Neither are gorgeous, powerful or awe-inspiring. Anyone who is in any way extraordinary is, by definition, not ordinary. Yet that doesn't stop a lot of us from compromising who we are to try to become who we think "they" want us to be.

At age 15, I had the lead in my school musical, "Damn Yankees." As Lola, a home-wrecking femme fatale, I had permission to practice every coquettish wink, seductive gesture and over-the-top innuendo I'd ever absorbed from pop culture— and got standing ovations for doing it "right." In the course of one weekend, I went from "brainiac" to hot commodity. And in the same weekend, I lost sight of who "I" was, drunk with the heady (hollow) popularity I suddenly felt.

So I flirted and toyed. While I never compromised my integrity or my intellect, I was most certainly a tabula rasa, trying on "costumes" and "lines." Yes, I got lots of attention and invitations; I also, unwittingly, opened the door to an eating disorder, an abusive relationship, wounded pride, deep depression and no sense of the authentic girl beneath the well-played persona.

There was, in the end, a very real choice to be made: lose myself totally or say, "No. No more. This is the part when I find out who I really am." Though very much afraid, I chose the latter and every goodness in my life is thanks to that fortune.

Recently, an artist sent me a collage which reads, "Tired of trying to cram her sparkly, star-shaped self into society's beige, square holes, she chose to embrace her ridiculous awesomeness and shine like the freaking supernova that she was." Yes, ma'am, she did. And now it's your choice: try desperately to fake "normal" and gain a fragile life based on lies *or*, decide to be a supernova, too.

We are not average. You and I can spend our lives "pretending to be normal" and we will always, always, always fail. We are not normal like they are; we are normal like we are. We are not beautiful like them; we are beautiful like us. No one has ever been remembered or admired or even loved for being "average." So don't aim for average. Aim for authentic. Trust your gut. Shatter boundaries. Transcend expectations. Change the world. Quietly, loudly, it doesn't matter. Unfold yourself honestly. Because if you don't believe in miracles, perhaps you've forgotten that you are one.

Anita Lesko

The thought never occurred to me to "fake it." Realizing at the tender age of four that I was different, I accepted that as my lot in life and simply carried on. For better or for worse, I was, simply, myself.

As I got older, being myself often got me in trouble because I would speak my mind and say it like it is, which hands down, didn't cut the mustard for developing friends or making life easy. But I just had to be me. And I still am, just nicer!

People watching has remained a fascinating pastime my entire life. Whether at work or out in public, I watch in wonderment the behaviors of "those people" as I call them, otherwise known as neurotypicals. I have a very keen ability to "see through" people who are not what they portray themselves as. I watch as they manipulate those around them, at which they are very talented. I wouldn't even have the foggiest clue how to be like that. Nor would I want to. I do not like those individuals.

I was never afraid to be myself. People either liked me or not. No in-between. For those who didn't like me, it was either because deep down inside they knew I could see through their façade, or because they simply couldn't handle someone so different.

Trying to fake it would seem very exhausting, but beyond that, you deserve better, *much* better. Stop trying to be something or someone that you think others *want* or *expect* you to be. They are not living your life, *you are*! We need to prevail in this world—we are a very unique species, one to be cherished and loved. In order for that truly to happen, *you* must believe in yourself, that you are worthy of such reverence. You have powers that others don't have, that laser focus for one.

I have this belief that Aspies were purposefully not given the area of social skills in their brains. Why? Because if we had those skills we'd be hangin' out with friends, accomplishing *nothing*. Instead, we are out there in the world blazing trails, doing exciting things and helping millions of people live better lives! My favorite quote is, "If you want to accomplish nothing, follow the crowd."

When in social situations, I watch what others are doing and try to do the same. Above all, always be polite and courteous, listen more than you talk, and keep the conversation light. Don't get into touchy subjects like politics, religion, or anything of a nature that will cause anger, make someone upset, and so on. Those topics are reserved for your closest friends whom you already know.

My friend, Alexis Wineman, has a saying, "Yes we are different, but why try to fit in when we were made to stand out?" That's exactly how I feel. Blind people are not expected to learn to see. Deaf people are not expected to learn to hear. Why do people expect *us* to change? Because we make *them* feel uncomfortable. That's how NTs react to different.

What I've learned is that people can overlook your quirks as long as you are a good person, do well at your job, are kind to others and animals, and are simply yourself. There's no need to wear a mask and hide behind it.

Don't dwell on the negatives, but instead focus on the gifts you've been given. Find other Aspies to surround yourself with, which will enable you to truly feel free to just be you!

Richard Maguire

I have heard from actors that playing King Lear is hard, partly because of how long the actor is required on stage during the play. Shakespeare has not given the actor enough time to relax from this demanding role during the play. On hearing that, I reflect on the autistic life and the hours in the day we need to act. At least an actor can finish the play, the role, and return to their non-acting life. Being autistic, it is not possible to do this. We are what we are, and we are a minority group of people, so acting and faking it becomes a daily necessity. I have to act longer and more consistently in life than if I were on the stage playing King Lear.

When at home, I mostly behave true to my autistic self, which is lovely. On going out, having guests and talking on the telephone, I put on what I call my shell. I have heard other autistic people say similar things and talk of putting on a shell to project an image and protect their inner autistic self from pain.

In the course of my life, I have not found another way of interacting, especially in social situations. I think it is something I must carry because I am so different and I need to interact with non-autistic people who are the majority of my human contacts. This is naturally tiring, and I do not know that non-autistic people know how tiring this is. This shell is added to all the autistic sensory issues and anxiety, and to be honest, getting through a day in non-autistic company is exhausting. I cannot tell you how to not be exhausted. I think it is our lot to deal with this because of who we are and how we must live.

There are things that help. One is to get some rest when you need it. I do like being able to tell people I am autistic and that I will need rest from company. That works with people I know and people who are sensitive to other people. I find them surprisingly accommodating of my need for rest and down time in between times of company. Most times though, people do not know how I operate and I risk problems if I tell them. In these circumstances, I will find space by going to the toilet, finding an excuse to go outside, offering to run an errand, fix something or get busy away from people for a while. People seem to find these reasons for breaking off contact acceptable. I like them because they buy me time and space to recover enough to go back into company. People also see these things as good, especially things they find helpful. This, too, relieves pressure, as people are apt to be more kind and lighter on me. They come to like my eccentricities and social mistakes. I think they see the whole as a package that is me. All this makes being out and in company less tiring, but not easy.

I have close friends in whose company I can be the quiet autistic me, and that is very good. Home with my family is a place I can rest from acting and faking it out in public.

I do not try to perform at my top level of faking it every day. I give myself days off to be quiet, stim and be my natural self. I do not think anyone can act and fake it all the time; lots do, and get over-tired and can be ill because of this. Try hard to connect with people. It really is needed. At other times be kind on yourself, and relax into your autistic life. Rest, recharge and be ready for the next time you need to act and fake it in public.

Ruth Elaine Joyner Hane

As a child, I did not know for certain if the rhinestone engagement rings at the dime store were real or fake diamonds. The rings were pretty and sparkled brightly. I remember trying the rings on my thumb, holding them up to the light, admiring their beauty. But the clerk said, "They're fake, sweetie."

Mother said she didn't know who I was. I was a fake, a pretender. Each day, I changed my mood and personality according to which friend I emulated. Not having an identity, I grew into a young woman who didn't believe she was attractive or talented. At midlife, my personality shifted like the weather. I was happy if the sun shone, and sad if it was cloudy or rainy.

After my first husband divorced me for being too controlling, a friend recommended that I see a good therapist she knew. At 43, with a new business and no support, I was depressed. After several months of therapy, and little improvement, the psychologist asked, "How do you feel? No, don't look out the window"—while tapping the center of her chest—"Check inside, in here."

"I don't know." There was no connection to my feelings.

The therapist tried again, "Please leave your 'I don't know' answers out in the waiting room. What are you feeling, right now, here—today?"

Lacking an honest answer, I quietly stood up and walked out of the session.

I was like a chameleon, a tree-dwelling lizard with the ability to change color at the whim of the environment. I said and did whatever pleased people and copied the personality of others. That afternoon, I walked around Lake Harriet with mothers, children, lovers, dogs and strollers, the sun glinting upon the pristine water. Looking at the white sails pushing the boats across the ancient lake, I determined to learn what my life was meant to be. I know that I aspired to be a better parent for my daughters, grow my clothing design business, live a happy life and learn how to make a difference.

The next week, I arrived at my therapy appointment ready to discover how to love myself and become a real me. The sessions were an opportunity to examine my life, as I had the rhinestones in the store, so I could know what was false and what is true.

I had no intention of misleading. When I was three years old, I thought I was a cat, and not a person. Cats were easy to understand, humans complicated. The neighbor's cat, Midnight, and I were best friends. I loved to pet her silky black fur, understood her language, and could communicate by mimicking her meows. Human words were elusive, the sounds mixed up and confusing. My mouth and tongue could not form the shapes necessary to make multi-syllabled words. I stared at mouths because they moved, not to learn enunciation.

Faking it, or pretending to be normal, is not unusual in the autism culture. Many others have a problem, as I did, with making eye contact and reading body language. We miss important clues about another's personality, their emotions and intentions. It is like attending a theatrical play with the curtain drawn. In *Ask and Tell*, I write: "I did not know what I did not know, that people glean useful information from facial expression."

Not everyone responds to psychotherapy as I did. But I'm happy to say that I did learn to love myself, as I am. I embraced my real personality, the one that was hidden.

REFERENCE

Shore, S.M. (ed.) (2005) *Ask and Tell: Self-Advocacy and Disclosure for People on the Autism Spectrum.* Shawnee Mission, KS: Autism Asperger Publishing Company.

Karen Krejcha

Have you ever heard the expression, "Fake it 'til you make it?" The idea behind this catchphrase is to imitate confidence or positivity when you're not feeling it, with the hope that by practicing this long enough, you actually will start feeling confident or positive.

As a human being, I have a preference for authenticity, loyalty and honesty. Faking it and not letting others see the real me seems disingenuous, yet I'll let you in on a confession. For much of my adult, and almost all of my teenage life, I have gone into social situations feeling like I was an actor in a play, watching myself from outside my own body as I wore a mask that hid my true self.

Although I wanted to be authentic in my communication and let out the real me (if I even knew who that was), unless I was with people I felt extremely comfortable talking with, I found it difficult to have meaningful conversation. I either stayed quiet or regurgitated what felt like mathematically programmed social responses, "social scripts" of sorts. I didn't think people would get me and believed that if people knew the "real me," they wouldn't like me or accept me for who I was. When I was a teenager and young adult, I never felt good enough.

The thought that I wasn't being true to myself bothered me. I tried to avoid social situations as much as possible, unless they involved my special interests. I'll admit that I was a pretty darn good actress socially, but the only acting I was interested in was on stage. Trying to be someone you're not for hours on end in real life is e-x-h-a-u-s-t-i-n-g.

I wanted to change but was scared, confused and uncomfortable. Then life threw me a curve ball and it was up to me to hit. After I learned that my children were both on the Autism Spectrum and I was diagnosed there as well, I realized that for all our sakes, I needed to just come out and try to live the most authentic social life possible.

It scared the heck out of me, but when I was called to found Autism Empowerment, I realized I would need to be in the public eye. God began putting me in places and situations where I would have conversations with people from all walks of life, all ranges of the Autism Spectrum. Anxiety would creep in and I'd want to run away screaming, but I would pray and persevere, and gradually it became easier. Not always. Not easy. Easier.

My advice is this. There may be times when "fake it 'til you make it" seems to work in the short term. In the long term, being true to yourself will be more effective, and the relationships you develop will be more genuine because they're built on honesty.

- Accept yourself for who you are, where you are. We all have strengths and gifts. We all have weaknesses and flaws. That's part of being human.

- Pray for guidance and strength. Pray often.

- Practice an attitude of gratitude. If you're in a social situation where you're uncomfortable, take your mind off your anxiety and focus on performing an act of kindness to someone else.

- Have you ever noticed that people often like rooting for the underdog? Embrace your inner underdog, because although things may not come handed to you on a silver platter, you will have the satisfaction of knowing that through perseverance does come strength. When you succeed, you are also more appreciative of what you have accomplished.

Mary Robison

I wore a mask of "normalcy" for most of my life. It was exhausting and pointless. People who know me best understood, long before I did, that I was on the spectrum. They allowed me to continue in denial because they knew that confronting me before I was ready would only upset me.

But I think I always knew. I surrounded myself with people on the spectrum. Those of my friends who are not on the spectrum all have significant relationships with other people on the spectrum; the neurotypicals of my acquaintance are all tolerant of ASD idiosyncrasies. I'm lucky that I have such a supportive network of friends.

The fact is there are many times when you may need to fake it—you must pretend to be someone who isn't on the spectrum. You must not flap or indulge in explaining your special interest; you must talk with inflections and engage in small talk. Maybe you have to attend the holiday party at work. It's hell. But you can practice beforehand what you will chat about. Go online to find a dozen or so non-offensive jokes. Think of some non-offensive one-liners to say about car repairs, birthdays, the weather, food, and a half dozen other topics. Prepare some generic questions about these non-offensive topics, also. You are all set, now.

Mingle—talk to one or two people, using your questions, lines, or jokes. Pick two from your repertoire. Listen to responses. Then, after chatting for a few minutes with them, move along. The key is to listen and find a break in a new conversation before you break in. Drinking is probably a bad idea, but making it obvious that you aren't drinking is equally bad. Drink something that looks like a mixed drink—a brown soda, a glass of diluted orange juice, or just some seltzer, on ice with a twist. After an hour or two, you should have made a complete circuit of the room and you can probably make your escape. You should have leftover things that you prepared—the idea was to have much more than you needed as chat-starters.

You can set your cell phone to ring at a certain time, making up a white lie beforehand that will allow you to leave after a socially acceptable amount of time. If you find that you are enjoying yourself, you don't have to use your white lie. After all, you still have more chat-starters!

The key to good faking is in preparation. You may find that the people you chat with have their own agendas and you don't need to use any of your own starters. That's all right—every group is different. You will know your chat limit, when you need to leave and collapse. Make sure that you can leave before that happens. When you are faking, the last thing you need is a meltdown. But worrying about the possibility of a meltdown can be a self-fulfilling prophecy. So don't worry; just have an escape plan as part of your preparations.

Dr. Tony Attwood's Advice on "Faking It"

"Faking it" is a survival strategy for those with an ASD that is effective and constructive, but there are concerns that "faking it until you make it" can be emotionally and intellectually exhausting. In the long term, it can have a negative effect on self-identity and self-esteem.

The person with Asperger's syndrome can begin employing this strategy in early childhood, by closely observing other children, to try to decipher how they seem to understand each other so well, and play together so enjoyably and harmoniously. This can involve trying to identify, by careful observation, the patterns and sequences in social behaviour and the unwritten social rules and conventions. Thus, some children who have an ASD become natural "child psychologists," frequently observing, and intellectually analyzing, interpreting and trying to predict the behaviour of their peers, family members and adults. This can include great attention to detail, from facial expressions to accents, and the creation of a mental "library" of "video recordings" of interactions for future reference. It is interesting that for some adults with an ASD, this has been the foundation of a successful career as a psychologist.

The next stage is to imitate a person who has been observed to be successful in a specific social situation. Some people with an ASD become talented in the art of mimicry, which can be intoxicatingly successful and an effective way of gaining social inclusion and acceptance. This can include mimicking someone's voice and body language, but also their clothing and attitude. These skills could be refined in drama classes during adolescence to a level that the person with an ASD could have a successful career as an actor. The ability to observe and analyze people in real-life social situations can also be supplemented by watching television soap operas to create a "wardrobe" of characters that can be activated in different circumstances, such that on waking, the thought may be, "Who do I need to be today?"

We use the phrase, "When in Rome, do as the Romans do," and this is applicable to those with an ASD who feel they are in a foreign or alien culture, and have to fake neurotypical to succeed socially. The strategy of acting and wearing different masks does work, but there are concerns. The first is that it is exhausting. The strategy can succeed for a certain period of time, but like Cinderella at the ball at midnight, it is suddenly time to leave the social gathering and subsequently suffer the consequences of intellectual and emotional exhaustion. The "faking it" strategy will require the creation of a range of "exit lines" when exhaustion occurs, and there may follow a social "migraine" which can only be alleviated by a prolonged period of solitude and tranquillity. Neurotypicals may not understand why the socialite now wants to be a recluse.

The question can then arise as to who is the authentic person? Acting neurotypical is certainly more appealing than being the defective person who is rejected and ridiculed by peers, but there can be powerful effects on the concept of self. The person with an ASD can believe that the "real me" has such despicable characteristics that no one must ever see the reality behind the mask. This can make the person who uses this strategy feel very sad and lonely, and only socially acceptable when taking on an artificial persona. This can contribute to a clinical depression or the diagnosis of Multiple Personality Disorder.

Shakespeare used the phrase "Life is a stage," and those with an ASD can learn the script and take on the role to act neurotypical. There are times when this ability is needed to succeed at school or work, but only temporarily. It is important to have the self-perception of being *different* and *not defective*, and not to hide the real person forever. Thus, in some situations, it is appropriate to be on stage and act, but when the "curtain closes" and the person with an ASD goes home from school or work, it is psychologically important to be true to the real self, and to be with people who accept and value the real person, people with whom that person can be natural.

Artwork (See Plate 10)

Painting: Faking It

Artist: Lea Morschel

Artist's Commentary: The world we live in is both beautiful and scary. She tries to adapt and blend in, yet has to wear thorns to guard herself from harm. I wanted to show the inner world she tries to hide away and protect. But faking it is difficult, because she cannot see the rules.

Painting: No Strings Attached

Artist: Nekea (Kea) Blagoev

Artist's Commentary: Many worlds, many frames, many figures, some controlled by others. Dimensions, acting and wooden faces. With no emotions, puppets controlling puppets. Strings attached or no strings attached. What are their intentions?

Painting: In a World of Billions

Artist: Michael Tolleson

Artist's Commentary: In my paintings that deal with persons on the Autism Spectrum, I always paint the figures *more* than their surroundings. This painting is about faking it in the world to fit in. The background is symbolic of the billions of people in the world while the dark figures represent the smaller community we operate within. Although we appear to be like everyone superficially, we are different, and no amount of acting, dressing, speaking like the world around us will make us like them. We are unique and this can cause us much distress.

CHAPTER 12

Getting and Keeping a Job

Stress Ranking: 12

Ranking of issue by stress caused

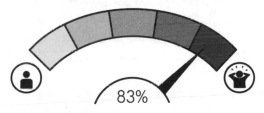

83%

Percent of respondents living with issue

69%

Many people with Asperger's/HFA have difficulty getting and keeping a job. Some examples of job-related issues include: "What kind of job would I be good at?" "How do I find a job?" "How do I apply for a job?" "Do I tell people I have Asperger's/HFA?" "How do I handle my sensory issues in the workplace?" Do you have concerns about getting and keeping a job?

Ruth Elaine Joyner Hane

The summer before my junior year in high school, I wished to dress fashionably but needed to earn more money. Even with a small clothing budget from my parents and all my babysitting money I couldn't buy the clothes I wanted. Some of my friends were applying for jobs as carhops at a new drive-in and golf driving range, called the Nineteenth Hole. Two teachers from our high school athletic department were co-owners. I made an appointment for an interview, but neglected to anticipate how a carhop dressed or what would be expected in the job they were offering.

I arrived for my interview wearing a lavender gingham checked dress with a long skirt and medium length sleeves, a style popular with my classmates. I made certain to be on time and answered all of the questions correctly, but showed very little enthusiasm for becoming a carhop. During my interview, the co-owner of the drive-in stood up from his desk and walked slowly around my chair. He looked at me carefully, then bent down to pick up a foil wrapper lying on the floor near my right foot, and casually looked at what little showed of my long slim legs. As he stroked his chin, he said, "I'll let you know."

When several of the girls were hired and I hadn't received a call, I asked one of them what they had worn to the job interview. "White shorts, very short," Rita said.

Rita suggested I check out the A&W Root Beer Drive-In, the Nineteenth Hole's competition. I ordered a frosty root beer and watched as carhops carried the trays and attached them to the partially rolled down car windows. I noticed their ponytails tied with bright colored ribbons. I eavesdropped as they talked about baseball and partying with the other customers. I knew I was good at pretending, or acting as if I were someone else, like a popular cheerleader or prom queen. Acting was normal for me. I could smile brightly and say, "Hey! What can I get you?" when I took an order on a small green notepad.

Since I knew I could pretend to be thrilled about serving teenagers a Coke, French fries and burgers on adjustable aluminum trays, that afternoon I stopped by the Nineteenth Hole to inquire if I had been hired. This time I wore white shorts and an attractive blouse, not intentionally sexy, but suitable enough for my future boss to notice I could fit in.

"Try out the new driving range tee while we talk." The partners conferred with one another, looking at me occasionally. I slipped a club from their merchandise display and swung a natural arch as I hit a golf ball high and true. "Okay, you're hired. Can you start on Monday?"

Doing a little research about the company or business you want to work for is necessary. Also, it helps if you know someone who is employed there. Seek out information about their expectations for computer skills, and other knowledge and experience required for the position. Be sure to learn about dress requirements. Is the employees' dress casual or formal? Is it a business or manufacturing environment, religious or entertainment? If it is difficult for you to access the information, ask someone you trust to help. Hygiene is very important. Wear an outfit that is clean and appropriate. And be aware that, while you do a little research about the job for which you want to be hired, the employer will research your profile, too.

Qazi Fazli Azeem

So here is what happens for most of us: we don't have too many or any friends, we love doing things in a repetitive manner, and have some things that we just love doing or working on most of the time we are awake. This is not a problem. It's an opportunity. The younger you start, the more time you put into your interest, hobby, or passion, and the earlier you move it towards a career, the better and faster you will make progress towards independence in your life.

Start young, think about all the things you love to do, the things that make you happy. In my personal experience, I loved drawing; I started with tracing dinosaurs from books, and then went on to trace other animals. I was introduced to play dough, and started making small animals out of it—the same ones that I was drawing when younger. This early involvement in the arts was something I continued with for a very long time, and eventually I used this ability when I became a teacher of design, digital art, and multimedia in my country.

I was exposed to computers from a young age, through educational games. Back then, I was able to edit the text variables in the Visual Basic English code on my Commodore 64 home computer, editing the text in games and putting my own name inside them. I had seen my older sister do this earlier, and I succeeded in doing it after a few attempts. The role of an elder sibling or mentor in demonstrating practical skills to a child on the spectrum is very important. We need to see the possibilities out there. We need to see at a young age what options and directions we can take.

We may miss out on or be delayed in our social networking, and not spend time with friends as much as we would like to, but this time can be an opportunity for your particular interest to turn into a potential career. My early interaction with computers and computer games allowed me to see and be impressed by computer graphics and animations.

Around the age of 14, I filled in for a graphic designer who was working for my father at that time, typing and checking spellings in a large manuscript. He had to back out at short notice, and I had seen him work, so I stepped in and finished his job twice as fast, with half as many spelling mistakes as he would have done. My family saw this potential and got me my own computer, which was used for playing computer games for a few years (where I learnt a lot about conversation by playing adventure simulation games by Sierra) but before long I had installed demo versions of professional graphic design software and was helping my father with his design work.

My father grew very sick when I was around 21, and I dropped out of the computer science program to work as a part-time computer graphics teacher at a local vocational training center.

This was one of the best decisions I could have made, since I stayed with them for around six years, studying in the morning, teaching in the evenings, and making myself better at teaching through practice. I was able to train thousands of students, who are now working across the world.

My desire and experience with teaching subjects of my interest developed professional skills that developed into a career. Teaching subjects that we love comes naturally to us, given time and practice, and so this is an area where more of us on the spectrum are needed.

If you have will, courage, skill and the desire to change lives and be remembered for generations to come…master your subject of interest and become a teacher. I look on my students as being an extension of me and my ideas. By teaching them, I am creating more people who think and work like I do. Even if you become a volunteer teacher and are able to teach others, that will bring purpose to your life, as it did to mine.

Richard Maguire

I am writing as an autistic adult who has managed to stay in employment throughout my adulthood, and managed, interviewed and hired people. I will write some of the things I have learned here. There is a lot to say, so I will use bullet points and keep the information short.

GETTING A JOB

- Find out what the job is about and what is required. Read the person specification and essential requirements. Base your application on these things.

- To get the job, you need to show the interviewers that you are the best person for the job. Your first way to do this is your application.

- We autistic people often find it hard to link these things together. Ask someone you trust to help with this so you can fully understand what the job is about and show exactly why you are the best person for that job.

- Describe your skills and transferable skills from other parts of your life and work.

- Your application should be easy to read and well written; don't write too much—be concise. The application is your way of getting an interview, and it is important to get it right.

- List all qualifications and relevant experience.

- It is normal and okay to be nervous in an interview.

- If you don't understand a question, ask for it to be repeated. Ask for an explanation of a question if needed.

- Answer the questions, and avoid talking about other things unless they support your answers. Don't go on too long.

- Be ready to ask questions of the interviewers. That exchange normally happens near the end of the interview. Your questions show you are interested. That is good!

- Greet the interviewers appropriately and make eye contact—get someone to coach you with this if needed. The interviewers will want to know how well you get on with people. Jobs are often social, and getting on with colleagues is important. Certainly, interviewers see this as important.

- Your aim is to show the interviewers that you are the best person for the job. They cannot guess what skills and experience you have, so tell them.

If you are offered a job, your next priority is to keep it. You can do this by being someone who is good to employ in that job. We autistic people have good things to offer that complement non-autistic employees. I learned to do what I am good at to complement other people's work. I can see different and important things and get them done. I am not good at team working, and very good at taking on special responsibilities and the things other people seem to dislike doing. This has helped me stay in jobs and be a valued staff member.

Take care to learn the job. Ask questions and get factual answers so you can build up a clear idea of the job and what you need to do. This is important, as if you are seen to be not learning the job, you will not have it for long.

Other important things include being punctual, and being well dressed and clean. Be polite, and don't get involved in workplace politics—we autistic people just won't do well at this type of politics. Employers will value our hard work, integrity and politeness. I have managed people, and good people are a pleasure to manage; they are also likely to gain the respect of their colleagues.

For more information, go to my website: autistmlivetraining. co.uk. Look for the job section where I explore the topics in this piece in more detail.

Debbie Denenburg

"Because I need to eat!" That is the response I gave a potential employer when they asked me why I wanted to work for them. Although it was the truth, it was the wrong answer. I was in my twenties, homeless, and trying desperately to find a way to support myself. That employer wanted a person who would do the specific job for which they had an opening. They didn't care that I needed food and shelter. The only thing that mattered was whether the job could be done, on time, every day, for as long as possible.

I have had many jobs over the years. I got most of those through temporary employment agencies. That is a very good route for getting jobs, because they get paid to keep you employed. I recommend them. Unfortunately, when the economy is doing poorly, the jobs are scarce and employers have the pick of the most qualified candidates. Competition is brutal.

Here are some tips for getting an edge. The two magic words are "volunteer" and "network." Do not mistake volunteering as simply working for free. This is your pathway to getting a real job. You will be expected to be at a certain place at a certain time and doing a certain function. This is priceless experience. In order to choose a suitable volunteer opportunity, it is important to follow your personal interests. If you love gardening, consider working on a community project that grows vegetables. If you love animals, you can do what I did for years and help in animal shelters. After you have done volunteer work for a while, you may ask for a letter of reference from your volunteer coordinator. This reference is just as good as an actual job reference. It is proof that you have the ability to assume responsibility and follow through with it. That's what employers want. It doesn't matter if you are on the spectrum or not. If you have proof of your abilities, that's what gets noticed.

The main benefit of volunteering is what the recipient gets from it. A perfect example is what is happening this very minute. By participating in this book, I have volunteered to write for *you*. I am not getting paid one cent for any of my writing or time or ability. I am doing this because I think you are a valuable person who deserves to have all the help in life that you want and need. The thing that I am gaining from it is that my life feels like it has much more value since someone else can benefit from my experience. You just can't buy that.

Finally, volunteering offers you the opportunities and network connections that you need. You can volunteer and stay with what you are doing or you can quit and go on to something else. You can keep doing this as much as you want. In doing so, you will discover your strengths and likes and dislikes. This is the way to test careers and find people who can help you along the way.

Temple Grandin

Make a portfolio of your work. You need to sell your skills instead of yourself. Try to avoid the normal interview route. I got many design jobs by showing a portfolio of my drawings to the right people. Today, portfolios of drawings, computer code, art, sculpture, math and writing can be put in your smart phone.

After you get the job, you need to keep it. Never talk about controversial issues such as sex, religion or politics at work. Ask only for accommodations you may actually need, such as a quiet place to work away from florescent lights.

Sometimes you just have to do what your boss tells you because he is the boss.

Freelance work is often good. I started my business one small design project at a time.

I have more information on employment in my books *Developing Talents* and *Different...Not Less.*

RECOMMENDED READING

Grandin, T. (2009) *Developing Talents: Careers for Individuals with Asperger Syndrome and High-Functioning Autism.* Shawnee Mission, KS: Autism Asperger Publishing Co.

Grandin, T. (2012) *Different...Not Less.* Arlington, TX: Future Horizons.

Mitch Christian

I was lucky enough to discover my passion for computers in high school in the late 1970s when my high school got in some PCs just as they were first on the market. As an art major in college, I never used a computer, and it was several years before I used one again, when I was getting my programming degree. When I first sat down at the PC I actually said hello, as if I were greeting a long-lost friend. My mother used to say computers were like a surrogate family for me, and she was probably right. I always knew they weren't really my family, though. I think that understanding my own skills and interests was key to finding a career path that was suitable for me.

I was able to turn my interest into a career with a job as a programmer at an insurance company. I work in an area that compiles the company's statistical information and sends it to an outside organization. My ability with numbers and math comes in handy, and being fast and efficient at my work is a big plus, too. An unexpected bonus is that my company has remained stable with only minor changes, so it provides an ongoing familiar environment for me. Also, being at a mid-sized organization keeps me from being around too many people during the day. So knowing my own need for a predictable environment and how much interaction I can tolerate has helped me find the kind of company I can work well in.

One of the biggest hurdles was the job interview. Selling myself to other people is not one of my strong points, and after half a dozen interviews I was feeling dejected. Over the course of the interviews, I had some feedback from my school's career placement officer about what the previous interviewers didn't like. So I was able to adjust my approach, and by the next interview I was feeling more at ease with the process. I was more relaxed and didn't get stuck on certain topics, and was more open to the give and take of the conversation. I had a second interview with this same company and ended up getting the position. The information that I got back from potential employers through the placement office was invaluable in helping me land this job.

Working in an office has the advantage of keeping me on a regular schedule in an environment where the rules are fairly clear. One of the problems can be having to interact with co-workers, as well as environmental factors such as lighting and noise. Generally in a business setting there are some common patterns to everyday chit chat which I eventually learned, and by talking to my supervisor and manager I've been able to arrange the amount of lighting I prefer, and to reduce some of the ambient noise levels. After working with the same people for a number of years, I've become comfortable enough with them to bring up the topic of autism and introduce them to some of the concepts surrounding the issue so they understand some of my quirks better. Being aware of my sensory needs and that I work well within an existing structure has been a great aid to keeping the position, and having leaders who are flexible enough to accommodate my needs has allowed my career to be a long-term one.

Charli Devnet

Like many Aspies, I have been unemployed or under-employed most of my working life. Despite the ever-present temptation to give in to despair, I kept plugging away alone. Eventually I learned to keep body and soul together through a patchwork quilt of part-time, off beat and freelance work. I am hardly "successful" in the conventional sense, but I did accumulate a bit of wisdom along the way.

- *Never get discouraged:* Do not let repeated rejections or terminations get you down. Neurotypicals get fired, too. They do not catastrophize the situation. They pick themselves up, dust themselves off and continue to knock on doors. Once you give up and say, "No one will hire me. I will never work again," it becomes a self-fulfilling prophecy.

- *Do not disdain temporary or low-paying work:* Frustrated by an inability to find a "suitable job," I decided to take whatever came along. My jobs included everything from legal research and serving process to walking dogs to assisting photographers at high school proms to handing out samples in the supermarket. Some of my jobs allowed me to use my intellect, some helped me develop social skills and some were absolute disasters. I learned from each one. Eleven years ago, I found employment as a tour guide in a historic house museum. I absolutely love my job. Yes, it is seasonal and the wages are modest, but it makes me happy. I finally have the opportunity to use my knowledge of Greek mythology, a childhood special interest, for here in the gardens are sculptures of Apollo and Aphrodite.

- *You cannot skate by on intelligence alone:* The conventional wisdom is that all Aspies are quirky geniuses. We know this is not true, of course, but even if you are a quirky genius— especially if you are—do not expect that your IQ will protect you from adverse experiences in the workplace. As in all avenues of life, some social skills will be demanded. Once I was severely reprimanded by my boss after I had corrected him in front of his clients, although my intentions were sincere. I was just trying to be helpful! One attorney fired me after I vigorously shook my head in open court at a judge's boneheaded decision. This particular judge was a moron, a political hack, and he completely misunderstood the issue. My superior knowledge of the law mattered not. I had made my boss look bad. I lost my job and the judge kept his.

- *Keep a good attitude:* You have a better chance of holding onto a job that you enjoy. If you are doing what you love, you will brush off minor inconveniences. You will try your best to conform your behavior to meet the demands of your boss, co-workers and clients. If your performance is criticized, you will improve yourself. If, on the other hand, you are doing work that bores, confuses or does not satisfy your heart, treat it as part of your education. Do your best while planning a change. If you allow yourself to be unhappy, sooner or later it will show. Small annoyances will become large problems. You will respond to criticism by sulking at your desk, muttering insults under your breath or having a meltdown. Disgruntlement is contagious. Your boss will harass you. Your co-workers will shun you, and your reputation as a fine fellow to work with will be damaged beyond repair.

Anita Lesko

My research indicates only 10 percent of Aspies are working. I'm hoping this is an incorrect statistic. But even if it's 20 percent, that's really bad. That means there is a huge percentage of Aspies collecting Social Security Disability Income. Funding for this is going to run out by 2016 according to an article I recently read. What are these Aspies planning on doing then? Their parents won't live forever to support them. And unless their relatives leave them a fortune, where will they end up? This might sound harsh but it is reality. Now is the time to start thinking how to get and keep a job.

Every time I talk to Temple Grandin on the phone, we talk about the young Aspies of today. About how so many of them don't work, won't work, or don't know how to work. We reminisce about our teen years when we both used to clean horse stalls. Temple shared with me that they nicknamed her "work horse," and my nickname was "Creepin' Jesus"! We worked hard shoveling out stall after stall. But that built our foundations for working later in life. It taught us responsibility, accountability, and how to have pride in doing our jobs well.

Temple and I both agree that the biggest factor in our success was having those jobs when we were young. "We need to get these kids working!" are Temple's very own words. Yes we do! And this fact is directed to the parents. It is up to parents to get their Aspie kids out there doing odd jobs. Whether it's cutting grass, walking the neighbor's dogs, delivering newspapers, working at the local burger joint, they must do *something*. *Anything*. It gets them out there, interacting with people and learning work ethics. There's no other way around this. If Temple and I did it, so can your child. It wasn't easy at times, but it was the best therapy in the world. For parents who home-school their Aspie child, this becomes all the more important. You can't keep your kid sheltered at home and then expect them to enter society without any social skills. Get them out working!

Building this work foundation early in life will help you throughout the rest of your life. Getting through the interview process is the first hurdle. First, you need to know all about the job you are applying for. Know the company as well. Then you need to practice interviewing. Find someone you know to do mock interviews. Remember to keep your answers efficient—that means to the point, in as few words as possible. During a real interview, remember to be polite and maintain some degree of eye contact. *Always* be on time, or even early. That allows you to collect your thoughts and calm down. Be positive but not obnoxious. Don't try to be something you're not.

Once you are hired, do the best job you can. Try to avoid office politics; you will get singled out as the bad guy if you do get involved, even though others may be doing the same. Just keep your energies focused on your job. If you need special accommodations regarding noise or lighting, do not hesitate to ask for them. Always be on time. Keep up with your personal hygiene. Be polite. Don't be afraid to ask questions if you are not sure about what is expected. People are usually more than willing to help you out.

Finally, avoid engaging in any controversial topics such as religion, politics or sex. Refrain from expressing your opinions about things, too—save those for your Aspie friends.

Dr. Tony Attwood's Advice on Getting and Keeping a Job

The Many Qualities of Someone with an ASD

The majority of adults diagnosed with an ASD are unemployed or under-employed, that is, their job does not match their abilities, qualifications and aspirations. This is despite those with an ASD having many skills which are sought by employers. These skills include: reliability, accuracy, persistence, attention to detail, enjoyment of routines and procedures, creativity in problem solving, extensive factual and technical knowledge, a strong sense of social justice, a preference for not allowing socializing to be a distraction, a talent for identifying errors for quality control, and a natural ability with cataloguing information and identifying patterns and sequences.

Appraising the Potential Workplace

The first stage is for the person with an ASD to find and apply for a job that matches his or her abilities, qualifications and personality. It is important to gather as much information as possible on the social and sensory aspects of the job and, if feasible, the attitude of the line manager and workmates or colleagues to someone who has the characteristics of an ASD. People with an ASD can sometimes have an uncanny ability to quickly appraise the social atmosphere of a new situation, and a positive or negative attitude towards ASD can become apparent on meeting the staff and seeing the work environment prior to or during the interview process. It is wise to trust that intuition.

Applying for a Job and Preparing for an Interview

There may need to be guidance in completing the application form, particularly in deciding whether or not to disclose the diagnosis. There are no clear rules on disclosure when applying for a job, and it is sometimes a personal decision based on whether disclosure would facilitate or inhibit achieving an interview. Once the interview stage is reached, it is important to decide what to wear, and to rehearse with someone who knows you well how to answer the anticipated questions during the interview. If you have stated in the application that you have an ASD, it may help to prepare a brief brochure on ASD and the resultant qualities you possess in relation to the position. The brochure can be attached to the application or given to those who are interviewing you.

Optimizing the Interview Process

A job interview is an intensely social ordeal. There is an expectation that you will be able to read the body language of those conducting the interview, and succinctly and honestly answer their questions. Many people with an ASD have difficulty "selling" themselves to a potential employer and knowing the social conventions in an interview. That is why it is essential that there has been some practice and rehearsal in interviewing techniques. It may also be valuable to have an informative portfolio of relevant work experience that can be the focus of the interaction, rather than have a group of people simply looking at you. If those conducting the interview know that you have an ASD, it will help if you are able to describe some of the difficulties associated with ASD. Stress that these are significantly fewer than the qualities, and that there are strategies to facilitate successful employment. Family members or job coaches may be able to provide guidance in how to answer questions about ASD.

Maintaining Successful Employment

Should the application be successful, there are strategies designed for those with an ASD to maintain successful employment. These strategies include having an assigned mentor (a colleague) who can explain not only the work requirements, but also the social dynamics and social protocols of the new work environment, and provide feedback and guidance on teamwork skills. There may also need to be more reassurance that work performance is satisfactory than would occur with a neurotypical, and there should always be prior notice of changes in job requirements. Fortunately, there are now several books on achieving successful employment for those who have an ASD, the majority being published by Jessica Kingsley Publishers.

The Benefits of Employment

There are so many benefits in achieving and maintaining successful employment for the person with an ASD. These include having a clear structure and purpose to the day, an increase in self-esteem and an effective antidote to depression. There is also the enjoyment of a greater income and financial independence, and an opportunity to make friends, as well as the satisfaction of being able to apply knowledge and abilities in a practical and lucrative way.

Artwork (See Plate 11)

Painting: The Interview

Artist: Marilyn Cosho

Artist's Commentary: In an interview, the mind is spinning and blank at the same time. With every question, this person, the interviewee, is thinking, "What do you mean? Could you give me an example? Am I even close?"

Painting: The Thirst

Artist: Michael Tolleson

Artist's Commentary: Even though I have an extremely high IQ, I personally have lived my whole life "under-employed." While most persons with Asperger's have average to high intelligence we tend to be very poor at the politics required to get and keep elevated jobs. I was touched when I saw a photo of the woman I painted in this portrait. Here she is dressed in a beautiful sari, yet she is required to do something as menial and manual as drawing water into a bucket and carrying it to where it is needed. I understand that frustration.

CHAPTER 13

Disclosing a Diagnosis

Stress Ranking: 13

Ranking of issue by stress caused

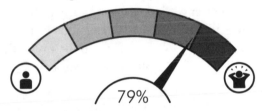

79%

Percent of respondents living with issue

73%

Many people with Asperger's/HFA have difficulty determining when it's right to tell others they're on the spectrum. Some examples of disclosure issues include: "Should I tell someone when I first meet them?" "Should I tell someone when they're interviewing me for a job?" "When is the best time to tell others of my situation (if ever)?" Do you have concerns about disclosure?

Richard Maguire

Q. How do you make sure a bad employer or prejudiced people do not make your life unhappy because of your autism?

A. Tell them about your autism.

It has been my experience that disclosing my autism has been an effective way of filtering bad people and jobs out of my life. On the other hand, when people are okay about my autism they are okay about me. They are people with good attitudes to life and people.

I have only been disclosing to people routinely for the past three years and I must say it has been good for me. Some people who thought I was being rude, offhand or just not trying socially have had a proper explanation of the way I live. Some people have said to me that they now see me in a better light. They like me, the way I behave and communicate. They used to struggle with me and wonder what I was really like. Some people said I was an enigma—I thought I was an enigma, too. Now they have the correct information, they like me better and feel better in my company.

I think there is another side to this. When I feel better about who I am, other people pick up on it. I seem more popular, and I wonder if this helps me feel better too. I haven't worked that one out yet.

I have been asked about whether to disclose or not by other people. I usually tell them of my experiences and the filtering effect. Then we discuss their lives and how they think disclosure will affect them. Exactly what to do becomes their choice and I do not judge them either way. Most people will disclose in their own time.

I used to get the wobbles in the early days of disclosing my autism. I think I had not rehearsed my reactions to others' reactions. Practice helps, as it does in so much of the autistic life. I needed to learn new gambits, replies and ways of talking about this new information and how people will relate to me when I use my new knowledge. I was taken aback by how many people had wondered if I was autistic, and by the people who were not surprised when I told them.

I did go to a couple of job interviews and got the impression that disclosure did put them off me, and I was not offered the jobs. I felt bad, but when I thought about it, I concluded that the rejections confirmed my suspicions about the lack of acceptance of autism, and I asked myself whether I would have been happy there anyway. The answer I gave myself was no, I would not have been happy.

That's all history now, as I became self-employed doing all kinds of autism work. Today, I sell my services as being from an autistic person. I know some people refuse me because of this and I am not bothered. If their attitude is that bad, I do not think my training would be well received or used. I do not give them any more thought. Instead, I concentrate my efforts where they will be appreciated and will do some good. That happens in nearly every case, which in turn increases my confidence in human nature. The autistic life is hard, and I have decided not to put any effort into chasing negative people—I want to build on the positive. If people want to change their minds about my autism and come with me, I am very pleased; if not, that is their loss.

Enjoy being autistic: it is possible, and I reckon part of this is disclosing and finding out who really does like you.

Qazi Fazli Azeem

I am Pakistan's first and only self-advocate for the Autism Spectrum. No one has ever come forward, not even since 2006 when I started giving my interviews on the local TV channels, and in newspapers and magazines. There are a handful of Aspies in South Asian countries like India and Bangladesh, but they are limited to their cities and associated with one particular special education school or center, and have not made many efforts to spread awareness in the entire South Asian region.

I have always seen myself as a human; my personal religious or national identity is secondary to my identity as a human. I see the autism community in South Asia and the world as being part of the same family and school of thought. I see others on the spectrum as having similar issues and similar solutions to me. This is why most of my efforts to raise autism awareness in my city, Karachi, my country, Pakistan, and my region of the world, South Asia, were never localized or intended to serve only a limited geographical or linguistic group.

My autism awareness efforts have been received and viewed in countries across the world, with many individuals and organizations acknowledging my efforts, from the United Nations World Autism Awareness Day website, to the Middle East and North Africa (MENA) region, to the United Nations and Inclusion International, as well as international advocates and researchers. I have documented everything, even putting English subtitles on my local interviews on Pakistani cable TV. I have shared most of my interviews on YouTube and most of my published interviews in PDF files on my website, and photographs on Flickr and Facebook. Most of my recommendations and posts for parents of children on the spectrum are free at the online forum of the Pakistan Autism Meetup Group. Sadly, any form of "disability" or "different perspective/ability" is a serious, taboo subject in South Asia, where there is little or no social awareness or responsibility towards children with autism. A lack of diagnosis together with superstitions are prevalent.

Since 2006 I have worked very hard and closely with parents, doctors, teachers, researchers and special educators, not only from South Asia but also from around the world, learning from them and teaching those who needed my help. I found out about my own Asperger's syndrome later in life, around age 25. Maybe this is why I already had an undergraduate degree and a respectable teaching job, and did not feel any fear about appearing on national and international media outlets to talk about Asperger's syndrome in Pakistan and the region. Would I have done things differently if I had the opportunity to do so? No, I would not. I am proud and pleasantly surprised at the support and encouragement I continue to receive from parents and special educators of children on the spectrum, not only from Pakistan but from all over the world.

I may now, at this point in my life, be higher on the spectrum, but this was not the case when I was younger. I choose to spread awareness so that I can help others, learn more about myself in this process, and eventually enable early intervention for children in my part of the world.

United we stand; we need more input from the South Asian region, and for people to work together for all of us. Citywide efforts are not sustainable, since we need regional examples and government-to-government resource sharing. Come forward, you are not alone, be proud of your difference. You join a growing number of self-advocates all over the world. Search our names online, learn from us, add to the global pool of knowledge and secure our combined future as the pioneers in the autism movement.

Henny Kupferstein

Disclosure is a personal journey, involving different bumps in the road for everyone. It all depends on the circumstances. Disclosure at college was an absolute necessity. In order for me to receive accommodations, I had to file my paperwork with the disabilities office. When I disclose, I usually get a few different types of responses. Most often, the person will immediately begin talking very slowly to me. Yes, that used to infuriate me, but I now understand that they are clueless, and not evil. The other type of response is usually a complete disregarding of what I have just said, merely because they don't know what to do with that information. At times, I still get the shocked gasp, "What? You?! Shut up!" Thanks to the media and advocacy from many individuals, that is no longer happening as often. Last but not least, there is always that person who will respond, "Oh, my nephew has that, and he's really cool." And then we're good. Those are the lasting friendships that I usually make.

Disclosure took a long time for me, and I could not do it. I could not say the A words for two years (neither Asperger's nor autism). I just couldn't. I couldn't say the word "disability" for three years. I struggled terribly to be understood, but then got upset and frustrated when I wasn't. I didn't understand that I should place the blame on myself for not disclosing while expecting the world to just magically read my mind.

Ultimately, my schooling took me far away from everything I have ever known. In a new county and almost a new time zone, I made a deal with myself to build a new identity, and start from scratch by freely disclosing. It turned into a very positive journey, mostly because of the amazing people I have encountered along the way. Not everybody has the luxury to just up and leave. So I would encourage them to pretend that they were newly born and starting over. If you are serious about this, you can pull it off. Disclosure will become the new and formulaic system for sorting through the wreckage of your life, and help elutriate the real friends from the rubble. It is totally worth it. And besides, you will eventually find people just like you, and they are the best ones in the world to hang out with. Even if you are all in your cave at the same time, it's nice to know that they are there for you in silence.

Dr. Know

I'm contributing anonymously (although Craig R. Evans and Dr. Tony Attwood know my identity). This in itself is a statement on my opinions about disclosure.

I have only disclosed information about me to a small group of people that I believed would:

- inform no one else about me

- view the information in a positive way

- obtain some net benefit from the information.

Disclosure is a complex issue and (like most things) depends a lot on individual circumstances. There are very few people that I think have the "right to know." In cases where the diagnosis is known by parents or caretakers, this includes first and foremost the individual. In cases with independent adults, I strongly believe that the individual has the right to decide who is to be given the information—I would say people in a lasting romantic relationship and offspring very likely should be informed. But there may be cases where it would be better to not disclose (at all or at least not right away).

Many things should be considered:

- Will there be a net benefit from someone knowing—otherwise, what is the point in disclosing? I think the population is in general too ignorant about the topic for full disclosure to provide a net benefit, so I suggest disclosing to only a few select people. When many (if not most) health professionals, including even psychiatrists and psychologists, have incorrect notions about autism and autistic traits, one should not expect better from the general population. Fortunately, some people (often those closer to you) will be motivated to educate themselves when you disclose, and that is a prime example of reacting in a positive way.

- Another point is the irreversibility of the disclosure. Once someone knows, there is generally no going back. When choosing whom to disclose to, you should consider also that some people just will not keep it confidential.

- Various ways of approaching the topic exist and you can fit the method used to the purpose and person(s) you are disclosing to. In most situations I would choose partial disclosure.

- In a professional context, you can simply describe whatever traits are relevant, and nothing else. For example, to an employer you could just mention any difficulties (such as sensory issues, or that while you don't typically look people in the eyes when they are talking, you are still paying attention). To some friends or relatives, you may want to explain whatever traits are relevant so they do not interpret them incorrectly.

- Briefly and accurately providing the relevant information is more likely to improve things for all involved. Giving a non-individualized "label" to people that may not have the motivation to educate themselves properly may lead them to acquire or strengthen prejudices, resulting in a harmful, rather than helpful, outcome. "Trait-based" partial disclosure is adaptable and a great pragmatic approach precisely because each situation is unique: Aspies are individuals, and neurotypicals (NTs) are individuals, too.

Ruth Elaine Joyner Hane

We need to decide what is significant in our disclosure of a diagnosis. Just as a good reporter collects facts for a news story, we should answer several of these questions: who, what, when, where, why and how? We might disclose fully to an immediate family member, medical professional, teacher and others who need to know, and only partially to casual friends and neighbors. At work, we disclose what is essential to a supervisor if we need a reasonable accommodation.

WORK

Disclosure of a diagnosis of autism entails sharing personal information to your supervisor or the Human Resources department to request a reasonable accommodation. Learning how to ask, in different ways, is important and needs to be practiced. You do not need to tell every aspect of your autism, only what applies in a particular job or position. Consider that what you reveal may have disadvantages in some situations and be beneficial in others. You do not need to share information about your autism if you can perform the "essential functions" of the job without the need for an accommodation, and can function effectively in all aspects of the workplace.

The cubicle assigned for me at Midway Training was in a high-traffic area. Naturally, the more social employees congregated near my desk, often sitting in my chair if I was not using it. I had fully disclosed my autism, so the employer was amenable, and agreed to honor my request to move to a different cubicle. The corner cubicle was away from the offensive florescent lighting, my desk was undisturbed, and I was not distracted by conversations, so I could get my reports in on time.

Some of us will need assistance in deciding what is problematic by consulting with someone in whom we can trust. This "helpful" person is someone whom you can be confident will have your best interest in mind and respect your privacy. If it is tough for you to judge who will be helpful, ask your immediate supervisor or someone in the personnel department to assign or suggest a mentor. This person should be respectful, honest and have worked in the department long enough to know the other employees and work culture.

COMMUNITY

When the pharmacist announces a prescription is ready at the Walgreens drug store, I startle because the audio is too loud. If I am at the checkout counter and need to protect my ears, I may say to the cashier, "Sorry for the delay, the speaker is too loud." If a similar incident happens in another setting, such as a restaurant, I may disclose to the waitperson or host, "I have sensitive hearing, and the sound is too loud. I'd appreciate it if you could lower the volume. Thanks!"

SCHOOL

School personnel can help you write your Individual Education Plan (IEP). Make sure to arrive at your IEP session ready to articulate the stressors in the classroom or school that are causing a hindrance for your education. When I was in fourth grade, I asked my teacher to wet-wipe the chalkboard so I could see the math figures. I could not see the chalk lines unless they *contrasted* with the background. When we understand our needs we can be clear about what accommodation will be helpful.

The following six questions will help you decide. Your "helpful" person can assist in completing these questions. Answer the following:

- Who do I tell?

- What do I say?

- When do I tell?

- Where do I make the disclosure?

- Why is it good to disclose?

- How do I say it?

Mary Robison

Since about a year ago, when I decided that being on the spectrum isn't the worst thing in my life, I've been pretty upfront about it. It is a part of me. I refuse to be embarrassed about it any more than I would be embarrassed about being female or left-handed.

The first time I told people that I was on the spectrum was as a panelist, in front of a large crowd *and* videotaped (the video is available on YouTube). I was shaking, literally, in my shoes. The audience was very receptive; most of them were also on the spectrum, although it wasn't an autism conference. As the hour went on, I grew more comfortable with "outing" myself.

I am an adjunct professor at a couple of local colleges. In the previous year, I have made it my practice to tell my students that I am on the spectrum. My purpose is two-fold. First, since part of my ASD includes prosopagnosia, or face blindness, I want them to know that I won't recognize them in the halls and that I need them to sit in the same seats for the entire semester. I sometimes ask if they mind if I photograph them, as I find that I can recognize people if I've studied their features in a photograph. Second, I want them to understand that everyone has learning deficits and to not be ashamed if they need some formal or informal accommodations. They just have to ask. When students see that I'm upfront about my issues, they are less anxious about their own.

So far, coming out to my students has been very successful. Coming out to my superiors has been somewhat less so. Still, I refuse to pretend, ever again, that I'm neurotypical. I'm successful as someone with ASD. I'm a fraud as a neurotypical.

I have told hiring committees about being on the spectrum twice. Once, I was not hired and once, I was. I don't have sufficient data to say if my admission prevented my being hired.

However, I can't avoid it; I behave in fairly stereotypical ways in front of a hiring committee. I don't know where to look. I laugh inappropriately. And I flap. Yet, I don't do these things when I am teaching in front of a class. It's because I know my discipline and I have other, more appropriate gestures and habits for teaching, but the hiring process is still something of a mystery to me.

Most academic or technical positions are tolerant, even encouraging, of those on the spectrum. Jobs that require a lot of interaction with the general public are much less so. The type of job I was looking for would determine how forthright I would be. In personal relationships, it shouldn't make a difference whether or not you are on the spectrum. Good relationships require effective communication, and since the spectrum inhibits good communication for you, explaining to your partner that you need additional cues is very important. But ASD doesn't excuse you when you act like a jerk! So don't.

Anita Lesko

Anyone with Asperger's syndrome wonders when and if they should disclose this fact. Unfortunately, our society has yet to grasp what Asperger's really is, even more so since the Newtown shooting by Adam Lanza. The media chose very irresponsible reporting on that event. They all began linking Asperger's syndrome to the killer mind. Nothing could be farther from the truth. This, of course, shed a dark shadow over people with Asperger's. This may perhaps make many of us even more cautious to disclose.

Regarding work-related issues, I think it's best *not* to disclose during a job interview. Simply put, you risk not getting hired. If you are qualified to do a job, that's what you are applying for. There is no reason to disclose at that time.

Once hired and working, there may come a time you need to disclose. That is when having a formal diagnosis comes in handy. You will have a letter from a psychologist to present to your employer. This conversation needs to be done in private.

Be prepared when you talk with your supervisor. Have printed materials to present to them, and point out your positive aspects: extreme focus, loyalty, and so on. Encourage them to ask you questions. State that Asperger's syndrome is on the Autism Spectrum, and is covered by the Americans with Disabilities Act. Familiarize yourself with this act at www.ada.org.

I have another point that is rather humorous. Even without your disclosure, everyone will recognize you are different! Disclosing only confirms it.

I personally found it to my advantage to disclose at my job for numerous reasons. It helps supervisors and co-workers better understand you. Again, educate them what Asperger's really is. Don't assume they know or understand the real facts.

For friendships and relationships I advise the same thing. No need to bring it up on the first get-together. Wait until the second or even third time together to spring the news. By then they will know you and should be more interested to learn more about you rather than want to flee! Instead of coming right out and saying I have Asperger's, I first ask if they have ever heard of it. If they say "yes," I inquire as to what they know. I'll then fill in the gaps. By then, they'll ask me why I'm asking—there's my opening.

As you get older, you get a feel for when that right moment arises. Be ready for when it does.

Karen Krejcha

In the computer security world, *full disclosure* requires that complete details of any vulnerability in the computer systems are disclosed to the public, including how to detect and exploit them. Fortunately, we don't need to give that kind of "full disclosure" when we talk about our spectrum diagnosis. Fear of rejection is bad enough. No one should be exploited.

The truth is, when you disclose your diagnosis, your experiences vary. Sometimes it goes very well and relationships improve. Occasionally a relationship ends abruptly. Often there are gradual changes.

You may be wondering how, why, when, where and to whom you should disclose your diagnosis. This essay focuses on "how."

First, a light-hearted sharing skills exercise:

Imagine approaching a co-worker or classmate in the hallway. That person asks how your weekend was. Which is your closest response?

A. Before entering the hallway, you hope no one sees you. When, despite all your best efforts to turn invisible, someone does see you and engages anyway, you mumble, "Fine, thanks," and subsequently get distracted by overanalyzing the situation.

B. Smile and say, "It was great, thanks. I had the chance to read a book I've wanted to read for quite a while. How was your weekend?"

C. Tell them about the book you read, and five reasons why you liked it. Give an analysis of how that book compared to another in the same genre that you read ten years ago that was made into a movie, which ended up having a sequel that was nowhere near as good as the original.

When stressed, I bounce between A and C. Answer B is what many neurotypicals consider socially appropriate. I *try* to be a B but that B buzz is rarely intuitive. I have to consciously practice.

In disclosing something as personal and important as your diagnosis, you'll need to practice the information you share. Here are suggestions. Please evaluate these in light of your personal situation.

1. Try to understand what your feelings are about being an Aspie. If you comprehend and are accepting of your differences, others you disclose to often see that. It helps them in renewing their acceptance of you.

2. Practice disclosure in advance. Write it out. Read it aloud. Did you convey what you intended? Too much information? Not enough? If so, edit and try again, noting that the content and amount of information you disclose will vary by person and situation.

3. Role-play your disclosure. I recommend doing this with both an Aspie and a neurotypical. Do this separately. Have

each person react to you in different ways, sometimes positive, sometimes negative.

4. Timing is very important. Never disclose during an argument. Be aware of the health and mood of the people with whom you want to disclose your diagnosis. (Easier said than done, right?) Pick a neutral or positive time.

5. Give others time to process their thoughts and feelings. Their initial reaction may not be long term, so respond to questions and keep communication open. Since no two people on the Autism Spectrum are the same, the person you disclose to may be confused and not really understand what your version of being an Aspie looks like. This is where role-playing possible scenarios in advance is very useful.

6. Do you have someone you want to disclose to in a more casual way? I like sharing *Dude, I'm an Aspie* by Matt Friedman and *All Cats Have Asperger's Syndrome* by Kathy Hoopmann.

7. After disclosing, realize that no matter the result, what you did was not easy. Give yourself credit.

8. Remember that the decision to disclose should be yours and is a gift of sharing an important part of who you are.

9. Finally, remember that we are each on a unique journey. When we compare ourselves to others, we often end up feeling inferior or superior; sometimes, a bit of both. Accept yourself for who you are, where you are, and let your light shine.

REFERENCES

Friedman, M. (2012) *Dude, I'm an Aspie: Thoughts and Illustrations on Living with Asperger's Syndrome.* Raleigh, NC: Lulu Press, Inc.

Hoopmann, K. (2006) *All Cats Have Asperger's Syndrome.* London: Jessica Kingsley Publishers.

Dr. Tony Attwood's Advice on Disclosing a Diagnosis

Sometimes the characteristics of ASD are conspicuous, such that a neurotypical may be confused and seek an explanation of certain unusual behaviours or reactions. It is difficult enough being different, but how do you explain that difference to neurotypicals? You have to make a decision regarding whether or not to disclose the diagnosis, and if that decision is made, how to explain the diagnosis. There are three options regarding disclosure.

The first is not to disclose the diagnosis and the characteristics of ASD, and hope that any confusion on the part of a neurotypical will soon pass. This may be a strategy with someone who is a stranger, and there may not be the time or the need to provide an explanation. However, those with whom you interact more frequently will probably start to notice a pattern of unusual characteristics and this may affect their attitude towards you. They may then use various derogatory words to describe you, such as aloof, rude, inconsiderate, weird, disrespectful or boring, both in their thoughts of you and when talking about you with other people.

The second option is to provide an explanation, but not to use an 'A' word such as Asperger's syndrome or autism. The explanation can be in terms of personality rather than a diagnosis, so that you say, "I am the sort of person who..." For example, where there may be confusion over your lack of anticipated eye contact, you might say, "I am the sort of person who tends to look away when you are talking. It helps me concentrate on what you are saying." Other examples might be, "I am the sort of person who is very enthusiastic about [insert special interest] and am not very good at reading the signs that someone is bored. If you are bored, please let me know and we can change the subject." Or, "I am the sort of person who sometimes says something that could cause embarrassment. If I have made you embarrassed, I am so sorry. I am trying to stop doing this. Can you be compassionate and help me overcome this problem?"

The strategy is to consider those characteristics of ASD that could be uncomfortable for, or misinterpreted by, neurotypicals. Without a satisfactory explanation they will assume a "moral" diagnosis, such as your being rude, self-centred or thoughtless. With guidance from family members and friends, you can create a spoken explanation that satisfies the neurotypical and prevents the development of a negative perception of you.

The third option is to explain openly to a neurotypical that you have an ASD. This is the bravest and perhaps the wisest option. This option would really be reserved for those who need to know of the diagnosis, and should be undertaken with great care. You will need to decide when and how to make the disclosure. During the disclosure, it may help to refer to literature on ASD for neurotypicals, and the Aspie mentors in this chapter have made their recommendations of books they have found informative and illuminating for neurotypicals.

Some adults with an ASD are quite open about their diagnosis, perhaps wearing t-shirts that boldly display a statement of being proud to be an Aspie. Other adults are shyer, and disclosure of the diagnosis is reserved for very specific people in their lives, with no open public disclosure. Disclosure is also easier for mature adults than it is for teenagers with an ASD, as neurotypical adolescents are notoriously intolerant of anyone who is different and whom they perceive as "defective." Having a diagnosis confirmed by a paediatrician, psychologi.st or psychiatrist can be used as a justification by others for rejection, humiliation and bullying. Thus, it is quite understandable that most teenagers with an ASD are fearful of having the diagnosis disclosed to peers.

Disclosing the diagnosis can be an advantage at a college or university, in order to be able to access student support services and to benefit from academic accommodations that are needed by students with an ASD. Jessica Kingsley Publishers have several books on the support and guidance needed for college students with an ASD.

Disclosure to an employer or line manager could facilitate greater understanding and guidance in work performance and expectations. There may also be a time when disclosure is an advantage in a friendship or romantic relationship, mutual understanding and honesty being the basis of long-term friendships and relationships. There is a genuine and understandable concern as to how each neurotypical will react to disclosure of the diagnosis, and whether the information will remain confidential with that person. It is a risk, but sometimes, as described by the Aspie mentors, it is worth taking the risk.

RECOMMENDED READING

Murray, D. (2005) *Coming Out Asperger: Diagnosis, Disclosure and Self-Confidence*. London: Jessica Kingsley Publishers.

Artwork (See Plate 12)

Painting: Freedom

Artist: Nekea (Kea) Blagoev

Artist's Commentary: A cruel tree is restricting my thought, a dark negative vein growing and expanding in the mind. A line bleeds and spreads into the mind, but I have a fight and that's when it becomes light and a little brighter to see, and I become free to just be me.

Painting: Don't Kill the Messenger

Artist: Michael Tolleson

Artist's Commentary: Darkness surrounds someone considering sharing information about who and what they are with family, friends and co-workers. Sometimes we feel like a dark messenger in the night as we explain that the person they thought they knew might actually be something else. Their concept as to why we behave the way we do and their perceptions of us may be shattered by the new information. We are fearful. The person in this painting has the task of giving what they feel is bad news to others. There is little hope or illumination symbolized by the single glowing lantern in a gray dismal scene. While a diagnosis may illuminate and explain much to us, sharing that information with others can be very difficult.

— CHAPTER 14 —

Bullying

Stress Ranking: 14

Ranking of issue by stress caused

77%

Percent of respondents living with issue

72%

Many people with Asperger's/HFA have been bullied. Some examples of bullying issues include: being verbally or physically assaulted in school or at play, and being threatened or intimidated by a co-worker. Do you have concerns about bullying?

Garry Burge

Bullying can be difficult to deal with for a person on the Autism Spectrum, and is often overwhelming and debilitating. I experienced bullying badly in school. Dr. Tony Attwood described bullying as a period of war service. I think Aspies are prone to being bullied because we are different and immediately obvious as targets. Our inability to understand the requirements of social skills and conformity causes us to be on the outer. In school, bullying can become a problem because teachers may not always be around and the schoolyard can be a place from where there is no means of escape. Also, teachers may not always understand the type of bullying behaviour that is going on, or know when to stop it. At school, I retreated to the school library because I knew I could be safe there.

Sadly, bullying does not always stop at school and it can occur in the workplace for the very few Aspies that can obtain a job. I have found that it is important to be aware of an employer that has anti-bullying policy, and to find a manager or work colleague who can understand and help you. An employment consultant could be involved to assist the employee to try to form a special working relationship with a supervisor or manager. This staff member needs to be aware of how the person with autism is coping, and to be available should there be any concerns or issues within the work environment. It is also important to report inappropriate or unacceptable behaviour immediately, and to inform the supervisor or manager of other staff members who may be difficult to approach or work with. This can help to make a big difference in overcoming levels of anxiety and stress that can cause issues with work performance and attendance.

Another thing that is important is to find ways of dealing with other employees' behaviours that the person with autism may consider inappropriate. The supervisor, manager or employment consultant can assist with support and advice on this matter, too. I have also found that joining a union can help ensure that any inappropriate or unsavoury behaviour does not continue. The union can stand up for the person and ensure that their rights exist within the work environment. I have had to consult the union when dealing with inappropriate or unacceptable behaviour which has affected me directly within employment. The union can be seen as a means of protection against exploitation and other factors that may impact on the person with autism and their work performance.

Bullying can be controlled within the work environment by simply complaining about any inappropriate behaviour. I have had to complain on some occasions to ensure that my rights are represented within the work environment, to help shield me from various difficulties.

Alexis Wineman

It is amazing how cruel people can be. The violence and teasing is sometimes more shocking than hurtful, but all we remember is the pain. I remember that in school I was teased for the funny way I spoke and because no one could understand a word that I was saying. The teasing was harsh enough that for the longest time I didn't want to have friends. I thought that everything that they said to me was true. I was useless, nobody wanted me around, and I wasn't worth anything. It got to the point where I was so used to it I became numb. No one wanted anything to do with me. I was just a punching bag to everyone and I accepted that.

I didn't really have any friends to have my back, like everyone else did. But the reason this kept happening was because I never told anyone. If I had told a teacher or my parents about the teasing it probably would have stopped. But instead, I kept it to myself. In fact, my parents didn't even realize that most of this happened until after I graduated from high school.

High school was where things started to change for me. Most of the bullies started leaving me alone, and I think it was because I had two older sisters who would have beaten anyone who messed with me. Not everything was perfect—I still had the occasional bully pick on me, but I was older and ignoring it was so much easier.

If I could go back in time, I would have stood up for myself, but I would do it in a way that kept me from becoming a bully myself. Make an effort to be nice to everyone, even the people you don't like. As clichéd as it is, my parents have always told me to "kill them with kindness," and when you do that, the bullies get bored because they are not getting the reaction out of you they wanted.

If you are the victim of bullying, you must seek out an adult to tell. Ongoing bullying rarely just stops: someone needs to step in.

Qazi Fazli Azeem

I doubt there are many people on the spectrum who have not been bullied at any time in their lives, whether in school, the workplace, out there in the public or even in their neighborhood. For a very long time, I gave up on all forms of public and social interaction with strangers, due to a few minor instances of bullying.

After studying books on human psychology, neuroscience and evolution, I better understood why this happens, and the territorial nature of the human primate. There is a direct link with what is accepted as socially normal or prevalent, and the difference expressed by the physical and verbal communication of the person on the spectrum. Some people may interpret this difference as a threat.

As the American president Franklin D. Roosevelt said, "The only thing to fear is fear itself." From this statement, I can infer that people are afraid of others that they do not understand. It is only through proper autism awareness in schools and workplaces that we can eliminate bullying and replace it with understanding and appreciation of diversity and change. There are some governments that discourage dissent by passing laws against difference of opinions and sharing those opinions in public. Bullying is the same, but at an individual level.

Physically confronting a bully never ends on a positive note and will get you in trouble. Neurotypical people get bullied too, just like we do. There is strength in numbers, so try to find others like you who are also bullied. Talk to them, move around together, share strategies on coping and becoming stronger as a group, and look out for each other in public. If you feel you are being bullied at school, immediately contact the student adviser or counselor or a senior teacher whom you trust, and ask for advice. If you are being bullied at work, consult your family or your caregiver and ask for advice, and if possible, consult your supervisor (unless they are the one who you feel is bullying you).

In my own case, my lack of eye contact is most likely what triggered the bullying. Try making eye contact with people that you talk to, since not making it might suggest that you are trying to hide something; this may not be the case, but it may be what others think.

There are national and international organizations now that help people on the spectrum to seek advice in cases of bullying. Bullying happens to most of us; be strong, you are not alone: ask for advice from others.

John Makin

I cannot say much about this from my own experience, having only been conscious of one occasion when I was bullied. There may have been, and probably were, other times when my peers attempted to bully me, yet were unsuccessful. I know I was notoriously slow to catch on to others' meanings and to pressures that may have been aimed at me.

The one time I was aware of it involved physical bullying—twisting my arms, shoulders, hands, and so on—by the boy who shared a double desk with me and was much larger and stronger than I was. This continued for some weeks, until I was refusing to go to school. I then had no qualms about relating the reason to my parents, who told me to respond to it, report it if necessary.

In the event I resolved it myself one day, when, while waiting to enter a classroom, he started to push me about. I stood square to him and told him off for what he was doing, for bullying me, there, right in front of the whole class. I told him that by picking on someone smaller and weaker than himself he was being a coward, that his behavior was uncivilized and unacceptable and that he should be ashamed of himself.

He never touched me again.

I had stopped it being something underhand and secret that others could turn away from, not see and ignore. I made sure that the whole class had it thrust in their faces.

Henny Kupferstein

Most of the time, I withdraw from conflict the moment it occurs. Experience has taught me that the way I react gives a free invitation to abusers to step right in and take full advantage of me. I usually don't realize how badly I am being treated until I am thoroughly humiliated and violated. Therefore, I run for the hills when I feel the heat. Literally. Physically, when my face feels red, I run.

Emotionally, I tell myself a few things: (1) Abusers abuse, because they can. (2) It takes two to tango, and a boxer needs a match to punch. (3) Sometimes, not answering leaves them powerless. This means that you retreat with dignity. And remember, it is not cowardly to retreat, if you are off to a better place.

I am the pseudoconflict meister! Every single miscommunication is due to my altered perception of visual, auditory and non-verbal stimuli. I have tried paraphrasing, which is supposed to show the neurotypical (NT) that you understood, but it just frustrated me even more if it didn't bring greater understanding. I have now learned a method that works better for me. I ask people to please "repeat that, using different words." This makes the perception fire up differently, so that I can get another picture of what is going on. Usually, that is all I need to fix a misunderstanding.

Richard Maguire

So far, every autistic person I have met has been bullied, and that includes me. I read biographies and the same painful pattern of bullying emerges. We begin young and the age gap between us and our peers is not too great. Things can be sweet. We can be cute. Then comes school, and bullying begins. Then secondary school, and bullying gets to a whole new level. By this time, we are way different to our age peers, so much so that they are not really peers any more. In our teens, the loneliness, bullying and pain of life get too much. Self-esteem, life, and the will to carry on collapse. Not all make it to adulthood.

I call the period between mid-teens and mature adulthood, 30 or more, the tunnel. It's dark and lonely, with little hope or comfort in there. I went through the tunnel between ages 14 and 37. People I mentor are in it for about the same time. And the bullies? They are with us on into adulthood. They can spot our poor posture, poor self-esteem and inefficient gait, our lack of social and protective skills, our sensitivity, our meltdowns and poor communication—they home in on us to practise their own vile take on social skills. I watch my son enter school, and his gait and the way he carries his body look so different. My heart breaks, as I know the bullies are in there. His school is very good and looks after him well, but the bullies have their ways, so I teach him his ways of showing confidence and taking control of how people interact with him. I believe this is the most effective way of dealing with bullying—don't be their target. Bullies are inadequate people; they cannot deal with confident people who will not be controlled by them.

There are things that can be done, and I have found that we autistic people have the most effective means of dealing with bullying within ourselves. Bullying stopped in my life when I learned that the way I present myself attracts them. I do not know what I did in detail, but in short, I stopped acting like I was nervous and apologizing for my existence in public. This was such a powerful realization. No amount of people looking out for me could be this effective. I put bullies off by changing myself, then after acting confident I became confident, and life is much better.

I help my son and people I mentor through this realization and process. How to do it varies from person to person, and at its heart it is looking confident, then growing and being confident. Slow down, don't rush, take and use space and time to be who you are and look like you feel okay about this. I recommend you read and view the work of Gok Wan. He is a British writer, television presenter, fashion consultant and designer. He was bullied for being fat and gay when younger. His work today is based on his self-realization that the solution to bullying was wholly in his control. It worked, and he shows other people how it can work.

I work with my son and many other people, beginning by infusing them with some hope, giving them cognitive exercises and encouraging them to seek positive feedback about who they are. This is hard and complex. People are coming from a low baseline. I work with an unconditional positive attitude. They are succeeding simply by engaging in the process. Success breeds success, the tunnel can be travelled, and a more confident person can come out the other end into a day where they feel they are dealing with life and steering their own future. They look physically larger. People comment about how well they look. This cements their progress and new life learning about confidence. The bullies start leaving them alone. The positive spiral is in motion.

Anita Lesko

Throughout my whole life I have been a bully magnet. I am convinced I am wearing a sign on my back that reads, "Bully Me!" It seems all people with Asperger's get bullied. We are different and don't fit in. That is great material for any bully right there. All through elementary school, junior high and high school, the bullies found me. College was different, I think because everyone is off doing their own thing. I enjoyed those years.

Worse than the school years, though, was workplace bullying. This is the worst kind because it can jeopardize your career. There is at least one bully in every workplace. I am convinced this is one of Murphy's laws. Doing mean things to someone else is what makes a bully feel good about himself.

Fortunately, there are measures you can take to stop a bully in their tracks. It may take several steps, but eventually you will win the battle. Just be patient.

For parents with school-age children on the spectrum: always encourage them to communicate. You need to know what's going on at school. If you discover they are being bullied, take action immediately. Start by making an appointment with the teacher; if nothing is done, then go to the next level. Continue up the ladder until you get the results you need for your child to be bully-free. There is no place for bullies in our society. We have all seen on the media the extremes it has gone to. It needs to stop once and for all. If you don't get results within the school system, then seek local law enforcement.

At one job, I was bullied for seven years by a co-worker. She tried everything on earth to get me fired. It didn't work. I left that job to pursue my special interest of military aviation photojournalism. Of course, within the first week on my new job, the workplace bully discovered me. This one spent the next ten years literally obsessed with me. It seemed as if every breathing second she was plotting the next evil thing to do to me. Everyone was well aware of what she was doing, yet no one stopped her. Looking back, it all made for making me a better person. I now see her as a very pathetic individual with many psychological problems. She no longer works there, and cannot come back to work at that institution. Funny how life works out.

Here is my advice to Aspies on the job. If someone is bullying you, go talk to your supervisor. Have documentation to back up your story. Once you recognize someone is bullying you, start writing down dates, times, who else was present. This will prove extremely helpful some time down the road. You cannot possibly remember all these details without writing them down.

Again, start at the most simple level: your supervisor. If that gets you nowhere, in most institutions there's a Human Resources department. Go visit them. If that doesn't work, there is the Equal Employment Opportunity Commission (EEOC), a federal government bureau. They can act as a mediator, and if they feel necessary, will also encourage you to file a suit. All being well, things can be dealt with at a lower level. If not, be comforted to know there are options. The Americans with Disabilities Act covers people on the Autism Spectrum. You should familiarize yourself with this act at www.ada.gov.

Don't tolerate bullying. It is your right to go to school or work without getting bullied.

Karen Krejcha

I was 16. It was my senior year of high school, and I was in the hospital for a gastrointestinal issue that even Sherlock Holmes would have been unable to deduce. My parents visited and brought an envelope mailed from "a friend," presumably get well wishes.

There was a boy I had a *major* crush on, so I was hoping it was from him. It was, but instead of declarations of love, there were potato peelings and a paper with one word on it: SPUD. I was devastated. Everything I was equated to a potato. Big, lumpy, plain, unimpressive…SPUD.

Why that word bothered me so much, I don't know. There had been many over the years. My maiden name was Pitsenbarger so I got "Pits with no ____" and "Pick some boogers." Someone once told me to say, "Sticks and stones may break my bones, but names will never hurt me." This *really* bad idea resulted in:

1. Kids who threw rocks and sticks.

2. Words that stung long after the pain of rocks and sticks subsided.

I wish I had the answer to make bullying stop. You can keep calm, be assertive, and share with appropriate adults. You can document behavior, be proactive in an Individualized Education Plan, and role-play conflict resolution skills, but there is no one-size-fits-all situation formula.

Especially when school age, it's important to understand that bullies may practice bad behavior but they are often hurting inside too. That isn't an excuse. It is possible to be both a victim and a bully. A person who bullied me in childhood ended up later learning he was an Aspie. He regretted his bullying days. It was later in life that he concluded his motivation was part defense mechanism, part mimicry and part wanting to belong.

Aspies often have trouble distinguishing between teasing and bullying. It feels very similar. Teasing behavior that is more likely acceptable is from someone you have a relationship with. It should be occasional and not based on bigotry. The intention is good-natured and not harmful. If you feel hurt and you ask it to stop, it should.

Bullying behavior has an imbalance of power between the bully and victim. It is often a repeated pattern, and the intent of the bully is to cause emotional or physical pain. It can negatively impact a victim's work performance, scores/grades, sleep patterns, eating and other functions of daily life.

Here are things to try when no one else is around to help:

- Unfortunately, you can't control what another person says or does but you *can* control how *you* respond. Focus on staying calm and keeping emotional response at a minimum.

- Bullies love power. They want you to be sad or lose your cool. Know this, and don't give that reaction. Practice facial responses that don't show great emotion.

- Be assertive with your body language and comfortable in your own skin. When you appear positive and confident, even if you feel the opposite, you're less likely to appear on a bully's radar. A side benefit is that by practicing this, you actually do become more positive and self-confident.

- Since a lot of bullying begins with verbal harassment, if you can defuse the situation early, you may prevent further occurrences. Practice your response plan.

Once you are away from the situation, talk to someone you can trust, get help if you need to and remember, bullying is not about anything wrong with you. It's about what is wrong with the bully. *You* are good enough inside and out and are deserving of acceptance and respect.

RESOURCES

Workplace Bullying Institute: www.workplacebullying.org
Pacer's National Bullying Prevention Center: www.pacer.org/bullying
stopbullying.gov: www.stopbullying.gov

Dr. Tony Attwood's Advice on Bullying

Why are those with an ASD so frequently, and at school almost daily, the victims of bullying? Why would a neurotypical enjoy causing distress to someone who is basically kind, innocuous and inoffensive? The reasons that those with an ASD are perceived as easy victims include:

- often being alone and not having a group of friends for protection

- having the posture and body language of someone who is insecure and vulnerable

- having low self-esteem and social status

- being perceived as a relatively "soft target," that is, someone unlikely to be assertive or able to retaliate in a way that could cause discomfort to the "predator."

There are many types of bullying, some overt and some covert. The obvious overt examples are threats and actions of physical violence and intimidation; but the more subtle and covert expressions of bullying are humiliation, derogatory gestures, mockery, sarcasm, malicious gossip, rejection, exclusion and teasing, practical jokes and "setting up" due to the victim's gullibility and lack of street wisdom.

For those with an ASD, bullying can occur not only at school, but in a local neighbourhood, at church, parties, family gatherings and any social occasion with peers. Unfortunately, bullying can also occur in the workforce during the adult years and sometimes can occur in a relationship.

The psychological effects of bullying are devastating. It is a major cause of school refusal and school suspension, often because the victim has become angry and reluctantly retaliated. It can be a contributory factor in the development of an anxiety disorder, due to constant fear of a bullying "attack" or ambush each day, and knowing that there is no way to prevent such painful emotional experiences. The derogatory and provocative comments and actions may be internalized and believed by the victim, contributing to low self-esteem and a clinical depression. As so many interactions with peers are associated with being bullied, and so few positive social interactions are experienced, there can be the development of a sense of paranoia that is based on reality.

By being so sensitive to frequent bullying and having difficulty reading the intentions of others, a person with an ASD may not be able to differentiate between friendly and unfriendly teasing, which can inhibit the development of a true friendship. Also, others may create a distance between themselves and the person with an ASD so as not to become targets themselves. This adds to a sense of loneliness and rejection. The person with an ASD may have few, if any, friends to provide not only protection and safety in numbers, but also to calm the anguish and dissolve the despair.

There may be no words or actions of support and compassion to create greater self-esteem, and put the event in perspective. Thus, the effects of bullying go deeper and last longer for those with an ASD than for neurotypicals.

There are additional concerns regarding bullying in terms of those with an ASD. They tend to have a limited range of options in response to bullying, sometimes only two: ignore, or retaliate with violence. There is then the very real risk of being caught and punished for the retaliation, while the perpetrator appears to be the virtuous victim. Another concern is when the bullying is not taken seriously by the relevant authorities, such that the person with an ASD regrettably "takes the law into their own hands," seeking retribution by violence. This is of even greater concern in countries that have easy access to weapons.

What are the motives of a person who engages in bullying? Again, there are many motivations, including the enjoyment of power and control through fear, the creation of greater self-esteem by destroying the self-esteem of others, and the establishment of an entourage of obedient "friends." It is interesting that research on the lifelong outcome of those who bully is that they are at greater risk of being convicted of a criminal offence, losing jobs and relationships and eventually suffering from issues of low-self-esteem themselves. Thus, both parties, the neurotypical who engages in bullying and the ASD victim, need rescuing, but how can they be rescued?

Strategies to Reduce Bullying

There needs to be a team approach when bullying occurs at school. The team includes the victim, and the person who engages in bullying acts, who needs to be informed of the long-term personal consequences of such actions. The team also includes staff and parents of all children or students; but the most important members of the team are the other children and adolescents who are not victims and do not engage in acts of bullying. They are the silent majority and must be encouraged to step in and stop the bullying, in order to rescue both parties. All students at a school have the right to enjoy a safe environment, and that includes all students being safe from acts of bullying.

The person with an ASD may need to learn and apply a greater range of responses to acts of bullying. While ignoring and walking away are constructive strategies, there is the possibility of the person who engages in acts of bullying increasing the intensity and frequency of those acts until there is eventually a negative emotional response. It is important that the child or adolescent with an ASD recognizes that "the name of the game" in bullying is to create a negative emotion in the victim, and once the negative emotion is expressed, the game is won by the bully. However, the person with an ASD can win by not becoming distressed or agitated. This is easy to suggest, but is actually very difficult for the person with an ASD to do in practice.

There will be a range of constructive responses to any act of bullying, so it is important to disclose what is happening to a parent or teacher. Together, the person with an ASD and the supportive people in his or her life can create an effective plan of action and reaction. Another advantageous response can be to train in the martial arts. This is not so much about learning how to hurt someone, but rather how to be calm, in control and assertive in a situation of confrontation. This can be a very powerful deterrent.

It will also be important to have safe havens away from known predators; for example, being able to be safe and secure in the school library, or attending clubs at school with like-minded individuals, such as the science club or information technology club, or rehearsing with the school choir or drama group. These are supervised situations that predators tend to avoid. Some situations, such as being on school transport, will generally need more supervision, and classroom teachers need to be aware of the vulnerability of the child or adolescent with an ASD. There must be very severe consequences for acts of bullying, because of the devastating psychological effects of such behaviour.

In trying to cope with acts of bullying, the person with an ASD may replay frequently and in great detail each event in order to try to determine the motives of the predator, and why he or she was chosen as a target. There is unlikely to be "closure," or an ability to forgive and forget, without an explanation of motives and choices. An adult, sometimes a psychologist, may be able to explain the motives of predators and why someone might enjoy causing pain, fear and despair; and they may offer reassurance that being a victim is not an indication of being defective and at fault.

When bullying occurs in the workforce, there are procedures and sanctions in employment legislation that can be used. For example, in the United States there is the Americans with Disabilities Act, and it is unlawful to bully or harass anyone in the workforce with a recognized disability. Thus, when it comes to bullying, disclosing the diagnosis is an advantage. Whether or not there is protective legislation, it is important that those acts are recorded in detail and reported to a supervisor or line manager, and to the Human Resources section of the organization or company. It is also important to make sure the employer understands that acts of bullying will affect work performance and attendance. There may also be advantages in being a member of a union, which may be able to provide advice and representation. If there is no satisfactory resolution, there is the option of finding another job with a more understanding and supportive employer and workforce.

Artwork (See Plate 13)

Painting: Brain in a Box

Artist: Marilyn Cosho

Artist's Commentary: Even in a box, this person's way of thinking is exposed. The wires represent things outside the person's control. Adulthood doesn't protect one from being bullied. It just takes on a more subtle form.

Painting: Red Badge of Cowardice

Artist: Michael Tolleson

Artist's Commentary: For those of us on the spectrum, the feeling and experience of being bullied is almost universal. The feeling and content of this painting is almost totally symbolic. I painted the figure in a dark corner. The world around him has grayed out since nothing but the attacks of the bullies has color value. The persons themselves are unimportant and need not be seen. The Red Hot insults and verbal attacks become their own entities as they pummel the child with hatred. The child has no value in his own mind, much like the garbage that also exists in the painting.

CHAPTER 15

Choosing a Career

Stress Ranking: 15

Ranking of issue by stress caused

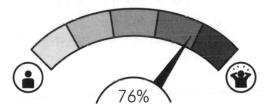

76%

Percent of respondents living with issue

58%

Many people with Asperger's/HFA have difficulties deciding on a career that's best for them. Some examples of career-related issues include: "Do I have a skill that people would pay me to use?" "How do I find out about my skill and what careers could I consider?" Do you have concerns about choosing a career?

Larry Moody

According to my Social Security records, my working life spanned 37 years. I have never been fired from a job. In almost all cases, I chose my jobs to match my skills and abilities. In a few cases, I chose jobs because I needed something quickly to pay my bills while I continued to hunt for a "better for me" job.

Ultimately, I believe it's largely a function of passion and zeal for your chosen profession that will drive you to get better and better at whatever you choose to do, and that will drive you to the top and ultimately to success. Although success is not guaranteed for anyone, neither is failure.

In my opinion, there are a few keys to choosing a career that significantly improve your odds of success:

1. IDENTIFY YOUR GIFTS...

For some few, this may be easy. But for most, this is likely to be the most difficult part of the whole process. "What? I have gifts?" you say. What are your general and "special" interests? And can you find a way to integrate them functionally into a job, and ultimately into a career path? Here are some areas to explore while searching for gifts through observation:

- What activities hold your interest?
- What subjects in school did you excel at?
- What jobs and tasks have you done well with?
- Do you have any skill-based hobbies?
- How do you most easily learn?
- Are you primarily a visual, aural or kinesthetic learner?
- What are your past and current "special interests"?

This is about *your* interests and *your* future, not what your parents or anyone else says you should or should not pursue as a career.

2. FOLLOW YOUR PASSION...

What do you really, really want to do? What are your special interests? There are two interesting little books I found that could help identify many more bizarre possibilities, and help you begin to think outside of usual roles. They are titled *Odd Jobs: Portraits of Unusual Occupations*, and *Odder Jobs, More Portraits of Unusual Occupations*, both by Nancy Rica Schiff.

3. DEVELOP YOUR TALENTS...

Da Vinci and Picasso weren't considered masters of their arts until many years after they began to practice and develop their skills under the tutelage of others. Einstein didn't create his theory of relativity overnight. Have you heard about the tourist that stopped a New Yorker on the streets of Manhattan and asked him, "How do I get to Carnegie Hall?" The New Yorker answered, "Practice, practice, practice."

It takes time and effort to develop your talents. Everyone starts at the bottom. I began my career in engineering as a draftsman, a surveyor, an engineering technician, a computer programmer and a designer. I logged seven-plus years of engineering-related work before receiving my BS in Civil Engineering. There is another book I recommend: *Developing Talents* by Temple Grandin and Kate Duffy.

4. YOU CAN LEARN TO DO ANYTHING YOU SET YOUR MIND TO DO...

As long as you are persistent and don't give up, if at first you don't succeed, try, try again. I earned my engineering degree over an 11-year period. There was a total of about 3 years of the 11 that I was working full time and not in college. I got discouraged and dropped out of college more than once, but I always came back. One of my required math courses (differential equations) I flunked four times before getting a passing grade. That's perseverance!

5. IDENTIFY APPROPRIATE TYPES OF EMPLOYMENT...

Here are some up-front questions to answer honestly for yourself before considering another job:

- What jobs have you had in the past?
- Were they related in some way?
- Which were you good at doing?
- Which were you bad at doing?
- At which jobs were you successful in the eyes of your employer?
- Why were you successful?
- Was it your ability, attitude, or both?
- At which did you fail in the eyes of your employer?
- Why did you fail?
- Was each failure due to a lack of skills, knowledge, or relationship issues?
- Are you easily distracted?
- Do you have specific auditory issues or sound sensitivities?
- Do bright or flashing or flickering lights distract you?

It's about identifying the types of working environments that will give you the best opportunity to succeed, and avoiding those in which you are likely to fail.

RECOMMENDED READING

Grandin, T. and Duffy, K. (2008) *Developing Talents: Careers for Individuals with Asperger Syndrome and High-Functioning Autism.* Shawnee Mission, KS: Autism Asperger Publishing Company.

Schiff, N.R. (2002) *Odd Jobs: Portraits of Unusual Occupations.* Berkley, CA: Ten Speed Press.

Schiff, N.R. (2006) *Odder Jobs: More Portraits of Unusual Occupations.* Berkley, CA: Ten Speed Press.

Richard Maguire

A career is not something that happens; it is made by you and is subject to many unforeseen and unknown events and people in life.

I have met many autistic people who have a singular focus on a particular career and a belief that it will happen, and no other options or jobs are adequate in their lives. Consequently, they have always been unhappy and unfulfilled. I will start by saying that a career will not happen like that unless you have a very saleable skill, such as the right sort of computer programming at the time of seeking a job. For everyone else, careers are made through hard work, experience, learning, making mistakes, having many unhappy experiences, being persistent, having and using social skills and keeping going even in the hardest times.

The best life and learning opportunities for me have been in work. I have never been proud or rejected a job because it was simple, low status or grotty; jobs have enabled me to meet a range of people I would not have met in my otherwise restricted autistic life. Jobs teach how to communicate effectively, get on with people and pursue someone else's priorities. A job exists because an employer created it. A job's only purpose is to do something the employer's organization wants done.

A job teaches you to be flexible, to get on with colleagues, to learn skills, to make priorities, to develop and share a sense of humour, to give and receive empathy, to grow as a person, to project yourself, to be on time, to initiate an activity at the employer's timing not your own, to look presentable, to have good personal hygiene, to make eye contact if you are serving customers, to deal with change, and to take instruction. In other words, jobs teach us autistic people most of the things we need to know to develop and get on in life.

A job provides opportunity for success and self-esteem—we must succeed at a job to keep it. Jobs are not about fun and that is a good thing; they are about commitment. Be prepared to be surprised at what you will find out about yourself in jobs. Jobs exist in the University of Life and this is where we all live, autistic or not. If you enjoy a job, that's great; if you don't, you will learn important things about life and persistence.

A job will test you and take you outside of your autistic interests and skills. That is good, as we can be too narrow at times, and a job broadens our outlook and takes us into the unknown, where we might be surprised at how good we are at things we never tried before.

Jobs are super ways of learning about where our future careers lie. It is even a good thing when a job is horrid and does not work out, because we learn something about which way *not* to go and how to get things better next time. And there will be a next time, as long as we have a positive attitude. No one will want to employ a moaner; individuals with a positive attitude are far more likely to be employed. An employer will more likely listen to you if you make positive contributions.

A series of jobs will provide invaluable information on how to make a career for yourself. There is time in your life to try out and learn. A career is an organic thing that has a life of its own within your life. Work at it and grow it and you can have a career.

My first job was pumping petrol at 16. I loved that job, and it taught me more about work and social skills than all my education to that point. Things I learned and friends I made in that job are still with me today, at 46. That job taught me so much about forging a career; I am forever pleased I had it.

If you cannot find a paying job, go and volunteer. You will learn and be better placed for a paid job in the future. I have mentored lots of volunteers who have gone on and succeeded at jobs and careers afterwards.

Lars Perner

I am one of those fortunate Aspies who actually gets paid (albeit not quite as much as I would like) for talking about my special interests in great detail. I even get to give exams, one of my favorite activities! (I can't say I enjoy grading them as much afterward, but that is another matter.) For someone who doesn't much like change, I sometimes can't believe that I pulled off never having to leave college—at some point, I just made a 180-degree turn in the classroom, and am now facing students. It doesn't hurt to be in a profession where eccentricity and absentmindedness are recognized as signs of genius.

In my case, I was fortunate that the supply of potential business school professors is somewhat less than is the case in the "basic" disciplines such as psychology, history and chemistry. Although I was aware when I decided to go into marketing rather than industrial/organizational psychology—which had been my earlier plan—that the job market was somewhat better in business than in the social sciences, I really can't take credit for having planned this well. But it worked out relatively well.

Those of us on the spectrum often mature somewhat more slowly than people in general. Even for ordinary people, it may be difficult to truly know in one's late teens or early twenties what one would like to do for the rest of one's life. Understanding the realities of what an occupation actually involves—as opposed to what we might have imagined—also takes time. Until I was a freshman in college, I had planned on becoming an attorney. However, as I took a course in legal research and learned more about the discipline, I began to realize that it was not for me. I am not sure if, at the time, I could have put this into words, but it seemed that the law was too spontaneous and adversarial for my taste. I did not realize at the time that I might have been able to go into appellate law, which might have been more to my liking. Instead, I decided that I wanted to become a professor.

When my psychology textbook mentioned, "A question that only a psychologist could ask" ("Why does an infant love its mother?") I was hooked. I knew that psychology was for me. I was not, however, particularly interested in becoming a clinical psychologist. I found a book published by the American Psychological Association titled *Preparing for Graduate Study in Psychology: Not for Seniors Only!* This book pointed out that only a minority of Ph.D. psychologists would actually get to teach in a university. That was one of the reasons why I ultimately settled on industrial/organizational psychology, since that was an area that had more potential for use in industry. I reasoned that I should probably know something about business to go into this field, so I decided to get an MBA on the way. It was here that I discovered marketing—and my field of consumer behavior in particular—

and realized that this was a better area for the application of my interests in psychology.

In my case, things were not as well planned as they could, in retrospect, have been. However, one important lesson is that I ending up choosing marketing, an area where there is less of an over-supply of job applicants than would have been the case in psychology. Often, it helps to look for alternative and less well-known areas of application for one's interests. For example, there is a lot of competition for jobs designing video games, an area that might be of interest to a lot of Aspies. However, those who go into the field of traffic engineering get to "play" with much cooler and more powerful computers to simulate traffic patterns. Finding out how to alleviate traffic congestion by simulating traffic flows can be much more interesting than playing an ordinary game. An Aspie may also have some unconventional but highly effective ideas on how congestion can be alleviated.

REFERENCE

Fretz, B.R. (1980) *Preparing for Graduate Study in Psychology: Not for Seniors Only!* Washington, DC: American Psychological Association.

Ruth Elaine Joyner Hane

Watching the clerk pile groceries into paper bags at the Red Owl, it was clear to me that I wanted to sell things. My first attempt at commerce was offering mud pies for one cent each. But none of the kids bought my produce. Not dispirited, I decided to try another tactic; I pulled my red Radio Flyer wagon, collecting empty pop bottles, and redeemed them at the College Grocery for two cents each. I was motivated by profit. I bought Nesbitt orange pop and Butterfinger bars.

The following endeavor included a "business plan." When the street department announced in the newspaper that our streets were going to be surfaced with asphalt, my friend, Janie, and I decided to become partners and sell Cool Aid to the workmen. We proposed a strategy to Janie's mother, who assisted in estimating the cost of a packet of powdered cherry drink, sugar and dish soap (for cleanup). She helped us learn how to calculate profit by cutting a paper circle into a pie shape to represent the costs of the Cool Aid.

The next day we asked the workmen, "Who do we talk to about selling Cool Aid?" The men motioned to a supervisor sitting in a truck. We pitched the concept of exclusively buying drinks only from us, by vowing to wash the glasses with soap and water and measure the sugar. At ten o'clock each morning we promised to bring the refreshments to their work site and charge five cents per glass. "You've got a deal," he said. We were industrious and sold enough drinks to host a neighborhood picnic, inviting all of the kids for hot dogs and chips at the end of summer.

When I was staying with my grandmother in Iowa at the age of nine, she taught me how to sew. I liked the vibration of the sewing machine as I passed fabric beneath the pressure foot, and sewed aprons, tops and shorts for my cousin and me. "What do you call someone who makes clothing for others?" I asked my grandmother. "A clothes designer," she replied.

My high school counselor suggested that a career in clothing design would involve taking Fashion Design at Parsons School in New York City. Since I could not afford the tuition, my second choice was to become a clothing buyer.

The On the Job Training program in high school was tailored for my visual, hands-on learning style. I apprenticed at the JC Penney store, gaining experience in the stock room, through accounting and sales. Then I studied retailing at the University of Minnesota, where I was selected Outstanding Student. I became an assistant buyer in junior sportswear and then a regional buyer in junior dresses.

In midlife, I returned to college for a degree in costume design, and apprenticed for a high fashion designer in New York City. I found hidden workplace agendas were an enigma; many of the buyers were socializing with upper management, gaining promotions and financial advantage.

After my children were born, I trained in interior design and became a design consultant for a Sherwin Williams Home Decorating center. After a few years, when I was refused a track for store management, I returned to college for a degree in costume design. I graduated with honors and was selected Phi Beta Kappa, a leadership fraternity. I opened a design studio, Ruth Elaine

Couture. After my diagnosis of autism, I began consulting with people who have health challenges in my Chi Field Healthcare business. Currently, I research face blindness.

With a rapidly changing world, we need to build skills for several careers, so we can prepare for emerging opportunities as communication and technology fields expand.

Anita Lesko

My career found me. I did not specifically go out and find it. It was a chain of events that led me to becoming an anesthetist. I think this is common for many people. Often your passion for something will lead you down the path to your future career. Always maintain an open mind and never fret over a missed opportunity. When one door closes, keep hunting for another to open. Don't always think in terms of a direct approach to getting your dream job. You may have to find an indirect avenue to arrive there.

Choosing a career is obviously a very important decision. You might be doing it the rest of your life. And you will spend a significant amount of time at your job each week. You generally spend more waking moments there than with your family. For that reason you need to like what you do!

One of your special interests might turn into a lifelong passion. This may be something that can earn you an income. Don't be afraid to talk to people who might be able to help you enter a career field. Plenty of people achieve their career goals through help from others along the way. No one makes it completely on his or her own. Someone gave them a break at some point.

Temple Grandin assembled a list of career choices that are best suited for people on the Autism Spectrum. It is a great list with numerous jobs. They are specific jobs that capitalize on our strengths and minimize our weaknesses. That list can be found in her book *The Way I See it*. Obvious jobs that might *not* be good choices would include those dealing with the public or large numbers of people, or jobs where there's lots of noise or bright lights; environments of chaos should simply be avoided. Having said this, the sensory overload that I just mentioned actually describes my job—I would not recommend being an anesthetist to a young Aspie! However, internet technology and "thinking" jobs done in peaceful surroundings are great choices. Physical jobs, such as landscaping, are also good.

Perhaps you are undecided about what career to choose. Spend a good amount of time researching careers that are in demand. Make a list of them. If you are in high school or college, talk to your guidance counselor. That's what they are there for. After you generate the list, analyze how someone with Asperger's would succeed at each job. Think about things like social interaction. How much would the job require? What would the environment be like? The very best way to truly discover what a particular job is like is to personally find out. Is there an opportunity to be a volunteer at the job, or to shadow someone there to see what they are doing? Perhaps there is some sort of internship program at a particular institution. Be assertive. Get your foot in the door. Once you have it ajar, you'll get in the rest of the way! Be persistent, and never, ever give up. If you want that job, by golly, go get it!

Don't be afraid to take a lower level job that allows opportunity to climb the ladder of success. Always remember: once you have your foot in the door you are halfway there. With perseverance you can make the other half happen. Believe in yourself, think positive and follow your dream, and never let anyone tell you that you can't do something. If they do, work twice as hard to prove them wrong!

REFERENCE

Grandin, T. (2011) *The Way I See It, Revised and Expanded 2nd Edition: A Personal Look at Autism and Asperger's*. Arlington, TX: Future Horizons.

Debbie Denenburg

I laugh uncontrollably when I get on this subject. I have always said I'll be dead of old age before I ever decide what I want to be when I grow up.

I didn't start out that way. When I was a little kid, I wanted to perform. I loved TV and the stage. I adored singing and dancing. At the ripe old age of four someone sat me down on a piano in a crowded restaurant. The pianist began playing a song I knew and I sang it for the whole place. I loved it! Nowadays I would still welcome the opportunity to perform, but I would want to act. I am enthralled with the thought of getting out of my own head and becoming an entirely different identity for a while. I would completely submerse myself in that.

Unfortunately, things didn't go the way I wanted them to as far as my career was concerned. I was completely discouraged from pursuing what I really wanted, so I gave up on it. I ended up letting others choose what I would do for a living based on what was available in the way of employment. It's been a very weird journey. I worked in so many varied jobs that I couldn't begin to categorize them into groups. One thing I learned is that when I have work, I throw my whole being into it. I love to work. I love to write and I am an artist. I love to sell stuff, so I am forever listing things on websites where I think I can make a buck. I am also enrolling in school again to go for a bachelor's degree in graphic arts.

When choosing a career, my advice would be to start with what you are passionate about. This is actually old advice going back many generations and preached by many people. The way to tell what you love is to recognize that you have no hesitation about it. No fear. You are ready to dive in headfirst and soak your soul in the satisfaction of just doing it.

Charli Devnet

This is an area where I wish that I had had better guidance in my youth. A nudge in the right direction would have saved me many years of turmoil and despair and resulted in a far happier and more productive life.

You see, early on, I was given a warped idea of what a career was. Shortly before I entered high school, the corporate giant IBM had built a headquarters in the remote rustic region of upstate New York where I was then living. IBM employed a lot of people, and the folks that worked for IBM earned the fattest wages of anyone in that backwater town. It was tacitly assumed that we scholastically advanced students desperately desired a career at IBM, or in some similar corporate environment. The less advanced students were offered more palatable options—farmer, auto mechanic, cashier, cook—but all that was dangled before my eyes was the ice palace of IBM. The prospect scared me to the core.

I was well into adulthood before I realized what should have been so obvious. Many people flourish and thrive in careers that do not involve a windowless cubicle or a three-piece suit.

What do I wish a mentor had told me?

- *Hold fast to your interests:* The right choice of career is already there inside of you, if you can find it. Growing up Aspie usually includes the hungry acquisition of facts in specific areas. You may well have become an expert in some esoteric subject, while lacking knowledge in more relevant concerns: how to fight off bullies, for example.

  As a child, I was fascinated by Greek mythology. I was a walking encyclopedia for the gods and goddesses of Mt. Olympus. This obsession of mine was occasionally considered a danger. Parents actually called the school to complain that I was spreading paganism among their sixth-graders! Most often, however, it was fobbed off as so much useless knowledge. "We're tired of hearing about Apollo and Aphrodite," said my parents. "Why don't you learn something that might lead to a job?" With a little encouragement, I could have parlayed my special interest into a career in museum work, in archeology, or teaching ancient history and comparative religions.

- *Consider the work environment and not just the paycheck:* Neurotypicals judge the worth of work by its salary. Jobs with the highest paycheck are deemed the most desirable. However, the bitter truth is that, leaving aside those scientists in Silicon Valley, the most lucrative jobs may not be Aspie-friendly. All companies have their protocols, and some place great emphasis upon projecting a corporate image or being a team player. When Michael Bloomberg was elected Mayor of New York, the media trumpeted Mr. Bloomberg's preference for the "open office." The mayor likes his employees to work together in one large room, constantly interacting, no separate offices, not even cubicles. When I heard this, I shuddered and murmured, "Not for a million dollars."

- *Who will your co-workers be?* Even if you do not excel at being a team player, you will probably have to spend time with colleagues and clients. For some, the socialization is desirable. However, if you absolutely cannot work with other people, you might want to select a career that allows you to do most of your work alone, such as writer, researcher or archivist. Or you might choose a field that allows you to work with animals, like veterinarian, rancher or zookeeper. Or you might be happiest in a career where people are more tolerant of your quirkiness, such as academia or the arts.

Dr. Patrick Suglia

Most successful people with Asperger's that I know (including myself) have always followed their instincts, which led them to their choice of career. Their interests started early on, either long ago in childhood or by trying out different hobbies and pursuits over the years. But where do you start when you haven't a clue? Indeed this is a source of frustration for college-aged students and adults who seemed to have fallen by the wayside. The absolute best place you can start is your local Workforce or Skills Assessment Center. There you will be able to receive, at no cost to you, skills assessments that will help you in determining what your strengths and weaknesses are. You may be surprised to find areas you are actually interested in, just as I pretty much stumbled upon areas myself over the years. You will be assigned a counselor who will oversee and guide your progress and will help you with finding the right job.

These centers, as well as your local community college, also offer free programs to give people the skills they need to make their own assessments. One very good self-assessment tool I recommend is the Clifton StrengthsFinder exam (Rath 2007; see also www. gallupstrengthscenter.com/purchase). The results will accurately point out untapped potentials you may have lying in your personality or psychological makeup that have yet to be discovered. An equally important tool is the Meyers-Briggs Type Indicator scale (www.myersbriggs.org). This test is often given among the myriad tests administered to diagnose your Autism Spectrum Disorder. This tool is very helpful at identifying your specific personality type and the strengths and weaknesses of that type. Many larger-named employers use the MBTI when considering candidates for certain positions. Therefore it's very helpful to know what they might find out about you ahead of time.

There is no one way to know what you would enjoy doing unless you actually do it. Don't feel bad about going through several jobs before finding something you feel comfortable with. Many people find out what they like through trial and error. Assessment tools and personality tests are mere indicators of what you would be good at. On-the-job experience is the best judge. As the old saying goes, "Do what you love, all else follows." Don't compromise your psychological and physical well-being just to have a "job." Although having a job to get yourself on your feet is necessary, having a career that you put your heart and soul into is what will assure your success.

In addition to centers for evaluation and self-assessment tools, you can always do things the way most people do early on in life, and that is to join a special interest group. Are you interested in astronomy, meteorology, carpentry, auto mechanics or computers? A great way to find like-minded people with similar interests in your area is to go online to www.meetup.com and find a group. You'd be surprised at what's out there. Over the years, when my business went through slow times, this website was the key avenue I found toward discovering other interests. If I didn't have a clue as to what I might be interested in, I simply guessed. Show up, give it a shot, and go from there. You never know until you try. One thing to keep in mind is that as you're going through the self-discovery process, doors might not automatically open. If you have an interest and you continue to pursue it, the right opportunities to make it your career will eventually show up.

REFERENCE

Rath, T. (2007) *StrengthsFinder 2.0*. Victoria Park, Western Australia: Gallup Press.

Dr. Tony Attwood's Advice on Choosing a Career

From my extensive clinical experience, over many decades, I have come to the realization that any job is possible for a person with an ASD, from astronaut to zoo keeper. The range of careers can include the expected ones, such as those in engineering, information technology, accounting and science, but also the less obvious, such as those in fine art, music, writing and involvement in all aspects of the film industry. I have known adults with an ASD who have been successful in the caring professions, from nursing and psychiatric medicine to veterinary science and zoo keeping, as well as the military, police force and politics. Thus, there is no automatic restriction on choice of career for someone who has an ASD.

How does a person make the decision on which career to follow? The first option may be to see if there are employment prospects related to a special interest or talent that is associated with the person's personality or profile of ASD characteristics. For example, a childhood special interest in Lego that develops during adolescence into an intense interest in the design of machines could become the basis and predictor of a successful career in mechanical engineering. There are certain careers where specialist knowledge is valued by an employer, for example academia, where the person with an ASD can actually be paid and encouraged to pursue a special interest. I strongly recommend, therefore, that adolescents have a detailed assessment of their abilities during their high school years to identify whether a special interest could be the foundation of a potential career.

Equally, a person may possess specific talents and skills associated with their ASD. For example, they may be able to sing with perfect pitch, draw with photographic realism, identify patterns and errors, or display a particular talent with logic. Any of these skills and more may benefit from being nurtured and enhanced, so parents may consider private tuition throughout childhood and adolescence to augment such skills, since they could well have employment potential in the future.

Whether or not a child shows talents and skills in a particular area, it is important that they are encouraged to develop social skills that will enable them to fit into a workplace in the future.

They will need guidance particularly in learning to recognize that criticism is a means for learning and improving; that a dull, boring task may not be your dream, but you can learn from it; that it is important to always do the best job you can no matter what it is; and that politeness, good hygiene and appropriate dress are essential factors in terms of acceptance in the workplace.

While certain areas of specialist knowledge may mean that a person with an ASD will be highly sought after for their expert advice, nevertheless most people will need at some point to go through the interview process to secure a job. The Aspie mentors offer some wise advice regarding this.

They also suggest that there is great value in volunteering (preferably in an area that is of particular interest), as it gives a person priceless experience in performing a given function, being punctual, working cooperatively and assuming responsibility. It is the pathway to getting a real, paid job, and at the same time provides a great opportunity and potential network connections.

In the past, before computer technology (and I often suspect that computers were originally designed by people with an ASD for people with an ASD!), those with an ASD often sought careers as craftsmen, such as watchmakers, jewellers, carpenters and so on; in other words, solitary pursuits where the emphasis was on high quality rather than mass production. There would probably have been relatively little stress at work compared to modern-day employment, where the emphasis is on production rates and social networking. Any career or specific employment position must be evaluated in terms of stress levels, including unexpected changes in the job requirements, the workload, and the social and interpersonal dynamics of the job. The person with an ASD will need to be well versed in strategies for stress management, as this will contribute significantly to their having a successful career.

The Aspie mentors also make frequent mention of the need for a good attitude regarding employment. This includes knowing how to be polite, take instruction, avoid workplace politics and keep opinions to oneself. Another important aspect that requires attention is the tendency by a person with an ASD to have a "one-track mind" regarding their choice of career. For example, they may have a strong belief that a particular career is the only one for them, and thus be reluctant to consider any other option. This approach will be disadvantageous, especially if the person does not have the necessary skills or ability to achieve the required qualifications for the job, or if the position is highly sought after and the number of applications far exceeds the number of job vacancies. It is wise, therefore, to be much more open-minded to all possibilities. Several career options should be considered—not forgetting that today it is very common to have several different careers during a lifetime.

The Aspie mentors have provided wide-ranging and wise advice and great encouragement for one of the more daunting aspects of adolescence and young adulthood, namely, "What career should I choose?"

Artwork (See Plate 14)

3D Graphic: Quiet Room

Artist: Derran Rootring

Artist's Commentary: I enjoy creating 3D graphics and animations with the computer, because of the unlimited possibilities. As a visual thinker, it enables me to communicate in a different way and helps me to give shape to my imagination. I often get into hyper-focus while working and get absorbed by the computer screen in front of me. The world around me seems to fade away and I'm able to escape in an infinite virtual world where anything is possible.

Painting: Fork in the Road

Artist: Michael Tolleson

Artist's Commentary: This painting tells an engaging story. Much like the Robert Frost poem "The Road Not Taken," here is a person who has reached a point in their life where decisions must be made. For the onlooker and the person standing, there is no right or wrong road. As we travel down the chosen road we can look back, but with any life-changing decision, we will never make that exact choice again. The color of the painting is bright, for all choices seem bright and promising.

CHAPTER 16

Improving Empathetic Attunement

Stress Ranking: 16

Ranking of issue by stress caused

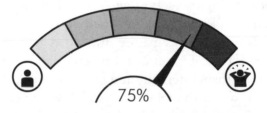

75%

Percent of respondents living with issue

58%

Some people with Asperger's/HFA are unable to feel empathy (an "emotional understanding") for others. Examples of this would be: not sensing if friends or family are uncomfortable or suffering; reading or hearing a news story about people involved in a tragedy or disaster and not being able to sense their discomfort; and witnessing a life-changing event such as the death of a family member and not having a change in feelings. Do you have concerns about empathetic attunement?

Dr. Patrick Suglia

Because of our straightforward nature, we Aspies tend to be accused of not having "feelings." People might think we are uncaring and cold and that we only think about our own needs. I learned to be more empathetic toward other people's emotions by monitoring and remembering my own at certain points in times. Then, I turned the tables, so to speak. When I felt pain from a specific illness or injury, such as when I had kidney stones, fear when I had my stroke, and sadness when my marriage ended and whenever a family member passed away, it is true that I didn't show a great display of emotions. But that didn't mean I didn't have them. I felt them internally and in my own way. Then I took such situations and I thought to myself, "What would another person be feeling in this same situation?" But it didn't end there. I then had to respond to the other person's concerns.

Our silence during emotional times may seem like an advantage to some, believe it or not. It shows that we are calm and that we have it together during stressful times. Because of this, we are often the ones who can continue on with what needs to be taken care of without feeling overly burdened. But for the people who are close to us, this is not what they want to see. They want to know that we care about the situation and that we identify with what they may be going through. For me, this was possible not only by identifying with my own experiences and placing another person in the picture, as I explained, but then taking the next step of responding with words of acknowledgement. One thing I came to learn as a caregiver is that the greatest thing people want and need from others is simply a word of acceptance of the fact that they are being affected, and that you support them in their plight. You don't have to cry with them or be in pain, too. You just have to say, "I understand, and I support you." This means so very much to a hurting neurotypical.

The genuineness of your words comes from the recognition that you once felt that pain, too. If your words are not true, the neurotypical will sense it. While you may not show much emotion at the time you are hurting, neurotypicals can be quite dramatic in their emotional expression. It is because we are wired differently that we do not exhibit such displays? Neurotypicals (NTs) need to understand that that doesn't mean we do not have the capacity to experience pain or recognize it in others. Being able to more openly show our experience of pain, and acknowledge it in others, are learned behaviors for us.

Usually we don't even know if somebody is being affected by a situation if they aren't telling us verbally or shouting out. If they do tell us, or shout, then it is obvious. Sometimes, people will become unusually still or quiet if something negative is affecting them. If you know the person and you observe this difference in them, that would be a good time to ask them, "Is everything okay?" We probably wouldn't normally be able to tell. But we can make it a rule of good social conduct to be observant for such a change. By doing so, we will certainly be rewarded in the end for understanding when something is wrong, and acknowledging that. This will lead to people opening up to us more, trusting us more, and thanking us for being so caring.

Debbie Denenburg

I am not empathetic—not according to the specific definition of the word. I do not take on the actual feelings or emotions of any other person. That said, I would clarify that, although I do not have this attribute, I do have a nature of compassion. I am affected by feelings. I can sense things like hurt, frustration, anger and sadness. I care about those things. I have had enough pain in my life that I hate seeing anyone else experience it. I have been accused of being callous. I have, at times, said nothing and done nothing. That didn't mean that I was oblivious to what was happening. It doesn't mean that I didn't respect the seriousness of the moment. I have learned that there are expectations in times of turmoil.

When someone is seeking empathy, I explain that I probably don't know what he or she is feeling, but I *do* care. If you find yourself in that position, try the following behavior: become their rock. That is someone who can be leaned upon for strength. Don't pass judgment on a person whose feelings have become out of control. Allow them to speak freely. That includes letting them get hysterical or angry. Listen without interrupting. Don't challenge anything they say. Be the person who allows them to vent, in a safe place, all that internal, volatile buildup. If they just want to be quiet, let them know it's okay.

When others are in a vulnerable position, they need someone who is strong to be on their side—someone who shows by example that it's possible to get through tough circumstances and still find peace. Be that person.

Richard Maguire

I do not hold the opinion that people with Asperger's are unable to feel empathy for others. I believe that we may have difficulty making the links and accessing what is there.

One thing that troubled me when I was accepting my autism was the image of us being cold, aloof, tetchy and unfeeling. I could not reconcile this with my ability to care, nor with that of the autistic people I knew and worked with. We are often the first people to know something is wrong with someone and often the last to know what to do about it.

I have learned to deal with this and have helped many autistic people deal with this over 30 years of work. What I have done is helped people learn about their emotions, name them, learn what they feel like (emotions are felt physically), where they are located, what they are and how to reference and name them. I have worked on the understanding that there is a lot of disconnection between the person, their emotions, consciousness of and ability to describe emotions and what to do about them. Most people, including me, have been scared and sought distance and distraction. Once these connections are made, I have helped people move on to an understanding that they are present in other people, emotional connections can be made and things can be done with reference to emotions.

This has been a revelation to me and others I know. It opens the way to being able to tune in to emotions and feeling in ourselves and other people. Thus, a whole new landscape of life, feeling and connection can be accessed. I always say that people have a latent empathic ability; I will strenuously deny they have no capacity for empathy. I think a lack of empathy best describes psychopaths, not autistic people. I believe empathetic attunement needs to be taught, unlocked and developed in many people. I also believe this to be true for non-autistic people, who may be more adept at covering up their lack of empathy with better social and communication skills.

Many autistic people work in social care, medicine, nursing and psychology, as these careers give structures to contact, show empathy, understand and care for people. This does not fit the computer geek, recluse or engineer stereotypes, but it is common in autism.

I believe every autistic person has as much love, joy, empathy and life in their heart as anyone else; what we often lack is the ability to make the connections and get this part of our life engaged and working.

Also important in this is getting our anxiety levels as low as possible. Someone carrying a burden of excess anxiety will find connecting with people hard, and showing empathy even harder. I know many people who are often the first to tune in to someone else's emotional state but are the last to know what to do about it. This is usually read as having no empathy and is often taught as such. I believe this does us a disservice and can cause people to overlook the possibility that a lot of us can make the connections and be overtly empathetic.

I believe we often need coaching from someone who knows the emotional and empathetic process to help us build up gestalts and routines for being able to tune in and then show empathy.

Larry Moody

Are you shy, tongue-tied or brain-locked?

As a teen, I always thought I was shy…almost terminally shy. There were times when I wanted to talk to girls but I couldn't. I just couldn't seem to be able to get the words out. I knew what I wanted to say but I couldn't, I just couldn't… That pretty well defined shy in my mind at the time. Little did I know that something very different was taking place.

As fathers go, I got lucky and have a good one. On the other hand, I was far from being the perfect son. Particularly problematical were my attention deficit disorder (ADD) and memory deficits, which were not diagnosed until much later in my life. I loved to build things to play with, and that involved using his tools while he was at work. All too often, I would leave one or another of his tools out wherever I had used it. In Florida where I grew up, leaving a tool outside almost always resulted in rust…a sure giveaway, even if I later remembered to put it back where it belonged. Punishing lectures were the norm. Sometimes I could not answer quickly enough when questioned after a thorough tongue-lashing, or could not answer at all. *A sure sign of defiance*…or so he thought. Little did either of us know that something very different was taking place.

About four years ago (circa 2009) I was one of two panel presenters speaking about autism at an evening meeting of parents and teachers at a school in Burnsville, MN. Having been asked a question about relationships, I was trying to relate something to do with my ex-wife and me, something that was very emotionally laden and I locked up mid-sentence… I could not speak! Nothing but gibberish came out before I went silent. I closed my eyes, went inside and self-calmed for a few seconds. I opened my eyes and continued, but nothing came out except more gibberish. Again I went inside. When I came back after a few more seconds I was able to finish the statement I was trying to make. I then changed the subject and told the group that I felt I needed to explain what had just happened with me.

I call it brain-locked. Someone else might call it a severe form of being tongue-tied. It makes no difference what you call it; it's still an uncomfortable feeling. With me, it only happens when my emotions are highly charged, and not often even then. My brain is racing. I know precisely what I want to say, but my tongue will not cooperate. No matter how many times I repeat it in my mind, when I try to speak, it either doesn't come out at all, or it comes out as gibberish… "Gaa, uh, ugh…oeirt erqg ajkeg…" You get the point. It's as though the connection between my brain and my tongue is lost for a while. My brain simply disconnects. For most of my life I would fight this inside myself. And the more I fought to speak, the worse it would get. Eventually, I developed for myself the technique of closing my eyes, going silent inside to self-calm for a few seconds, and then returning. Usually I can then continue with what I was saying. If I can't continue, I simply repeat the process until I can.

Well, after my explanation, the program continued for about 20 more minutes and ended. As the parents and teachers were filing out of the rows of seats and heading for the door at the back of the room, one woman turned directly toward me instead. I have a significant deficit when it comes to appropriately interpreting facial expressions. So when I saw tears running down her cheeks, I knew something was amiss, but I did not know what I had done. Do I stand, or do I run? Well I stood there… From bravado, or more likely a deer in headlights, I'm not sure which. She walked right up to me and wrapped her arms around me in a hug as I stood there silently, and she said: "Thank you, thank you…" And she proceeded to tell me her story:

She has a six-year-old autistic son. Earlier, when I went into what I later explained as brain-lock, she instantly recognized that that is what happens with her son occasionally. She said she had always thought he was being defiant and evasive, refusing to answer her, and she had punished him for it many times…but will never again! She thanked me once again, turned and left. I never knew her name.

To have that kind of positive impact on the lives of even one parent and child makes all my efforts and occasional embarrassing goofs as a speaker worthwhile. That's why I speak out. That's why I do this and other things to help improve understanding and acceptance of us by the neurotypical population.

Paul Isaacs

I believe understanding others is the key to getting on in life with relationships, friendships and even with workmates. It's an important attribute that can affect people around you. I think that the myth that autistic people lack empathy is not correct. I have met many giving people all the across the Autism Spectrum from non-verbal to verbal...all of whom have wisdom and empathy.

My parents, who are both on the Autism Spectrum, are also very empathic souls who give a lot of time to others such as friends and family. I likewise do the same. I like to help other people in times of need and stress. To be a good friend, you must be there for others and treat others how you would like to be treated in certain situations. It builds trust, stability, emotional connectivity and binds you and the other person.

My parents were always helping with broadening out the awareness of others. I lived in a sensory-based world and was non-verbal for a long time. I had love for my parents and people I like—I just didn't show it a typical way. But as I got older, I developed ways of showing my love and support for my friends and family. There is no "wrong" or "right" way of showing pure empathy; it is a about building bridges of understanding between both parties to gain a mutual understanding.

Here are some tips and advice I have learned from parents:

- Shake hands when greeting friends and family members for the first time (depending on preference, sensory issues and situation).

- Ask that person how they are (this concept of questions will build up over time as you get to know them).

- Be aware that other people have thoughts, feelings, beliefs and ways of life that are different from yours.

- When you are having difficulties, talk about them to friends and family members.

- When your friends and family are having difficulties, be there for them.

- Think of others' feelings, not just your own.

Ruth Elaine Joyner Hane

Lack of empathy is common in today's fast-paced culture. Our daily media sources flash grotesque images of murder, war, disasters, accidents and violence so often we become desensitized. Whatever feelings of empathy we may have become lost in daily exposure.

The nurse who checked my blood pressure during a post-surgery visit to my doctor asked, as she charted my numbers, "How are you doing?" "Not well, I have a lot of pain and I can't tolerate the pain medications the doctor prescribed." She answered with her back to me, "Yes, that surgery is painful, that's what they all say." I knew that recovery would be difficult, but had expected more empathy from the nurse. I felt as if she was indifferent.

Even though the nurse's response was factually correct, and she was taking care to enter my weight and blood pressure accurately, she was ignoring empathy. With increasingly heavy patient loads, medical professionals are challenged to take time to use caring touch and kind words that convey an understanding of pain in recovery from major surgery.

We lose our humanity if we as a culture fail to develop an understanding of another's suffering. I recently saw media coverage of a man who slid onto a river that had partially frozen over, leaving an open patch of water where his sled landed. Instead of immediately calling emergency services and expressing concern by assuring the stranded man that help was on the way, the onlookers stood at the edge of the ice and laughed hysterically. This was a life-threatening situation. Fortunately, one woman realized this in time to secure a rope to a branch and rescue the man.

One of the ways I have learned to develop empathy is by observing people who have a generous supply. These people notice others in need and naturally offer assistance and words of assurance, and are good listeners. I believe the nurse who was too busy, in the example I gave, was at a loss to understand how to respond to my problem with pain medications. If she had paused in her charting, turned to look at me and simply expressed empathy by saying, "I'm sorry," I probably would have felt better.

Empathy is taught very early in life, from the kind care given when we are infants. When I was born, I could not tolerate touch, being held or scratchy, rough clothing and blankets. The message my body sent was pain, as if I had burns all over. A neighbor, who was good with babies, discovered that I relaxed in very warm water baths. She securely held my body beneath the water with just my face exposed while she cooed a singsong nursery rhyme. She used empathy and compassion to help me reduce my tactile anxiety.

Most people learn empathy, sympathy, compassion and understanding incrementally, but it does not come naturally for a person who lacks the ability to take another's perspective. Next time something happens, and you are unsure how to respond, ask yourself these questions:

- How would I feel if this happened to me?

- What would I like to hear or have done for me that would make the situation better?

- Would this person like the same thing as I would, or some other remedy?

- Is doing something the best option or could words of sympathy be better? Or both?

If you freeze in indecision and there is someone present who has skills for showing empathy, pay attention to what they do and say. You will have more skills for understanding when an opportunity for empathy arises again.

Mitch Christian

There's a kind of instant subconscious reaction to the emotional states of other people that I've understood better in myself over the years. If someone approaches me for a conversation and they're full of worry, fear, anger or joy I find myself suddenly in the same state of emotion. That's probably why I have such an intense dislike for people with negative attitudes. Sometimes I react without knowing it to the other person's emotional state, for instance, if they're upset for some reason, then I sense it and I may feel guilty for no apparent reason, or if they're exuding anger, I might feel anxious and want to get away from them.

On the other hand, I don't often respond to someone else's situation just from hearing the words that describe it. So, if I'm listening to a news program that's discussing a tragedy, I won't feel anything at first, until they reveal personal details about the people affected. At that point, I can start to feel overwhelmed and need to stop listening. To me, it makes sense that I would only genuinely feel for someone else if I know something about him or her as a person.

My stronger emotional reactions are often delayed. It took about two months before I cried after my grandmother died. While I was watching a movie I found myself sobbing when an elderly lady died, and I realized that it was actually my grandmother I was thinking about. A few years later, when my mother died, I had a similar reaction but it happened sooner and without warning. It was the next day, early in the morning, when the feelings rose within me, and for a couple of minutes I cried more intensely than I ever had. A few minutes later it happened again, only not as strongly.

Sometimes it's overwhelming to have too much bad news in my personal life and I will block out part of it. While my mother was dying of cancer, I heard that someone I knew had major heart surgery due to severe blockage of the arteries. It must have been too much for me to handle, and apparently I blocked the news from my mind, because months later I heard about it again, and realized that I had forgotten to ask anyone about how he was doing.

At other times, I will express what looks like an inappropriate response, especially to a stressful event. While I was at work one time, a co-worker started choking on some candy. I had an urge to laugh and looked at him with a big grin. Someone else had called for help, and by that time the candy had dislodged from his throat. He was upset with me, so I made up a story and told him that I thought he was just kidding around. I think it was the stress of the situation that made me react the way I did.

Thinking back over these situations makes me realize that my emotional responses, or lack of a response, will often seem out of place to many people. From my point of view, my reactions are actually stronger than normal, but to others they don't occur when expected or in the manner that is expected. It helps to be aware of these differences in order to develop a sense of self-acceptance and to understand that other people will not realize that I am an empathic person, just in a different way. In some situations, it may help to explain that to the other people involved.

Anita Lesko

I am always the first one to pick up on something amiss with another individual. I am able to distinguish very subtle facial cues that others would not see, or it might be a feeling I pick up from them. In any case, I'm aware there's something different. The only problem is, I don't know what to do about it! I get extremely uncomfortable and my first and only reaction is to avoid it.

Recently, a co-worker's son was killed in an accident. I felt absolutely horrible for her. For a parent to lose a child is devastating. She was out for a while. Upon her return everyone was going to her to hug and console her. I felt so very uncomfortable and awkward that I just avoided her, and didn't go anywhere near her for months. When I did have to talk to her, I would totally avoid the topic. I realize this is a terrible cop out. I feel very badly inside, but it's the best I can do. I have no clue how to make my face and voice seem like I mean it. If I said something in my monotone voice, it wouldn't sound right. And my inability to make appropriate facial expressions would come across as inappropriate. Avoidance thus becomes my best coping mechanism.

The only good news is that I can recognize another person's feelings and have compassion for them. In fact, I think I feel more compassion than most NTs. So many people are totally wrapped up in their own lives, and barely notice things around them. However, I notice *everything* going on around me, especially the news. I admit that I am a news junkie. With that comes exposure to daily tragedies happening around the world, all of which sends me on the emotional rollercoaster of life. I am often troubled for days after hearing something sad on the news. Yet if I mention it to others, they blow it off. This is my gauge of my compassion for others.

Another thing I can now do is recognize that I have upset others. This generally doesn't occur until after the fact. I didn't realize that I was going to make them mad or upset before I said or did something. Once I've done that, I can then see their reaction to it. Then I can look at the whole picture and see *why* I made them upset. The best I can do is say I'm sorry, and use the experience as a learning tool. Next time I might be able to draw from it and approach things differently, all being well, with a better outcome!

Since learning of Asperger's, my perspective has greatly changed. It has enabled me to see how the choices I make affect others. I am still a work in progress. I still make others upset or angry—I hope I'm doing it less and less. I don't intend to hurt others, and I certainly don't like it to happen to me. Because it's not natural to me to recognize these things, I really have to work at it, which is what makes it so easy to mess up. I aim to look at things from the other person's perspective. Once you start training yourself to do that, it gets easier to figure out what you did wrong. I'll never get perfect at this or anywhere close, but I'm on the right track. That's what is important. I do recognize what others are feeling, and I feel for them. I'll just keep trying to get better at showing them how I feel.

Dr. Tony Attwood's Advice on Improving Empathetic Attunement

People who have an ASD are often accused of lacking empathy, being callous and not caring about other people. However, some of the kindest people I know have an ASD. Why is there such a contradiction? Psychologists divide the concept of empathy into three components: cognitive empathy (to know); emotional empathy (to feel); and compassionate empathy (to respond). Those with an ASD can have difficulties with each of these three components of empathy.

Cognitive Empathy
This is the ability to read body language in order to reocognize when someone is distressed and determine the degree of distress. Those with an ASD are often able to read "the headlines," that is, they are aware of the obvious signs of distress, such as noticing that someone is crying. The difficulty is in the "fine print," that is,

reading the more subtle and transitory expressions and contextual cues that help to precisely determine what someone is thinking and feeling. People with an ASD take time to cognitively process information conveyed non-verbally, and the signs may be fleeting and confusing. Neurotypicals rarely "freeze" a facial expression or body posture, and can be oblique in speech; for example, when being asked, "Are you okay?" may reply, "Yes," but are not actually feeling okay.

If the signs of distress are subtle and not recognized, then there will not be the anticipated response indicating empathy, hence the accusation of a lack of empathy and callousness. It is, therefore, a question of not reading and being uncertain of the more subtle body language cues that indicate distress, not necessarily a lack of caring and compassion.

We tend to think of the ability to "read" what someone is thinking or feeling as an ability to read facial expressions, tone of voice, prosody of speech and contextual cues. Research has confirmed that these cognitive aspects of empathy are impaired in those who have an ASD. However, from my clinical experience and having read so many autobiographies, I have observed that some people with an ASD seem to have an emotional "sixth sense," that is, an intuitive ability to accurately perceive a negative "atmosphere" on entering a social situation, or instantaneously knowing the negative mood of someone they know well. Psychologists have yet to explain this characteristic of ASD. My advice is to trust your "sixth sense" intuition in such situations—it is probably accurate.

One very significant problem for those with an ASD is not a lack of emotional sensitivity, but rather an oversensitivity to the negative emotions in others. This can cause the person to avoid social situations in which the prevailing emotions are negative, due to their being exceptionally vulnerable to "bad vibes."

Emotional Empathy

This is the ability to "feel" someone's distress. Neurotypicals have the intuitive and immediate ability to "put themselves in someone's shoes," and to resonate with and absorb someone's feelings. While people with an ASD may have emotional empathy for experiences that they themselves have been familiar with, they may have difficulty being empathic with emotional experiences they have not personally known. The mental process for the person with an ASD is to remember the feelings they experienced and to be empathic. Without personal experience of those feelings or the depth of emotion, they experience confusion in trying to identify the other person's emotion, and have difficulty achieving empathy.

Compassionate Empathy

This is the ability to know how to respond to someone's feelings, especially distress. Neurotypicals expect a response that is appropriate in terms of intensity and efficacy. This can be difficult for someone with an ASD, who may be able to read the signals and appreciate the depth of feeling, but is unsure how to respond. This is compounded by fear of making a mistake or rejection when deciding how to respond and with what intensity. Sometimes it feels as though there is less risk of making a mistake or rejection by doing nothing.

Neurotypicals usually anticipate words and gestures of compassion and affection, but the problem for those with an ASD is that these may not be their own most effective and preferred emotion repair strategies. Their preferred repair mechanisms can be solitude or the distraction and enjoyment of their special interest. When the neurotypical, therefore, is deliberately left alone to recover, or the person with an ASD starts talking about their special interest in an attempt to lighten the mood, the perception by the neurotypical is that the person with an ASD is lacking compassion and empathy.

The solution here is for the neurotypical to state clearly both his or her feelings and the depth of those feelings, and what actions would alleviate the distress; or for the person with an ASD to ask exactly what he or she can do to help the person feel better.

Accusations of a lack of empathy and not caring can be made in relation to the ability to express the conventional signs of grief. Neurotypicals express and alleviate their feelings of grief at a funeral or family gathering by communal crying. The person with an ASD may not be able to resonate with this "infectious" method of expressing grief, and they may then be assumed to be callous. There may well be deep grief, but often not expressed in the way anticipated by neurotypicals. Grief can be expressed by a temporary increase in the characteristics of ASD, such as isolation and social withdrawal, engagement in the special interest (as an antidote to feeling sad), and an increase in anxiety and sensory sensitivity. Neurotypicals may not recognize these characteristics as signs of grieving.

One of the characteristics of expressing emotional empathy is attentive listening with emotionally empathic comments to someone's personal experiences, such as saying, "Oh dear," or, "How sad for you," or sounds such as "Mmm" or "Tut tut." There can also be body movements and gestures, such as nodding or shaking the head, or making a facial expression consistent with the feelings of the neurotypical in a particular part of the narrative. Neurotypical women in particular are expected to engage in such behaviour to indicate emotional empathy. However, the person with an ASD may be listening attentively to the story line, but not apparently giving an indication of empathy for the circumstances and experiences being described. This is especially conspicuous when women who have an ASD are listening to a conversation or story with a female companion, friend or family member. Again, this can lead to the neurotypical making the false assumption that the person with an ASD lacks empathy.

It is possible for those with an ASD to eventually, perhaps over decades, learn the subtle cues that indicate when an expression of empathy is required, and to recognize the depth and intensity of response expected by the neurotypical. Because it is a difficulty reading body language, and not an indication of a lack of ability to care or express compassion, the person with an ASD needs guidance and encouragement rather than criticism and rejection.

Artwork (See Plate 15)

Painting: Trying to Read Between the Lines

Artist: Marilyn Cosho

Artist's Commentary: Trying to understand another person is like trying to see the whole picture through a keyhole. No matter how great the effort, the edges will still be out of view.

CHAPTER 17

Should I Be Tested for Asperger's/HFA?

Stress Ranking: 17

Ranking of issue by stress caused

67%

Percent of respondents living with issue

61%

Where some people diagnosed with Asperger's/HFA may feel relief or liberation, others have issues with the label. Some examples of these issues include: feeling sad, feeling depressed, feeling hopeless, and feeling angry at "being different." Do you have concerns about your diagnosis?

Charli Devnet

Aspies diagnosed in midlife speak of their sense of relief to finally have a label to apply to themselves, their liberation from the shame of the past, the empowerment that self-knowledge brings, the freedom to be proud of themselves at last. It is as if they have found the missing piece of the puzzle, the clue that solves the mystery, and the roadmap that leads home. This is how it was with me.

When I was a child in the 1960s, the diagnosis of Asperger's was unknown in the United States and the term "autism" implied "mentally retarded." No one believed that a person with a high IQ could actually be autistic. Nevertheless, I always knew I was different from the other kids. My teachers knew it, too. They called me a "gifted child" because of my intelligence, but I was also referred to as a behavior problem, emotionally immature or, simply, a misfit.

All too soon, this little savant fell flat on her face. With no diagnosis, my shortcomings were ascribed to character flaws. As a child, I was annoyed and angry to be persistently misunderstood. It was all *their* fault. However, as the years unwound and my losses piled up, I began to internalize the comments I heard. No friends, no dates? No job? Is life one disaster after another? It must be all *my* fault. Sure, I am selfish, stubborn, lazy and rude. Pride flew out the window. I shuffled through life, eyes downcast, shouldering a heavy burden of shame, a loser in life's lottery.

Diagnosis allowed me to hold my head up again. That is the experience of a late-diagnosed Aspie. However, had I been diagnosed as a child, I would certainly not have felt that way.

As a child, I did not like being singled out, either for praise or condemnation. I did not even like being called "gifted." My one desire was to be considered just one of the kids. "Being different" was hard to bear. That was why the bullies chased me, on the one hand, and why the teachers sent me to the principal's office, on the other.

Thus, I can understand how receiving a diagnosis of Asperger's before one is ready may make one feel stigmatized. It cuts off the prospect of one day blending in. You are sentenced to a lifetime of uniqueness.

For those who have been diagnosed before their time and found it unsettling, I offer this advice: diagnosis does not make you an Aspie. It's like switching on a light in a dark room. The light allows you to see, but does not actually change what is already in the room.

It's always better to know than not to know. We Aspies like acquiring knowledge...and self-knowledge is the root of all wisdom. Once you know and accept yourself as you are, you can move forward with your life and flourish. You need not waste valuable years, as many of us did, trying to fit yourself—a square peg—into a round hole.

If your goal truly is to be a face in the crowd, it may still be possible. I know adult Aspies who seem to me almost neurotypical. They have steady jobs, stable marriages, friends and families. I am tempted to ask them, "What makes you an Aspie?" (It is impolite to ask that question.)

Moreover, labels don't matter as much as you think, out here in the real world. Tell people you have Asperger's and half of them will stare at you blankly. Others will smile and say, "You must be a genius, then."

Qazi Fazli Azeem

There is no greater feeling in the world than to know that you are not alone...that there are others out there like you—others that you can meet and learn from. We are a community, an international one. We exist all over the world, in all cities and countries, and come from all religions and groups of people, and we are growing.

We are Asperger's, and we will change the world together.

Ruth Elaine Joyner Hane

Leaving my session with a psychologist who specializes in autism, I had mixed feelings. I was happy to have a diagnosis, but sad to have lived so long without knowing about my neurological difference. As I pressed the down button for the elevator, another woman joined me. It was Friday afternoon on a beautiful summer day in Minnesota. The attractive person standing next to me, I guessed in her late twenties, seemed anxious. "So, do you have exciting plans for the weekend?" she asked, as we stepped into the elevator. "No, do you?" "Yes! I'm going to a rock concert!" I contemplated, given my new diagnosis, what I would have said if she had inquired if I had plans for *the rest of my life*.

It was because of doubters who told me that I probably did not meet the criteria for autism that I made an appointment. My psychologist disagreed with the critics, saying she had never been more certain because I met almost all of the criteria for High Functioning Autism. She asked, "How have you learned to accommodate so well?" I considered the question, "I don't know, but I'll think about it."

Nearly 20 years have passed since my diagnosis. I believe I have learned to accommodate my differences because of the guidance of others. I grew up in a small town where reasonable variances were accepted and tolerated. My excessive energy, insatiable curiosity, undiagnosed dyslexia and resistance to change were just the way I was. Many of our neighbors were professors at the local college. When I had a question, I just asked. If my question was not in their field of study, they referred me to a colleague. I learned about horticulture, home economics, animal husbandry, English, biology and mathematics by asking questions. After I heard a song about the bones of the body, I asked, "What is a back bone?" Dr. Grebe showed me a skeleton in his biology lab and I touched the bones of the spinal column.

My greatest challenge is social. It takes an effort to attend social events, reciprocate with neighbors and foster friendships. After I get to know someone, I usually disclose my diagnosis. I have learned that no matter how much effort I put into acting normally, I omit something or offend another person. I become especially sad when I cause rifts in our family. Usually, miscommunication is from not using enough words, making assumptions, or not understanding another perspective.

I enjoy a challenge. I was happy to receive a diagnosis because it gave me an opportunity to learn all that I could about autism. I began to read, research, meet professionals and learn how to make my life easier. I volunteered, gave workshops, wrote and started social groups. I learn from others diagnosed with autism at conferences, in groups and on the internet.

I feel fortunate to have developed friends among my peers. To an observer, it would appear as if autistics are casual acquaintances, since we tend to omit the usual social niceties, and progress to an exchange of information and ideas, usually standing apart at arm's length. Many on the spectrum do not tolerate hugs or touching, while others seek deep hugs and some prefer light pressure. We learn to directly ask before we assume how to greet or touch one another. The unspoken bond of experiencing life differently connects those of us with autism.

Scientists are developing subtypes in autism. With a more specific diagnosis, we can find others who are like us. And, perhaps, find many lifelong friends.

Henny Kupferstein

Those who do pursue a formal diagnosis find it to be life altering, in a good way. After the inevitable grieving process, one discovers that among like-minded adults there seems to be a rambunctious group of delightful people. If you do have the luxury to meet up with them, your experience will be a pure delight. Newly diagnosed people discover that indeed they now belong to a sub-culture, one they are very much comforted to be a part of. Therefore, I highly recommend a formal diagnosis to boost-charge that social connection and deep emotional bond with others.

Another reason for a formal diagnosis is for paperwork stuff. You might find it helpful to apply for social security based on disability if you are in desperate financial straits. This can be a temporary process until you can get yourself on your feet again. With over 90 percent of us being unemployed, I would say this is a wise step. I mention this, because you need to tell your evaluator that you plan to apply. They will then know exactly what kind of information to evaluate for, and how to write the report accordingly.

Quite similarly, if you plan to continue your education after high school, you will need this formal diagnosis. But you also must tell your clinician that you are applying for college, and would like to be assessed for accommodations. This is very important because you must submit all this paperwork to your college, and they do not have to employ experts to evaluate you. Additionally, the college will only accommodate exactly to the letter of the written accommodation recommendations. So make sure you mention it to the clinician. They are well skilled and knowledgeable on what worked and what didn't for others, provided that you land by the office of an expert skilled in diagnosing Asperger's. Otherwise, you set yourself up for a long string of disappointments and horror stories.

James Buzon

I suspected for a long time that I was different in ways that didn't just amount to being "unique." I think my first moment of realization was when I was in kindergarten. I remember the odd sensation of not quite being able to understand what other children were saying, like I was trying to grip something slippery that would not stay still. I remember being called weird. It was my first experience of things just not feeling right.

I had seen *Rain Man* with Dustin Hoffman as Raymond Babbitt. Once or twice, I thought about what autism was, and sometimes wondered if I was autistic. I didn't have those special talents that seemed to be displayed by him. I just knew that I felt different, and my way of interpreting the world was different. To those observing me, I just needed to work harder, to grow up and to "apply myself." The phrase "everyone has bad days" seemed to apply to every day.

I kept pushing, and somehow made it through my required years in public schooling. All the while, I was reading self-help books, and to others, I seemed to have many friends going through high school. I had quite a few friends, and was happy to feel wanted. However, I still felt different. No matter what was happening around me, I felt disconnected.

It wasn't until I went to college and really began to address my feelings of anxiety and depression that I found a therapist who knew about Asperger's syndrome. I read up on Temple Grandin, and started to see that I could very well be autistic. At the time, I didn't take it seriously; I was still trying to take care of my self-esteem. The gap between how people viewed me and what I felt inwardly seemed to grow wider. That disconnect was still there.

After college, things went downhill very quickly. I couldn't afford to attend a graduate school. On top of being unable to follow the path I had chosen to become a college professor, I was hospitalized for having what was labeled a "psychotic episode." I started falling further into my depressive state, further exacerbated by the fact that those who believed they were helping me were unwilling to listen to me. I felt like I was talking to a brick wall. Even after getting a neuropsychological test, my doctor and therapist still kept trying to apply labels that didn't fit.

Finally, I happened upon a book about Asperger's syndrome. The title was *Look Me in the Eye* by John Elder Robison. I read that book every chance I could get. Once again, I felt that spark of recognition, and decided I had to try to get some sort of help. My doctor and therapist weren't helping matters by throwing labels of "schizoaffective" and "schizophrenic" in my direction in hopes they would stick (the two most common psychiatric labels, I later discovered, to be confused with AS). I eventually risked going off of my medications and leaving therapy to prove to myself that they were incorrect.

The next step took a bit longer, mainly because I wasn't aware of the next step to take. The only thing I knew was that I was neither "crazy," "stupid" nor "retarded": my grades and intelligence spoke volumes about my abilities. I finally got the courage to ask my vocational counselor about being retested for AS. Mainly, I wanted my psychiatric label wiped from all paperwork. It was erroneous and misleading. I was given the name and number of a professional familiar with administering neuropsychological tests, and soon had an appointment. As it turned out, my psychiatric label was erased, and I was diagnosed with an Autism Spectrum Disorder.

I was over-the-moon excited! For once, I felt I had triumphed over everyone who had ever told me I was wrong about myself. I felt vindicated. I also felt a bit bewildered, because all of a sudden, I was unsure of what to do next. I had my suspicions confirmed, and I had answers. I suppose that was what I was looking for. I still felt a bit lost.

In time, however, I've come to realize that I can use my diagnosis to my advantage. I don't view it as a "get out of jail free" card, nor any sort of excuse. What I do have is someone on my side in helping me get work when I get back into the "real world" after college. I have a counselor who can be a mediator if I ever need that assistance. In short, I have a lifeline. Anyone on the spectrum needs a lifeline. It may mean the difference between getting fired for being "weird" and keeping that job. Having an actual assessment means that there are services to help when it's needed.

Most of all, the diagnosis means I'm no longer "weird" or "creepy"; it means I have a different way of seeing the world. It legitimizes my very existence. It lets me ease up on myself when something doesn't go well socially. It means that I can finally join a community of others like me and use that commonality for support. I recommend those seriously struggling to find themselves to seek out others on the spectrum. I know when I've had a bad day that I have friends who know *exactly* how I'm feeling, because they have been there. I'm no longer alone in my struggles.

REFERENCE

Robison, J.E. (2008) *Look Me in the Eye: My Life with Asperger's*. New York, NY: Three Rivers Press.

Jeanette Purkis

I was born way back in 1974. The Asperger's diagnosis was first available in the English-speaking world in the late 1980s. If you've done the sums you'll see that I couldn't have had a diagnosis when I was in primary school. In fact, I went through 13 years of schooling without an Asperger's diagnosis. This meant that school was often very unpleasant, as I had no idea why people didn't seem to like me and picked on me.

It was very important to me to be popular and included in a group. However, this eluded me for almost all my childhood and teenage years. I had the occasional friend, but I was never quite sure what to say to them or how to behave and they usually gave up and left me alone again. When I was a teenager, I thought that the only way that anybody would like me was if I belonged to a group that they also belonged to. First of all, I belonged to my parents' rather uncool church. That didn't do it for me, so I joined an extreme left-wing political group, the International Socialists. I loved being in this group because all the members were older than me. This wasn't the best group to belong to, though, as I often drank alcohol, used drugs and got aggressive at political rallies.

My need to belong to a group was far stronger than my sense of morality or ethics, and I ended up belonging to a very negative club indeed—that of criminals. I thought that if I did things my criminal friends liked I would be "cool." It was at this time that I got my Asperger's diagnosis. Even though that little description of the world as experienced by me and all the other Aspies could have changed my life, it took me over seven years before I accepted that I did, in fact, have Asperger's syndrome.

I spent those seven years doing stupid and dangerous things just to impress my "friends." Eventually my life became so chaotic that I decided to make some changes. I did some therapy and enrolled at university. When I was about to start my second year of university, I accepted the truth. I did, in fact, have Asperger's syndrome. It was a description of the way I experienced the world, of how I saw things and really, of who I had always been. Rather than thinking that the diagnosis was a way for my parents to make excuses for my poor behavior, or that Asperger's was essentially a diagnosis of "geek," as I had for years, I now knew that it was correct.

My acceptance of my diagnosis was an acceptance of myself. It was probably the most important step in my maturity, and I'm so glad that I can now proudly say "I am an Aspie."

TIPS FOR ASPIES

- The Aspie club is an awesome club! There are so many cool people who have the diagnosis. We're smart, interesting, honest and good. Never be ashamed of who you are!

- Finding out that you are an Aspie when you're young is fantastic and liberating. Treasure it, as it means that you can make the most of life from an early age.

- People will, and do, like you for who you are. You don't have to follow a negative group to be accepted. Friends are everywhere. You may wish to start with other Aspies if you're having difficulties making friends.

Anita Lesko

The decision to seek formal testing is a very personal choice. This may depend on several factors. I personally only see it necessary for work or school purposes. After learning of Asperger's, I then thoroughly researched it. I knew without a doubt that I had Asperger's. I'm sure this is the same for everyone else. You don't need a psychologist to confirm it.

I would definitely see the need for a parent to have their Aspie child formally diagnosed. This would be necessary for the school system to make special accommodations for the child. It also serves the faculty to better understand the behaviors. What might seem like an unruly child might instead be recognized as one who is experiencing sensory overload. That can make all the difference in the world. This would hold true throughout elementary, junior high and high school. In many colleges and universities, they now have special services for students with special needs. You would need your official diagnosis for that purpose as well.

The workplace is the most crucial area of need for the formal diagnosis. People on the Autism Spectrum are protected under the Americans with Disabilities Act. An employer must accommodate any special needs you will have. By having a letter from a psychologist stating you do in fact have Asperger's, those needs must be met. It will also protect you from being bullied on the job.

Other reasons for seeking a formal diagnosis would be for health insurance reasons, or for being eligible for disability allowance. Obviously the diagnosis is warranted.

Look for psychologists who have a lot of experience with Asperger's. Not every therapist really knows what it is or how to deal with it. That person is the one ultimately interpreting your test results, so do your research prior to making an appointment, and don't be afraid to ask questions. Even a visit to the office to inquire in person will help—and that goes for any kind of doctor, for that matter.

I found the several hours of testing that took place over three days both irritating and amusing! I could not believe some of the bizarre tests I was presented with, most of which seemed totally worthless to me. However, these tests are designed to determine how your brain thinks, so just forge ahead and do them, no matter how silly they appear.

Once all test results have been obtained, it will be several days before your psychologist reviews them. They will then talk with you about the findings, and they will also talk with you to make the final conclusion: that you have Asperger's! You already knew that. Now you have a piece of paper to prove it.

I highly advise everyone to become familiar with the Americans with Disabilities Act. Go to www.ada.gov. This is for both individuals and parents of children with Asperger's.

Richard Maguire

My view of getting a diagnosis is that we are logical people who need to have things in a framework that we can work with. Getting a diagnosis helps us lots and gives us framework, affirmation and assistance in working out where to go in life.

Behind all this are a lot of personal, life and timing issues. Receiving a diagnosis, even if it is not a surprise, leads to a journey of emotion, discovery and re-negotiation with oneself and other people. A diagnosis is a substantial piece of information and life event. Don't think it will be easy even if you are keen to be diagnosed. It is good, but not easy.

I experienced a sense of grief over what might have been and how I might have lived and developed my life. I had a confirmation of what I had believed for 25 years before the diagnosis. But until the diagnosis, there was a vestigial notion that I might be wrong. I spent years knowing, but not wanting finality. I do not know why, I just did.

I have spoken to several adults about their quest for diagnosis, and they reported having a time of knowing and waiting before seeking a diagnosis. What we had in common was a life event that triggered us to seek a diagnosis. Some people attend an autism event, hear about themselves, and then feel strongly they want a diagnosis and confirmation of where they know they are in life. If I had a pound for every time I was approached after training people, speaking at an event or discussing autism with someone, for my opinion about whether they should get a diagnosis, I would have enough money to buy a good meal out, with drinks, for me and my family.

I consistently come across people who have known for years and were making their journey towards a diagnosis. I sometimes join them on their journey and help them decide what to do. A diagnosis works for many people; however, there are a significant number who are content to know they are autistic without seeking a diagnosis. These people always have a reason: a mother who will put everything she has into her autistic child and does not want a distraction from her mission to be the best mum she can be; an elderly person who is happy to have the peace of understanding in their later years; the successful, self-driven person in a busy career who knows they are autistic and feels they are living well— maybe they will seek a diagnosis in future decades? And there is the person who is fine with living as they are and does not see an advantage in a diagnosis, just as there are those who are too busy with life, family and job to take time out for a diagnosis.

I feel for the ones who are so crushed and frightened that they cannot disturb the fragile life they have with the emotional input a diagnosis involves, and the ones who have had bad experiences in education and growing up from being stigmatized because they were different and struggled. These people need love, quiet support and affirmation.

My advice to you would be to reflect on where you are in life. Where would a diagnosis fit into your life? What could your life be like post-diagnosis? What might your family feel? Would a diagnosis help them? You have time to decide. A diagnosis is significant, and life will be different afterwards. I support you whatever decision you make.

Dr. Tony Attwood's Advice on Being Tested for Asperger's/HFA

There are distinct advantages in having a diagnostic assessment and confirmation of having an ASD such as Asperger's syndrome, as outlined by the Aspie mentors. These include:

- having an explanation for being different and therefore experiencing relief in knowing you are not mad, bad or defective, despite the "psychological assessments" of predatory peers, and self-evaluation based on those derogatory comments

- acquiring a framework to understand your difficulties and abilities, and to use that framework to explain those difficulties and abilities to others

- gaining access to services and support at school or college, and guidance from literature on finding and keeping a job that matches your abilities and qualifications

- ending a sense of isolation and loneliness by identifying a culture of like-minded individuals who have had similar experiences; members of that culture can become valued friends

- gaining more insight into the positive characteristics of ASD

- knowing where to go for further information and advice on any aspect of ASD in published literature and on the internet, such as Autism Hangout (www.autismhangout.com)

- benefitting from the advice of Aspie mentors who are the wise elders of the tribe of ASD

- acquiring greater self-acceptance, and confidence in being true to your real self.

The road to acquiring a diagnosis is not always an easy one. There can be reluctance in teenagers and adults who have the characteristics of an ASD to seek an assessment by a psychologist or psychiatrist, fearing a diagnosis of being "schizo" or "psycho." For adolescents at high school, there can be some reluctance due to fear of rejection and teasing by neurotypical peers, who have a remarkable intolerance of someone who is different and perceived as having a "mental" condition.

There may also have been a successful "mask" created to hide the real self, and thus a fear of the vulnerability and rejection that might result from exposing the real self. Sometimes creating the mask and acting neurotypical can be so successful that others will challenge the diagnosis as they do not perceive the amount of effort that went into acting neurotypical, or realize that the real self was hidden.

It is essential that the clinician conducting the diagnosis has training and considerable experience in the assessment of adolescents and adults with an ASD such as Asperger's syndrome. This is particularly important for girls and women with an ASD, who are often more skilful than the boys and men in camouflaging their ASD characteristics. They tend to compensate for their difficulties using strategies such as acting neurotypical, which can continue to occur even during the diagnostic assessment. You must be honest, therefore, in answering questions and explaining abilities and experiences. By creating a false impression or trail, the only person who is being deceived and denied is you. It is also important not to use the diagnosis as an excuse to avoid appropriate consequences and responsibilities. Equally, you must not assume that certain abilities will be impossible to achieve. The Aspie mentors have clearly stated that some apparently elusive abilities and experiences, such as a successful career and happy, long-term relationship, can be achieved by those who have an ASD.

The diagnosis does not change who you are, but does explain *why* you are who you are, and may provide access to guidance on how you can achieve your ambitions and become the person you would like to be.

Artwork (See Plate 16)

Painting: Coming Out

Artist: Marilyn Cosho

Artist's Commentary: Being diagnosed at the age of 54 was like coming out of a dark hole. The stairs represent the long journey. The diagnosis also gave me the courage to share my art, which I had kept hidden in the dark.

Painting: The Exam

Artist: Michael Tolleson

Artist's Commentary: This person waits to be examined by the doctors. The area where she waits is full of color while a cold, clinical gray surrounds the doctors. Her head hangs in fear and her arms are folded and protective of her and her nakedness. She knows she is soon to be laid bare in front of alien eyes. It's as if the very blood in her body is draining out of her and onto the seat and floor. The doctors suck in her discomfort like vampires feasting on her blood.

About the Aspie Mentors

Qazi Fazli Azeem

 Year of birth: 1981

Country where I am currently living: USA (on Fulbright Scholarship till 2014; originally from Karachi, Pakistan)

Favorite part about being Asperger's/HFA: People coming up to me and saying that they have never met anyone like me in their life.

Least favorite part about being Asperger's/HFA: The internal struggle and battle that I have to go through every time in social settings, and making "light" conversation with neurotypicals, to make sure I don't scare them because of my intense interests in arcane subjects. I have to "keep my gloves on" and wear a mask of conformity.

Last completed level of education: Pakistan's first multimedia design undergraduate in 2006. I am currently enrolled in the MFA (2012–2014) for Dynamic Media Communication Design at the Massachusetts College of Art and Design in Boston, USA, through the Fulbright Scholarship.

Current job: Graduate teaching assistant, Massachusetts College of Art and Design, Boston.

One line of advice I would give to someone with Asperger's/HFA: Wear the mask of conformity as you practice and get better at what you do. Eventually, you will find others like you; join them, and change the world.

One line of advice I would like the world to know about Asperger's/HFA: The story of one with Asperger's is as old as the story of science, math, art, language and creativity. We have enabled innovation, and push the boundaries of technology every day. A day will come when there will be more Asperger's and fewer neurotypicals, and then the world will understand that Asperger's syndrome is human evolution in action.

Garry Burge

Year of birth: 1972

Country where I am currently living: Australia

Favorite part about being Asperger's/HFA: It is a means of identity and understanding.

Last completed level of education: Bachelor of Arts degree.

Current job: Service support assistant, University of Queensland library.

One line of advice I would give to someone with Asperger's/HFA: Don't deny you have Asperger's syndrome, as it only makes the world a much harder place to live in.

One line of advice I would like the world to know about Asperger's/HFA: Accepting people into the world makes for a much better, more diverse and interesting place.

James Buzon

Year of birth: 1984

Country where I am currently living: USA

Favorite part about being Asperger's/HFA: My imagination.

Least favorite part about being Asperger's/HFA: Sensory issues.

Last completed level of education: BA English.

Current job: Currently pursuing a BS in Graphic Design.

One line of advice I would give to someone with Asperger's/ HFA: Individuality is a very precious commodity. Love your individuality, and things will begin to fall into place.

One line of advice I would like the world to know about Asperger's/HFA: I would tell everyone that we can change the world dramatically (and for the good, might I add), if we are given the chance.

Bob Castleman

Year of birth: 1958

Country where I am currently living: USA

Favorite part about being Asperger's/HFA: My penchant for non-linear thinking.

Least favorite part about being Asperger's/HFA: People not understanding my non-linearity.

Last completed level of education: College junior.

Current job: Database administrator.

One line of advice I would give to someone with Asperger's/ HFA: The universe is bigger than you. Step outside of yourself and discover it.

One line of advice I would like the world to know about Asperger's/HFA: Educate yourself before you say anything about autism and Asperger's. You very likely know only what flows through mass media. Would you like *your* life defined by the internet? Neither do people with an Autism Spectrum Disorder.

Mitch Christian

Year of birth: 1962

Country where I am currently living: USA

Favorite part about being Asperger's/HFA: Remaining reasonable when confronted with overreactions.

Least favorite part aboutz being Asperger's/HFA: Hyper-sensitivity to sound.

Last completed level of education: Four-year college degree.

Current job: Computer programmer.

One line of advice I would give to someone with Asperger's/HFA: It's going to be okay.

One line of advice I would like the world to know about Asperger's/HFA: You need us.

Debbie Denenburg

Year of birth: 1958

Country where I am currently living: USA

Favorite part about being Asperger's/HFA: I'm usually right! I love researching and giving factual information. This has the result of people trusting what I say.

Least favorite part of Asperger's/HFA: Not being understood. I feel like I say things straight up, but neurotypicals (NTs) seem to think that there is always something unsaid instead of taking my words at face value. This leaves me confused and frustrated.

Last completed level of education: High school.

Current job: The disability benefit is my main income but I always work. I am an artist and I have an Etsy shop online where I sell mostly vintage items. I have also written a movie screenplay.

It is in the hands of a filmmaker, but there has been no action on it yet.

One line of advice I would give to someone with Asperger's/ HFA: Believe you can be loved for who you truly are.

One line of advice I would like the world to know about Asperger's/HFA: By opening your mind to allow a knowledge of Asperger's, you will be increasing your opportunity to understand a bigger picture of humanity.

Charli Devnet

Year of birth: 1954

Country where I am currently living: USA

Favorite part about being Asperger's/HFA: Being unique.

Least favorite part about being Asperger's/HFA: Loneliness.

Last completed level of education: Postgraduate degree.

Current job: Tour guide.

One line of advice I would give to someone with Asperger's/ HFA: Know yourself. Without self-knowledge, you can acquire a passel of college degrees and never be wise.

One line of advice I would like the world to know about Asperger's/HFA: Give us a chance. We're a lot more fun once you get to know us. We may seem anti-social, rude, stubborn, immature and uncaring, but this may well be due to the painful experiences that many of us have endured in our youth. Sometimes you have to break down the walls to get to us, but it's worth it.

Temple Grandin

Year of birth: 1947

Country where I am currently living: USA

Favorite part about being Asperger's/HFA: My logical thinking.

Least favorite part about being Asperger's/HFA: Anxiety, until I took a low dose of antidepressants.

Last completed level of education: Ph.D.

Current job: Professor of Animal Science (since 1990).

One line of advice I would give to someone with Asperger's/HFA: Find something you are good at to turn into a career.

One line of advice I would like the world to know about Asperger's/HFA: Aspies are smart, hard working, and can solve problems.

Ruth Elaine Joyner Hane

Year of birth: 1940

Country where I am currently living: USA

Favorite part about being Asperger's/HFA: My unusual sense of humor reveals the lighter side of life.

Least favorite part about being Asperger's/HFA: Sensory overload is most challenging. People expect me to respond and function well in spite of loud environments and major distractions.

Last completed level of education: Bachelor of Science/Home Ecology, magna cum laude.

Current job: Research in vision/prosopagnosia (face blindness).

One line of advice I would like the world to know about Asperger's/HFA: Live fully in this precious moment.

Paul Isaacs

Year of birth: 1986

Country where I am currently living: United Kingdom

Favorite part about being Asperger's/HFA: I like that I can see the world from a different perspective.

Least favorite part about being Asperger's/HFA: Stress levels and anxiety.

Last completed level of education: General National Vocational Qualification (GNVQ) (NVQ Level 2); Information and Communications Technology (ICT) Intermediate Course.

Current job: Autistic speaker, trainer and consultant for Autism Oxford.

One line of advice I would like the world to know about Asperger's/HFA: Do not fear people with autism, embrace them. Do not spite people with autism, unite them. Do not deny people with autism, accept them for their abilities. And they will shine.

Dr. Know

Year of birth: Withheld

Country where I am currently living: Somewhere in Europe

Favorite part about being Asperger's/HFA: I would rather think about the favorite part of being myself. I like being who I am. I guess I am particularly fond of my high intelligence.

Least favorite part about being Asperger's/HFA: I would rather think about the least favorite part of being myself. Again, I like being who I am, but I can identify parts I want to work more on: not getting so angry sometimes (even if I am being provoked), and getting better at not hurting the feelings of people I like (it is not intentional, but it still happens).

Last completed level of education: Ph.D.

Current job: Postdoctoral researcher.

One line of advice I would give to someone with Asperger's/ HFA: Depends so much on the individual Aspie, but I think the following quote is something that a good chunk of Aspies should consider thinking about: "What do you care what other people think?" Arline Feynman reportedly asked this question often to her husband, the famous scientist Richard Feynman, when he was worried about what his colleagues thought about his work.

One line of advice I would like the world to know about Asperger's/HFA: There should be no doubt that Aspies have been contributing a lot to the world. Neurodiversity is strength in societies, analogous with biodiversity, which is known to be a significant strength in nature. The world benefits greatly from having so many different individuals in it—Aspies together with NTs.

Karen Krejcha

Year of birth: 1967

Country where I am currently living: USA

Favorite part about being Asperger's/HFA: Better understanding of my neurological wiring has helped me with acceptance and self-esteem. I appreciate my creativity and quirkiness and enjoy the opportunity to connect with others on the Autism Spectrum.

Least favorite part about being Asperger's/HFA: My social naivety when younger led to some traumatic life experiences with long-lasting pain. I hope by writing and speaking candidly about my past, I may prevent other Aspies from falling into similar situations.

Last completed level of education: Majored in child and family development at California Polytechnic University, San Luis Obispo.

Current job: Executive Director and co-founder of Autism Empowerment, a vibrant 501(c)3 non-profit charity founded in 2011 that is dedicated to promoting Acceptance, Enrichment, Inspiration and Empowerment within the autism and Asperger communities locally, regionally and worldwide: www.autismempowerment.org

One line of advice I would give to someone with Asperger's/HFA: Accept yourself for who you are, as you are and be authentic to yourself in all relationships.

One line of advice I would like the world to know about Asperger's/HFA: We're human beings, wonderful and flawed and just like you. We desire acceptance, love, respect and life with meaning.

Henny Kupferstein

Year of birth: 1977

Country where I am currently living: USA

Favorite part about being Asperger's/HFA: Intense concentration abilities, perfect pitch and synesthesia.

Least favorite part about being Asperger's/HFA: Sensory issues.

Last completed level of education: Bachelor of Science, Music Leadership in Society

Current job: Composer, researcher

One line of advice I would give to someone with Asperger's/HFA: Make peace, accept that the sky might be green for others, and be submissive when you tell them that.

One line of advice I would like the world to know about Asperger's/HFA: Behind a highly articulate person is an individual who struggles greatly to communicate, despite their gifted orations.

Anita Lesko

Year of birth: 1959

Country where I am currently living: USA

Favorite part about being Asperger's/HFA: Diversity and my "laser focus." Thanks to my Aspergian gifts, my life has included: administering anesthesia; jumping horses over six-foot-high fences in competition; ice dancing; becoming an internationally published military aviation photojournalist; learning to fly a helicopter; writing my autobiography—*Asperger's Syndrome: When Life Hands You Lemons, Make Lemonade*—in two weeks by writing 16 hours each day; heading the development of a hippotherapy center at the world's largest Snoezelen complex; and starting the Flying High with Autism Foundation.

Least favorite part about being Asperger's/HFA: Asperger's is an invisible syndrome, yet how is it that neurotypicals "see" it immediately, even before you say one word?

Last completed level of education: Proudly graduated from Columbia University in New York City in 1988 with my Master of Science in Nurse Anesthesia.

Current job: I have been working as a Certified Registered Nurse Anesthetist for the past 25 years, and have been at my current job for 15 years.

One line of advice I would give to someone with Asperger's/HFA: Don't focus on the fact that you have Asperger's. Get out there and use your extraordinary gifts to make a difference in this world!

One line of advice I would like people of the world to know about Asperger's/HFA: Aspies feel like we're from another planet because neurotypicals *make* us feel that way by their reactions and behaviors towards us. I'd like the world to know that we are real people too, and find it in their minds and hearts to allow us into their world, so we're not always on the outside looking in. Two powerful words of advice: *accept difference*.

Richard Maguire

Year of birth: 1966

Country where I am currently living: United Kingdom

Favorite part about being Asperger's/HFA: It's an adventure, fun being different and being an original thinker.

Least favorite part about being Asperger's/HFA: Anxiety, tiredness and socializing.

Last completed level of education: BA in theology and religion from Oxford Brookes University, January 2010.

Current job: Self-employed, running my own business, Autism Live Training, providing training and mentoring, speaking and autism advice from the point of view of an autistic person.

One line of advice I would give to someone with Asperger's/ HFA: Learn to enjoy being Asperger's, take control of your life and make your own luck.

One line of advice I would like the world to know about Asperger's/HFA: We are lively, emotional, feeling people; please become still enough to hear us. We are good to have around and have much to share.

John Makin

Year of birth: 1950

Country where I am currently living: Scotland

Favorite part about being Asperger's/HFA: Thinking. My ability to think and reason, and my desire to learn all about everything I come across. My ability to solve problems.

Least favorite part about being Asperger's/HFA: Difficulty in understanding what people want of me or are asking for.

Last completed level of education: High school.

Current job: Retired.

One line of advice I would give to someone with Asperger's/ HFA: Look outwards, not in. If you take no interest in those around you, they will ignore you.

One line of advice I would like the world to know about Asperger's/HFA: We have been here throughout history, and were considered part of the richness of the human race. Only now are we labelled.

Larry Moody

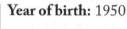

Year of birth: 1950

Country where I am currently living: USA

Favorite part about being Asperger's/HFA: I routinely think outside the box, and I'm not overly concerned about what people think of me... I know who I am and what I'm capable of. I march to a definitely different drum!

Least favorite part about being Asperger's/HFA: I just can't seem to appropriately interpret people's facial expressions, thus I miss out on a lot of the unspoken communications around me, resulting in many social faux pas.

Last completed level of education: Bachelor of Science in civil engineering.

Current job: I retired early from engineering, at age 50, successful and wealthy. I am currently on the Board of Directors of two non-profits, the Autism Society of Minnesota, and Autism Works. I also function as a speaker and advocate on autism issues.

One line of advice I would give to someone with Asperger's/ HFA: Be persistent. If at first you don't succeed, try, try again!

One line of advice I would like the world to know about Asperger's/HFA: We are different, not defective... Whatever your estimate of us is, it's wrong! If we can discover our gifts and talents, and can find the resources to develop them, watch out! We will astound and amaze you with what we can do.

Lisa Morgan

Year of birth: 1963

Country where I am currently living: USA

Favorite part about being Asperger's/HFA: I think differently than others and I like the way I see the world.

Least favorite part about being Asperger's/HFA: Being misunderstood.

Last completed level of education: Master's degree in the art of teaching in special education.

Current job: I am a teacher of children with special needs.

One line of advice I would give to someone with Asperger's/HFA: Be your own wonderful self, have confidence in your abilities, take good care of yourself, and stay positive!

One line of advice I would like the world to know about Asperger's/HFA: People with AS are a very creative, blatantly honest, extremely loyal, fair to a fault, intelligent group of people who can add many innovative insights to the world.

Jennifer Cook O'Toole

Year of birth: 1975

Country where I am currently living: USA

Favorite part about being Asperger's/HFA: Being able to sense and articulate patterns—in experiences, in people, in ideas—that the rest of the world seems to miss.

Least favorite part about being Asperger's/HFA: Missing the patterns that the rest of the world sees! Thinking (time and again) that I finally have my footing, and discovering, instead, the carpet being pulled out from underneath me.

Last completed level of education: Graduated with honors from Brown University and have since studied at the Graduate School of Social Work at Columbia University and Graduate School of Education at Queens University.

Current job: Author, educational consultant, speaker, CEO, MOM!

My one line of advice I would give to someone with Asperger's/HFA: Whatever you do, wherever you go, whether you are loud or soft, bold and glittery, or subtle and strong…don't forget to be *awesome.*

One line of advice I would like the world to know about Asperger's/HFA: Beneath our bravado, ideals and intensity, we are so very afraid of…so much; please be kind with your advice, be gentle with your rebukes, and be ever-generous with your patience, creativity and love.

Lars Perner

Year of birth: 1954

Country where I am currently living: USA

Favorite part about being Asperger's/HFA: Having a novel way of looking at the world.

Least favorite part about being Asperger's/HFA: Sensory vulnerabilities.

Last completed level of education: Ph.D., Marketing, University of Southern California, 1998.

Current job: Assistant Professor of Clinical Marketing, Marshall School of Business, University of Southern California.

One line of advice I would give to someone with Asperger's/HFA: Each individual on the spectrum is unique. You may differ significantly from most others on the spectrum on certain variables. Many of us, for example, are anything but visual thinkers!

One line of advice I would like the world to know about Asperger's/HFA: Many people with AS have rather unique skills to contribute to the world and may come up with new ways to look at things. The important thing is to identify the potential of the specific individual.

Jeanette Purkis

Year of birth: 1974

Country where I am currently living: Australia

Favorite part about being Asperger's/HFA: Being honest, moral and trustworthy.

Least favorite part about being Asperger's/HFA: Knowing that I miss out on most of the meaning when I'm talking to someone.

Last completed level of education: Masters degree in visual arts.

Current job: Public servant, author.

One line of advice I would give to someone with Asperger's/HFA: You can do anything! Don't let your diagnosis stop you from doing anything.

One line of advice I would like the world to know about Asperger's/HFA: We are capable, intelligent, and have a lot to give. If everyone were the same, the world would be a boring place.

Mary Robison

Year of birth: 1957

Country where I am currently living: USA

Favorite part about being Asperger's/HFA: Being able to concentrate with one single purpose for hours or days on end.

Least favorite part about being Asperger's/HFA: Being able to concentrate for hours or days on end and forgetting to eat or sleep as a result!

Last completed level of education: Ph.D.

Current job: I have several. I am an adjunct professor, a tutor, the president of my electronics business, and I'm a writer.

One line of advice I would give to someone with Asperger's/HFA: Persevere! Don't give up just because the world doesn't understand you. Go out, find your niche, and thrive.

One line of advice I would like the world to know about Asperger's/HFA: We've always been here and we are the creators of everything that makes your lives easier—all we ask is tolerance.

Steve Selpal

Year of birth: 1950

Country where I am currently living: USA. But I was a Canadian until age 20, which explains a lot.

Favorite part about being Asperger's/HFA: It's a huge improvement over my lifelong diagnoses. From 1970 to 1979, my diagnosis was paranoid schizophrenia and from 1979 to 2006, it was bipolar manic-depression. I took lithium carbonate for 21 years. When I quit in 2000, nothing happened. In 2006, it was ascertained that I was born this way. Besides Asperger's, I probably am mentally ill. I've always double checked my work and tried to reflect if I am acting crazy or sick.

Least favorite part about being Asperger's/HFA: None personally.

Last completed level of education: Bachelor of Fine Arts in 1979.

Current job: President of Steve Selpal Art Production, Inc. That's just illustration, graphic design, murals, selling paintings, shaking money out of trees, whatever I can. I do my job well.

One line of advice I would give to someone with Asperger's/ HFA: Don't kill yourself. Always know that this too shall pass. You can do what they do (NTs) and even reiterate what they do in more ways than they have patience for. Use the KISS principle: Keep It Simple Stupid!

One line of advice I would like the world to know about Asperger's/HFA: Don't be surprised if they are cleverer than you are. Never ask them, "How are you?" You might get a long-winded ontological analysis and that's your fault, not theirs.

Dr. Stephen M. Shore

Year of birth: 1961

Country where I am currently living: USA

Favorite part about being Asperger's/HFA: Experiencing the world and our community.

Last completed level of education: Doctorate in Special Education.

Current job: Assistant Professor of Special Education.

One line of advice I would give to someone with Asperger's/ HFA: Find a way to use your often considerable strengths for success!

One line of advice I would like the world to know about Asperger's/HFA: The potential of people with Asperger's is unlimited – just like everyone else.

Dr. Patrick Suglia

Year of birth: 1962

Country where I am currently living: USA

Favorite part about being Asperger's/HFA: The creative ways my mind figures things out.

Least favorite part about being Asperger's/HFA: Not being able to get the social clues and making myself look clueless in more ways than one.

Last completed level of education: Professional doctorate.

Current job: Chiropractor.

One line of advice I would give to someone with Asperger's/HFA: Don't sweat the small stuff, and it's all small stuff. Don't take anything personally, and remember that you are never the cause of someone else's frustrations.

One line of advice I would like the world to know about Asperger's/HFA: This isn't going away. We aren't going away. If we did, there'd be nobody around to save your butts when you get into a bind.

Liane Holliday Willey

Year of birth: 1959

Country where I am currently living: USA

Favorite part about being Asperger's/HFA: My mind wraps itself up in ethics, honesty, objectivity, dependability and pragmatism. I think these are the cornerstones of a healthy and kind society, and the ingredients of living a fulfilling life.

Least favorite part about being Asperger's/HFA: I wish I was not such a literal thinker. I do get annoyed and dismayed, not to mention confused, on a daily basis trying to figure out the real message behind everything from television commercials to personal conversations I engage in.

Last completed level of education: Doctor of Education.

Current job: Owner, Kirkshire Farm.

One line of advice I would give to someone with Asperger's/HFA: We are not broken; we are otherwise fixed as wonderfully unique thinkers.

One line of advice I would like the world to know about Asperger's/HFA: People with Asperger's can be as capable and able as anyone else so long as the world accepts that differences in behavior and thinking are the keys to a truly great society.

Alexis Wineman

Year of birth: 1994

Country where I am currently living: USA

Favorite part about being Asperger's/HFA: Being able to mimic everyone.

Least favorite part about being Asperger's/HFA: The frustration.

Last completed level of education: High School.

Current job: Miss Montana.

One line of advice I would give to someone with Asperger's/HFA: Autism doesn't define you. You define it!

One line of advice I would like the world to know about Asperger's/HFA: Never underestimate us, because we will surprise you.

Contributing Artists

Michael Tolleson

 I have Asperger's and I am an artistic savant, which accounts for my ability to paint proficiently and effectively without formal training. June 2013 marked two years of actively painting and creating 350 gallery-worthy paintings (no mistakes, including my first painting). With each new painting, I continue to evolve, develop my own style and progress because of an aptitude that I attribute to my Asperger's.

While I can paint as an artistic savant, I have other deficits such as face blindness (inability to remember faces if they are "out of location context" or if clothing or hairstyle has significantly changed). I can do complex math in my head, but cannot fill out forms, reports, schedules, or balance a checkbook. Asperger's has for me its pluses and minuses…such as, I have the tendency to be very, very, very verbal (I talk a lot).

My art travels between two paths; one more realistic and the other more abstract and soul based. The opportunity to create for this book presented itself at a time that I was painting with my impressionistic, loose style. My typical subjects were not as emotional as the subjects and stress points I tackled for this book. With each chapter's title, I had to reach deep within myself and explore how I personally felt when I experienced that stress point. Then I asked myself how the stress points would look if I created on canvas and thus put in a visual context the feeling within these subjects. When I create, I paint feelings. So the ability to create a visual depended on how deeply I felt the stress point in my soul. Because of the time I took to really feel each subject, I was able to explore and create visual definitions for the feelings that sometimes are hidden within ourselves or that we refuse to discuss. For this opportunity to create 14 unique and cohesive paintings, I will be thankful for the rest of my life.

When I examine my ability to paint, every stroke is instinctual since I have no training. And I rely on the use of the huge amount of observed and retained information stored in my Asperger's mind.

Each painting I create, regardless of size, is painted in less than one hour. When photographed during the process of creating a finished piece of artwork, my hand appears as a blur due to the speed of movement. This is the genius of a savant mind with Asperger's. In many ways I feel possessed during the actual act of painting, and I am reluctant to take credit for the finished work resting on the easel when I am done. The finished outcome is always a surprise to me.

My actual process is very interesting. The use of a reference photo that I lay beside my easel in many ways dictates what my autistic mind will perceive as the approach for the finished artwork. For each painting that was done for this book, I researched photo after photo of subject matter that had "feelings" of the stress point I was attempting. Each reference photo had to speak to me. I had to have an emotional connection to the subject, colors or design placement of the photo.

The actual process toward the finished piece can go in many directions, but ultimately my subconscious mind takes the photo and transforms it into my own version of the subject in the photo. Imagine taking a simple photo and punching up the colors on adrenaline. That is what happens in my subconscious mind.

Although my hand, brush and palette knife movements are quick and almost manic, the application of the paint is somehow calculated. Color and emotions that pour from the finished canvas draw viewers deeply into the implied "story" of the art. Ultimately, I hope the paint on the canvas provides a doorway into understanding a world within autism and will ultimately capture my desire to touch another receptive soul.

Michael Tolleson lives in Seattle, Washington with his artist partner, Jack Carl Anderson, who also has Asperger's. Together they have an art gallery that displays artwork from about forty challenged artists, many with autism. They also have an autistic art mentoring center that provides one-on-one instruction for art students on the Autism Spectrum.

Other Artist Contributors

Nekea Blagoev, Australia (www.getsmashedart.com)

Marilyn Cosho, USA

Debbie Denenburg, USA (www.debbiedenenburg.com)

Jennifer Healy, USA (www.jennifer-healy.com)

Lea Morschel, Germany

Charlotte Poe, United Kingdom (www.taxidermae.com)

Derran Rootring, The Netherlands (www.derran.nl/en)

Stephanie Tihanyi, St. Martin, Caribbean (www.stephanietihanyi.net)

Kimberly Gerry Tucker, USA (ravenambition.wordpress.com)

Victoria Ingemann van Rooij, Denmark (http://vikseivr.deviantart.com)

The Survey Questionnaire

The survey was constructed by Craig R. Evans and administered from January 17, 2012 to March 19, 2013 through Survey Monkey at: www.surveymonkey.com/s/Aspiequestions. The address of the online survey was distributed globally to associations and databases of known individuals with ASD. An open invitation to others on the spectrum (either confirmed with a diagnosis or suspected) was broadcast via a video at Autism Hangout. Three hundred and twenty-two (322) surveys were completed.

Those surveyed were first asked whether a particular issue affected them. The occurrence of the issue was tallied from their responses. Later in the survey, all respondents were then asked to rate the 17 issues on a scale of 1 to 5, where 1 indicated that it caused them minimal or no stress and 5 indicated that it caused them a great deal of stress. Those figures were then converted to a mean percentage of stress caused by each individual issue. This measurement allowed for an accurate ranking of the 17 stressors within the responding population.

The following graphs show the demographics of the survey participants.

Now we need some information about you. Are you...

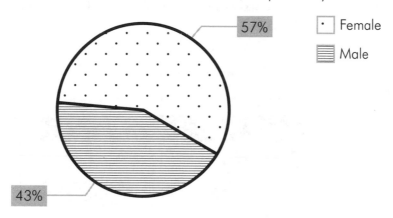

Which category below includes your age?

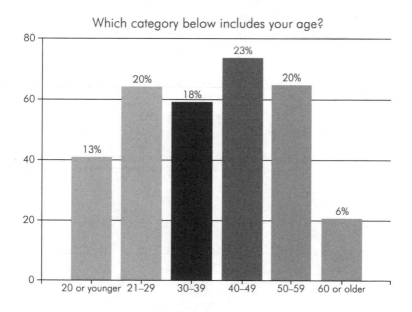

What is the highest level of school you have completed or the highest degree you have received?

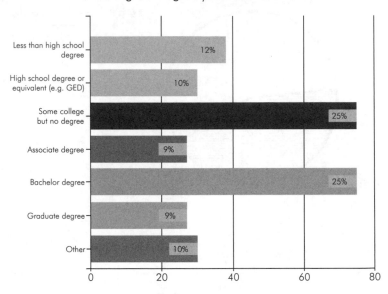

What is your living situation?

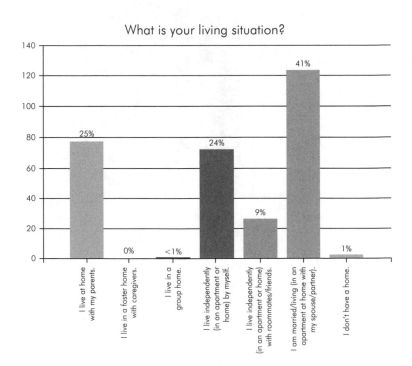

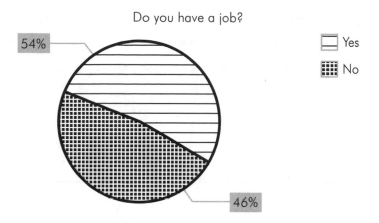

Do you have a job?

54%

46%

Yes

No

The stressors/issues were assembled from books, articles, and conversations with people on the spectrum, autism experts, seminar notes (on the subject), videos and blogs found at news sources, YouTube postings (and follow-up comments), personal websites and autism forums. To assure the completeness of this list, an open-ended question was asked of survey respondents for "other categories" that may have been missed by the 17. There were many helpful suggestions—most dealing with specific "how to accommodate" issues. Among them:

- How do I live an autistic life in a neurotypical (NT) world?

- How can I explain autism/Asperger's in two sentences so that people understand?

- How can I discover my gifts and talents?

- How do I care for myself?

- How do I raise my children to understand both autism (me) and an NT world?

- How do I help NTs understand me?

- How can I recognize (stop) people from taking advantage of me?

- How do I get support to help me be me?

- How can I learn to be more flexible?
- How can I find peace and love?

These issues and more will be considered for future research and book projects.

Editors' Websites

Dr. Tony Attwood's site: www.tonyattwood.com.au

> This website is a guide for parents, professionals and people with Asperger's syndrome and their partners.
>
> In this site you will find issues related to Asperger's syndrome, resources, resource papers Tony has authored, related topics and Tony's presentation schedule.

Craig R. Evans at Autism Hangout: www.autismhangout.com

> Autism Hangout is an online discussion forum that reports news, complies facts and community-submitted personal experiences and invites ongoing discussion to discover insights on how best to deal with the daily challenges of autism.

Anita Lesko at BornwithAspergers: www.bornwithaspergers.com

> Meet leading Asperger's advocate Anita Lesko, and learn of her journey through the first 50 years of her life when she didn't know of Asperger's, and how she tackled it once discovered! Join in on her weekly live show, where you can call in or email questions, and hear from other leaders from the world of autism. Learn about Anita's not-for-profit organization, The Flying High with Autism Foundation, which will enable those on the Autism Spectrum to soar to heights they never dreamed possible.

Mentor and Artist Index

"In addition to it being my honor to share my ideas with my community of people with Asperger's in this book, I continue to be amazed at the nuggets of information, brilliant in their simplicity, that would have made my life immeasurably easier if I had only known. The good news is that this resource, full of hard earned experience and advice of those with Asperger Syndrome is available as an important key to leading a fulfilling and productive life."

—*Dr. Stephen M. Shore*

"All of the unanswered questions of my life would have been answered with this book. Readers will feel like they have a best friend and support system, and advice that will save them from many mistakes, and instead lead them down the path of happiness and success!"

—*Anita Lesko*

"Hindsight is always 20/20—except when it's completely-usable-today insight, and then it's superhero vision! That's this book. It is where you ditch the 'should-haves' and 'could-haves,' and sense the possibility of NOW. It is, ironically, finding that, as Aspies and as people, our greatest strength is being different…together."

—*Jennifer Cook O'Toole*

"Because those of us on the spectrum vary greatly in the specific challenges we face, it is helpful to have a huge treasure chest of coping strategies to draw from."

—*Lars Perner*

"With the help of a few friends, life is always easier. This book is a best friend for everyone on the spectrum and I am very happy the stories shared, helped me feel better about me!"

—*Liane Holliday Willey*